THE STATE OF BLACK AMERICA 1998

Published by National Urban League

THE STATE OF BLACK AMERICA 1998

EDITOR

Lee A. Daniels

ASSOCIATE EDITORS

Dachell McSween

Rose Jefferson-Frazier

**DESIGN, PRODUCTION,
SALES AND DISTRIBUTION**

Image Partners

CREATIVE DIRECTOR
John Shearer

ART DIRECTOR
Lisa Weber

SALES
Dave Weiner and Associates

Copyright© National Urban League, 1998
Library of Congress Catalog Number 77-647469
ISBN 0-914758-99-3
$24.95

NATIONAL URBAN LEAGUE

Our Children ⊜ Our Destiny

JONATHAN S. LINEN
Chairman

HUGH B. PRICE
President and Chief Executive Officer

MILTON J. LITTLE, JR.
Executive Vice President and Chief Operating Officer

PAUL WYCISK
Senior Vice President and Chief Financial Officer

M. GASBY GREELY
Senior Vice President, Development and Communications

MILDRED L. LOVE
Senior Vice President of Operations

Cover: Naomi Campbell, Women Model Management
by Albert Watson

THE STATE OF BLACK AMERICA 1998

TABLE OF CONTENTS

Continued on next page

Pathways to Power:
The State of Black America 1998

By Hugh B. Price

Last summer President Clinton said America must honestly examine its racial problems if it is to avoid being crippled by them.

His central question—are we ready to become a robust, multiethnic democracy?—is not rhetorical. It is the fundamental challenge of America's future.

At first glance, there may seem to be little to connect the president's plea for inclusiveness to the health of the political economy of Black America and to the fostering of economic power among African Americans.

But in fact, they are inextricably connected. The world is living with a new economic order now, one that promises to be harshly unforgiving of economic weakness—as the economic turmoil in Asia has unmistakably shown. That the region was only recently touted with such certainty as an economic wonderland underscores how important it is that nations—and their citizens as well as businesses—discipline themselves to be well-prepared, economically vigilant and properly active, so they can have the best chance to be prosperous.

America won't be strong unless it is strong economically, and it won't be strong economically unless the opportunities for economic success are shared far more broadly than they are today.

Black America won't be strong, either, unless it is strong economically—unless it can help inspire more of its "human capital" to take advantage of the opportunities in the American and global free market.

If Black America isn't strong economically, America can't be.

That's the new American reality.

That is what the essays in this latest volume of *The State of Black America* are concerned with: What must be done to fully equip Black America for the economic challenges ahead, in order to enable America to successfully negotiate the new economic order. Together the essays present a compelling check-off list, if you will, we can use to gauge our present state of readiness.

As a group, African Americans have made enormous progress in the three decades since the victories of the civil rights revolution ended legal support for segregation and discrimination. But our authors' words and data leave no doubt that the challenges before us and the nation at large are very serious and will demand all the determination, inventiveness, and power we can muster.

Our authors say: America cannot afford African Americans to be asset poor, to be so bereft of wealth. America cannot afford so many African Americans to be so trapped within our inner cities, isolated from the mainstream of society, chained to poverty by poor education and a low level of skills. America cannot afford so many African-American youth to be so deprived of an effective, enabling education by outmoded curricula, disorganized schools, and too many poorly trained teachers. America cannot afford the present-day—and eventually—far-greater costs of leaving so many African Americans out of the technology loop, too far back on the information superhighway to take active part in the high-tech society of the 21st century.

WHY CAN'T AMERICA AFFORD THESE INADEQUACIES?

Aside from the obvious moral response, the pragmatic answer is: because the complexion of America will change dramatically over the next several decades. By the middle of the next century, the U.S. population will be half Caucasian, half people of color. Americans must come to terms with this reality once and for all if our nation is to prosper and prevail.

We must understand that any dialogue about race and ethnicity ultimately must look to the future if it's to make a difference: That's why blacks, whites, Hispanic Americans, Asian Americans and Native Americans all belong at the round table of the national discussion about race. And any national conversation about race must quickly be followed by national commitments to open wide the doors of opportunity, once and for all.

For institutions and individuals in White America, that reality means committing themselves to affirmative action, locking the gates of opportunity in the open—not closed—position. It means universities and employers committing themselves to inclusion, even in the face of continuing assaults on affirmative action. It means labor unions including everyone in their ranks, from bottom to top. It means government acting responsibly to build a foundation of employment for its citizens most in need.

Yes, American industry has made great strides toward inclusion. But it still has a way to go to get it right. America has not yet entered a "post-civil rights era." The headlines of last week and yesterday and today make it clear that African Americans and other people of color all too often still have to fight for the right to be treated in a non-discriminatory fashion. The patterns of exclusion and abuse of African-American workers persist. The backlog of tens of thousands of cases at the federal Equal Employment Opportunity Commission is proof that encouraging inclusion up front is more effective than hoping that overburdened enforcers can catch up to bigots after the fact.

That encouragement is what affirmative action offers: It is both a set of tools to remedy discrimination and a philosophy practiced by institutions determined not to revert to the days of tokenism and de facto segregation. And it is a necessary pathway to opportunity and economic and political power.

African Americans must pursue economic power—the endgame in a capitalist democracy like ours—with greater vigor. This is a civil rights challenge on par with the epic struggles of the past against segregation in public schools and public accommodations. It is so because African Americans and their allies must again, by their success and determination, compel the white majority to make the moral choice. For we are still struggling over the issue of inclusion, and that remains a moral issue—albeit one whose guise now is how to manage the rules of a healthy capitalist economy so that all Americans get the chance to play the game.

Individual self-sufficiency, as important as that is, cannot be the ultimate goal. No ethnic group can prosper by setting such modest limits on its

11

aspirations. Black folks must push past that and go for economic power.

We African Americans have part of the human "resource base" we need to take our people to an entirely new plateau of economic power. We have scores of management consultants, plant managers, product managers, salespeople and even a smattering of senior executives who've worked inside corporations in the core lines of businesses. We have more and more community organizations rebuilding the infra-structures of their neighborhoods by attracting increased private and public investments to their communities—refurbishing parks and resi-dential housing, building and managing shopping centers, creating ven-ture capital funds, brokering opportunities for black and Hispanic (or all non-white) entrepreneurs.

We have a deep pool of talented MBAs, attorneys and undergraduate business and marketing majors who—thanks to affirmative action—have been able to show they have the requisite skills and ambition to get ahead, not just in minority markets, but in mainstream markets, too. And we have a growing corps of micro-entrepreneurs, working in an economic sector where business savvy and a reputation for reliability and quality work are equally critical to success.

We have a long, challenging march ahead. But this is one that, given the dividends economic power pays, must be made.

The fact of the matter is that black-owned firms are much more like-ly to hire inner-city residents for the jobs they're qualified to train for and do. Economic power provides the resources for exercising the polit-ical clout at the local, state and national levels that is crucial to African Americans' success: For mobilizing our ballot power so that politicians who covet our vote don't take us for granted. For influencing national election outcomes, which, as we've learned the hard way of late, shape the composition of those federal courts that ultimately rule on issues close to home, like affirmative action and contract set-asides.

Economic power will also generate the increased wealth African Americans must amass to make black philanthropy an even more potent force for good. In recent years spectacular gifts by people of modest incomes—like Oseola McCarty and Matel "Matt" Dawson Jr.—have shown us that it is not only wealthy donors who can give gifts that have a huge impact. African Americans must consider new strategies that individuals, church groups, and community organizations can use to build a philanthropic fund and effectively distribute grants so that black-oriented organizations as well as those of the larger society benefit.

The foundation for the surge we must make toward economic power, of course, is rooted in giving our youth the education that will enable them to play by society's rules and prosper. We must make certain that today's minority youngsters, who'll constitute half of America's adults by 2050, are fully prepared to pull their weight tomorrow. Never before has their education—both in meeting present-day scholastic standards and in learning how to learn—been so important to our future. Many African-American children, from poor as well as middle-class and affluent families, do understand that. But too many others have not caught on. Even though we recognize that many of them face the most daunting obstacles to success, we simply cannot accept using the existence of those obstacles to excuse their failure—nor the inaction of the adults who bear the responsibility for their guidance.

Unless more African-American youth get the message that learning is important, their chances of earning the income that will enable them to construct productive lives for themselves will range from slim to none. And that will augur a very dim economic and social future for African Americans. We need to invest in producing more of the human capital that will capture the economic capital we need to be strong. This issue of *The State of Black America* identifies clearly what that investment will require to get our schools and our youngsters on track—recommendations that are reinforced by the impressive results in mathematics the innovative EQUITY 2000 program has already achieved with thousands of youngsters across the country.

Given our robust economy and the confidence with which Americans at almost all income levels are rushing to invest in it, the prescriptions for future success our authors delineate can be met. Indeed, the unprecedented spread of prosperity to larger numbers of Americans than ever before—and their reinvestment of some of these gains into the economy—show what will happen once America distributes opportunity even more. We've got a lot of work to do. But we do know what that work entails.

Let's get started.

The Racial Asset Gap*

Melvin L. Oliver and
Thomas M. Shapiro

THE AFRICAN-AMERICAN COMMUNITY AND THE MEANING OF ASSETS

At the dawn of the 21st century, the African-American community harvests a mixed legacy of progress and despair. On the one hand, we celebrate a growing and increasingly prosperous black middle class, while on the other hand, we lament the increasing persistence of a small but consequential underclass. These depictions are based in part on indicators like income, job status, and behaviors (e.g., marital status, fertility, crime, etc.). Considering racial inequality and the meaning of African-American economic status through these prisms provides an incomplete and often inaccurate picture. *Black Wealth/White Wealth* (Oliver and Shapiro, 1995) developed a perspective on racial inequality that is based on the analysis of private wealth. A change in focus from income to wealth shifts our perspective on racial inequality and the economic position of African Americans as they face a new century—by revealing deep patterns of racial imbalance not visible when viewed only through the lens of income.

The basis of our perspective is the analytical distinction between wealth and other traditional measures of economic status and of how people are "making it" in America (for example, income, occupation, and education). Assets are a particularly important indicator of individual and family access to life's chances. Income refers to a flow of money over time; wealth is a stock of assets owned at a particular time. In other words, wealth is what people own, while income is what people receive for work, or from a retirement pension, or from social welfare.

Wealth signifies the command over financial resources that a family has accumulated over its lifetime, along with those resources that have been inherited across generations. Such resources, when combined with income, can create the opportunity to secure the "good life" in whatever form desired—education, business, training, justice, health, home, comfort, and so on. Unlike income—which most families use for food, clothing, and shelter—assets are used more often to create opportunities, secure a desired stature and standard of living, or pass class status along to one's children. Wealth taps not only contemporary resources but material assets that have historic origins. Private wealth thus perpetuates inequality that is the product of the past. Viewing racial inequality through the lens of wealth, then, revolutionizes our conception of its nature and magnitude. A focus on wealth sheds light on the historical and the contemporary impacts of not only race but class.

Increasingly, as government support for the poor and disadvantaged are withdrawn, African Americans will have to depend more on their stored assets to provide educational opportunities for their children, shelter for their families, retraining for work in an international economy, and access to medical care. True economic status cannot be gauged without a focus on assets. Measured from this standard, the African-American community has far to go and is still hampered by the combined effects of a racially biased past, persistent racial bias today, and the class bias that promotes asset accumulation by the well-off at the expense of the poor.

THE GREAT RACIAL WEALTH DIVIDE

African Americans have not shared equally in the nation's prosperity. They earn less than whites, and they possess far less wealth. Table 1 [all tables and figures referred to here begin on p. 34 ; the editors] presents data on income along with median wealth figures. The black-to-white median income ratio has hovered in the mid-50 to mid-60 percentage range for the past 20 years or so. Fluctuations have been relatively minor, measured in tenths of a percent. In many ways, American society became accustomed to this benchmark of inequality. In 1988, results from a large survey of American households, The Survey on Income and Program

Participation (SIPP), showed that for every dollar earned by white households, black households earned 62 cents.

A new perspective starts to emerge when wealth is examined. The wealth data expose far deeper inequalities. Whites possess nearly 12 times as much median net worth (all assets minus liabilities) as blacks—$43,800 versus $3,700. In even starker contrast, perhaps, the average white household controls $6,999 in net financial assets (not including homes and vehicles) while the average black household retains no nest egg whatsoever.

The 1988 ratio of black-to-white median household income reached 0.62, but the median net-worth ratio stood at 0.08. Moreover, a comparison of net financial assets shows the enormity of blacks' wealth disadvantage—white households possess nearly 10 times as much mean NFA as black households. Half of all white households have at least $6,999 in an NFA nest egg, whereas nearly two-thirds of all black households have zero or negative NFA.

Of course these are averages; many whites as well as blacks command larger wealth portfolios than these figures suggest. And just as many control fewer resources. However, the asset deprivation to which blacks are subject, both absolutely and in relation to whites, reverberates throughout their economic circumstances. Let's look at the numbers to see what assets, and lack of them, mean in the lives of black families.

One family—Eva and Clarence Dobbs and their three children—now live in a neat, two-story craftsman home in the working-class area of South Central Los Angeles known as the Crenshaw District. The Dobbs are a perfect example of a family "struggling" and "surviving." Both adults, full-time workers, together earn close to $50,000 annually, but are asset-poor and, in fact, live in the shadow of debt. Clarence, an occupational therapist, works with stroke patients at a number of hospitals. His work is not steady and doesn't pay much. Eva is a personnel assistant in a Fortune 500 company. While she has been on a career ladder and done well, the corporation is in the midst of outsourcing its personnel functions, and her job may last for only a couple more years.

The Dobbs' lives are organized around church and children. The kids

17

go to a private Christian school to "protect them from the streets" and to give them the kind of education that will "teach their souls as well as their minds." For Eva, the $3,000 tuition fee is high but not excessive "if you think about clothes they would need in public school."

Their rented home is sparsely furnished. They have two cars, which they need to get around in a city whose public transportation is notoriously inadequate. Eva and Clarence are very proud of their oldest son, who has received a scholarship from a private university in the Midwest, although they are somewhat concerned about finding the money to help him out. But this is a family that will survive.

In their everyday struggle to make ends meet, there is little left over to save. In fact, Eva and Clarence have no savings account. They once had about $1,500 in savings, but withdrawals for "emergencies" and "nickel and dime" things soon depleted these reserves. Their most fervent hope is to save enough to purchase a home. The housing market in Los Angeles, however, plays havoc with that desire. A median-priced home costs $220,000, and the $44,000 down payment seems way beyond their reach. Furthermore, years of struggle have left a trail of bad credit reports that will hurt their chances of qualifying for a home loan.

What few assets they have are in Eva's 401(k) account at her company. For the past two years, Eva has been regularly making deposits—half of which are matched by company contributions. She now has about $4,000 in this account. The high tax penalties for early withdrawal have prevented the Dobbs' from drawing on these assets in their battle to survive.

Meanwhile, the Dobbs' have begun to attack their credit woes. A $2,500 loan from their credit union helped consolidate Eva's credit card debts. Unfortunately, Eva also owes $1,600 that she borrowed to help pay for her auto insurance ("which is usually about $1,400 for one car [the other car is not insured], because of the area I live in"), her state income taxes, and her son's college-related expenses. Because both Eva and Clarence come from very poor backgrounds and have no family assets to draw on, Eva's mother bought her car for $6,000, a sum that Eva is determined to repay. Thus, when the ledger is balanced, the Dobbs' have no assets and are, in fact, in debt.

The Dobbs' asset poverty is well represented in the data from SIPP. Henry Terrell reports (1971) in his *Wealth Accumulation of Black and White Families* that the average black family held $3,779 in mean net worth in 1967, a figure that by 1984 had risen to $19,736. In 1988 the average black family's net worth had increased to $23,818. Yet this impressive progress among blacks pales somewhat when matched with wealth gains among whites. The average white family's mean net worth in 1967 stood at $20,153 and rose to $76,297 in 1984. By 1988 it had increased to $95,667. Although there were impressive absolute gains for blacks between 1967 and 1984, the wealth divide widened by $40,000 during those years, and by 1988 it had reached a gaping $71,849.

Theories of wealth accumulation emphasize income as the pre-eminent factor in wealth differentials. Indeed our own work clearly shows that wealth accrues with increasing income. Since black households earn less than two-thirds as much as the average white household, it only makes sense to ask, to what extent can the gross wealth disparities that we have noted be explained by the well-known income inequality between whites and blacks? Examining blacks' and whites' wealth at similar income levels provides a clear and direct way to respond to this question. Standardizing for income permits us to test whether the black-white disparity in wealth holding emanates from income differences.

The data is very convincing in one simple respect: Differences in observed income levels are not nearly sufficient to explain the large racial wealth gap. The black-to-white wealth ratio comes closest to equality among prosperous households earning $50,000 or more. Even here where the wealth gap is narrowest, however, blacks possess barely one-half (0.52) the median net worth of their high-earning white counterparts. For net financial assets, the mean ratio ranges from 0.006 to 0.33. The highest earning black households possess 23 cents of median net financial assets for every dollar held by high-income white households. One startling comparison reveals that poverty-level whites control mean net financial assets nearly as great as the highest-earning blacks, $26,683 to $28,310. For those surviving at or below the poverty level, this data indicate quite clearly that poverty means one thing for whites and another for blacks.

The general conclusion to be drawn from these straightforward yet very revealing tabulations is that the long-term life prospects of black households are substantially poorer than those of whites in similar income brackets. This analysis of wealth leaves no doubt regarding the serious misrepresentation of economic disparity that occurs when one relies exclusively on income data. Blacks and whites with equal incomes possess very unequal shares of wealth. More so than income, wealth holding remains very sensitive to the historically "sedimenting effects" of race.

An examination of wealth concentration also compares the wealth distribution within black and white communities. When wealth "pies" are placed on the table, very few black households are served. Sixty-three percent of black households retain zero or negative net financial assets, in comparison with 28 percent of white households.

Although many researchers, led by William J. Wilson, who wrote *The Truly Disadvantaged*—correctly point to increasing economic differentiation as the reason for growing economic inequality in the black community, a comparison with white households provides a different perspective. In our analysis, $43,000 in net worth situates a household smack in the middle of the white community's wealth distribution; but a household with the same net worth in the black community ranks among the wealthiest one-fifth. Similarly, a small nest egg of $2,000 in net financial assets places a black household in the richest one-fifth of the black community, whereas the same amount puts a household only in the fortieth percentile among whites.

What accounts for these stark differences in the distribution and concentration of wealth between blacks and whites? Why is the wealth portfolio for blacks and whites of equal stature and accomplishment so drastically different? We address this question in three stages. The first stage investigates the extent to which human capital and sociological and labor-market factors explain the racial wealth disparity. Our analysis must address how much of the racial wealth difference can be explained by a multiple set of factors—education, income, occupation, and so on—working together. We want to determine how much of the existing wealth gap between blacks and whites is related to the fact that blacks do not share the same social and demographic characteristics as whites and how much can best be explained by race itself.

The second stage brings institutional and policy discrimination from the public and private spheres into the analysis. This section focuses on one institutional and policy arena—the mechanisms surrounding home ownership, most notably, housing and mortgage markets. Home ownership is a crucial social area for several reasons. In many ways, owning a home represents the sine qua non of the American Dream. Yet racial segregation still characterizes neighborhoods and housing patterns in America. The effects of racial residential segregation go far beyond the mere restriction of blacks (and other minorities) to central-city ghettos and a few isolated communities elsewhere in the metropolitan area. Racial segregation also denies African Americans and minorities access to jobs and high-quality schools, consigning these groups to socially and often spatially isolated inner-city ghettos. For most Americans, excluding the very rich and the very poor, home equity represents the only major repository of accrued wealth. This section explores the ways in which the denial of access to mortgage and housing markets on equal terms severely constrains blacks' ability to accumulate assets.

The third stage adds a historical dimension to our analysis. By examining the intergenerational transmission of inequality we are able to empirically document how an oppressive racial legacy continues to shape American society through the reproduction of inequality, generation after generation.

GENERATING CONTEMPORARY INEQUALITY

Individual factors like income, education, occupation, family status, and age affect racial wealth differences. A regression analysis allows a more complete understanding of the impact of a multiple set of variables, enabling us to isolate those factors having the most influence on changes in wealth, while simultaneously controlling for the effects of all others. For example, regression can examine the effect of education on wealth while simultaneously holding all other important variables constant. [1]

The regression results vividly show the continuing importance of race in the wealth accumulation process. To make our findings even more graphic, we can "decompose" the results of our analysis; that is, we can take the regression results for whites and blacks and insert the characteristics of whites (e.g., mean income) into the black wealth equation. This procedure assures that blacks and whites have the same level of human capital and other factors. By recomputing the black results using white levels of income, education, occupation, and so forth, we can arrive at a hypothetical level of black wealth and compare it with the actual white one. Wealth differences will no longer relate to any disparities in the wealth-associated characteristics of whites and blacks, but to the way these characteristics contribute to wealth differently for blacks and whites; in other words, they will reveal "the costs of being black."

Figure 1 illustrates the results of our decomposition for the entire sample. As is clear, if blacks were more like whites with regard to the pertinent variables, then income parity would be close at hand. The average (mean) racial income difference would be reduced from $11,691 to $5,869. This robust reduction in income inequality is not repeated for wealth. A potent $43,143 difference in net worth remains, even when blacks and whites have had the same human capital and demographic characteristics. Nearly three-quarters (71 percent) of the difference is left unexplained. A little over three-quarters of the difference in net financial assets is also unaccounted for. Taking the average black household and endowing it with the same income, age, occupational, educational, and other attributes as the average white household still leaves a $25,794 racial gap. Clearly, something other than human capital and identifiably important social characteristics is at work here. We cannot help but conclude that factors related to race are central to the racial wealth gap, and that something like a racial wealth tax is at work.

The sharp critic could easily respond to these results, however, by pointing out that we have not included in our analysis a central factor that may very well account for a great deal of the unexplained variance:, namely, marital status. The furor over marital status in relation to the economic condition of black America rages daily. Poor economic fortunes of black families are consistently linked, in both popular and scholarly discussions, to the disproportionate share of black female-headed households. If black households are poor, it is because they are headed by single women who have not made the necessary human capital investments and who have not been active earning members of the labor force. To demonstrate the relevance of these ideas for wealth, we conducted similar decomposition analyses for black and white married and single households. If married blacks shared income, educational, family, occupational, regional, and work experience characteristics with whites, they would still confront a deficit of $46,294 in net worth and $27,160 in net financial assets. If white and black single heads of households were to share the same characteristics, blacks would find themselves at a $32,265 net worth disadvantage, and their NFA shortfall would amount to about $20,681. Thus, even when we examine racial differences as a function of marital status, huge wealth gaps persist.

Since contemporary social, locational, demographic, and economic factors fail to explain the vast disparities in wealth between blacks and whites, the other two stages therefore need to be layered into our analysis.

INSTITUTIONAL AND POLICY FACTORS GENERATING WEALTH INEQUALITY

HOUSING

Federal housing, tax, and transportation policies once effectively reinforced residential segregation. These flagrant official policies ceased in the late 1960s, yet an extremely high degree of segregation persists in America's residential communities today. In *American Apartheid* (1993), Douglas Massey and Nancy Denton report just how segregated American neighborhoods are: to desegregate housing entirely, 78 percent of blacks in Northern cities and 67 percent of blacks in Southern cities would have to move to new neighborhoods. Although there are more blacks in suburbia, no significant desegregation of the suburbs has taken place. By 1993, 86 percent of suburban whites still lived in places in which blacks represented less than 1 percent of householders. Continuing segregation is not a choice blacks freely make; rather, it is a social condition that results from racial steering, redlining, hostile white attitudes, and lender discrimination.

How does this enduring residential seclusion affect the buildup of housing wealth among blacks? Our discussion will emphasize three key

23

points at which institutional and policy discrimination often intervene to restrict blacks' access to housing and to inhibit the accumulation of housing wealth. First, access to credit is important, because whom banks deem to be credit worthy and whom they reject may delineate a crucial moment of institutional racial bias affecting access to home mortgages. We need to link the results of discriminatory processes in housing and mortgage markets to how racial wealth differences are generated. The second area of potential discrimination concerns the interest rates of loans for approved home buyers. Any significant institutional bias in mortgage-lending practices and rates carries serious implications regarding who has access to the American Dream and the cost of that dream. Third, as is well known, housing values rose steeply during the 1970s and early '80s, far outstripping inflation and creating a large pool of assets for those owning homes. Did all homeowners share equally in appreciating housing values, or is housing inflation color-coded?

MORTGAGE LOAN REJECTION RATES

In 1990 and 1991, according to Federal Reserve Bank studies, black and Hispanic applicants were denied mortgage loans two to three times more often than whites in some cities. Banks turned down high-income minorities more often than low-income whites. The publication of this information helped trigger a renewed and spirited debate on whether discrimination occurs in the home-mortgage market. Community activists, pointing to these discrepant denial rates as prima facie evidence of discrimination by banks, urged immediate redress. Bankers insisted that none of their lending practices could be considered discriminatory, claiming that the studies did not take into account information on creditworthiness, credit histories, loan-to-value ratios, and other financial factors.

The Federal Reserve Bank of Boston augmenting previous Federal Reserve reports, gathered information on 38 other factors that possibly accounted for the racial gap in mortgage denial rates (*Mummell, et al,* 1993). Taking bankers' objections seriously, the study specifically analyzed the previously unexamined area of creditworthiness. The study showed on average that minority applicants, did indeed have greater debt burdens and weaker credit histories, and that they were less likely to buy single-family homes than white applicants. These negatives accounted for a large portion of the difference in denial rates, reducing the disparity between minority and white rejections from the originally reported 2.7-1 ratio to roughly 1.6-1. After controlling for financial, employment, and neighborhood characteristics, the report found that black and Hispanic mortgage applicants were more likely to be turned down roughly 60 percent more often than similarly qualified whites. [2]

The Boston study offered some keen insights into how and why the large differences in mortgage rejections had come about. Loan officers were far more likely to overlook flaws in the credit records of white applicants—and to arrange creative financing for them—than they were in the case of black and Hispanic applicants. Everything else being equal, whites benefited from a general presumption of creditworthiness that black and Hispanic applicants did not, so that lenders were more willing to overlook flaws for white applicants than for minority applicants.

INTEREST RATE DIFFERENTIALS

Studies clearly demonstrate banks' discriminatory practices in approving home loans. The Federal Reserve system is now sending pointed messages to member banks, encouraging them to implement remedial programs. To this emerging picture we can now add information that suggests the existence of racial barriers to wealth accumulation, even for those able to obtain home mortgages. Using information from SIPP, we investigated the mortgage interest rates banks charge their white and black customers.

Table 2 displays tangible racial differences in mortgage rates that were uncovered by our survey. Overall, blacks pay a 0.54 percent higher rate on home mortgages than whites. A half-point discrepancy may not seem like much, but consider its long-term effects: a half-point difference on the median black home mortgage of $35,000 adds up to $3,951 over the course of a 25-year loan. Thus, every black homeowner is deprived of nearly $4,000, money that potentially could have been invested in financial instruments earning interest and accruing further capital.

The interest-rate numbers for blacks tell a story, but not the whole story. We are not alleging that blacks or other minorities pay higher interest rates because of intentional, sweeping discrimination. Loan rates are announced, posted, and even advertised; loan officers do not raise rates when a minority borrower fills out a home loan application. Bankers speculate that variations in mortgage rates occur because customers purchase different loan "products," fixed- and variable-interest-rate loans, for example. Certainly not all customers go into a bank knowing the entire array of available loan products, and not all leave with the same information.

As for whites, they may be purchasing variable-rate loans, refinancing, or making larger down payments more often than blacks. Also, whites are in a position more often than blacks, to use their assets to secure loans at lower interest rates by paying higher "points" on their mortgages.

Many bankers suggested that young white couples, are more likely than blacks, to receive parental help in buying a first house. Given the superior financial position of middle-aged and older whites, it is not surprising that the parents of young white couples are more apt to be in a position to help. The likelihood of similar parental assistance for young blacks is minimal.

This finding is substantiated by our interviews. Parental assistance often comes in the form of gifts, interest-free loans, or loans that are never paid back to help with down payments and closing costs or to help reduce the interest rate by enabling young buyers to pay higher points on their loans. Preliminary findings from the "Los Angeles Survey of Urban Inequality" indicate that white home buyers are twice as likely as blacks to receive family assistance in purchasing a home.

This form of intergenerational wealth transfer, we believe, is crucial to any explanation of racial mortgage—rate differences. Families who have few assets and cannot call on parental assistance probably pay higher interest rates. While the role of white parents in their children's purchase of a home somewhat moderates the notion of intentional institutional discrimination by bankers, black mortgage holders still end up paying more.

The discriminatory process may have come full circle. Because assets are a component of creditworthiness, banks regularly either refuse loans to blacks with financial profiles similar to those of whites or write higher interest-rate mortgages for them. As a result, blacks tend to accumulate assets at a lower rate than whites.

Home equity is more important in black wealth portfolios than it is for whites: it constitutes 63 percent of all assets held by blacks. Thus biases in mortgage markets clearly and severely depress the total assets in the black community.

Institutional practices, it appears from our research, exact a very heavy toll on the asset accumulation process in the black community. We projected the penalty blacks will pay for mortgage rate discrimination through the year 2011. In stark terms, the half-point penalty that blacks regularly pay currently adds up to $10.5 billion in extra payments banks receive from black borrowers. Using the costs paid by current black homeowners, we project that the "price of being black" will be about $21.5 billion for the next generation of black homeowners.

RACIAL INEQUITY IN RISING HOUSING VALUES

Racial differences in housing values have not come under the same scrutiny as home-ownership rates or home-mortgage practices. Federal government actions principally financed and encouraged suburbanization and residential segregation after World War II. Taxation, transportation, and housing policies promoted suburban growth. Discriminatory policies locked blacks out of the greatest mass-based opportunity for home ownership and wealth accumulation in American history.

How does residential segregation affect the value and appreciation of homes? In general, homes of similar design, size, and appearance cost more in white communities than in black or integrated communities. Their value also rises more quickly and steeply in white communities. In theory, then, whites pay a premium to live in homogeneous neighborhoods, but their property appreciates at an enhanced rate. While this may mean that blacks find relative housing "bargains" in segregated communities, their property does not appreciate as much. We have already seen that blacks do not have the same access to mortgages as whites and that those approved for home mortgages pay higher interest rates. We shall

27

now consider how these disadvantages are compounded by racial differences in housing appreciation.

Among those with mortgages, the mean value of the average white home increased $53,000 compared with $31,100 for black homes, from 1967 through 1988.[3] This $21,900 difference is a compelling index of bias in housing markets that costs blacks dearly. It accounts for one-third of the racial net worth difference among all homeowners with mortgages. [4]

Inflation and speculation in housing markets benefited all homeowners, but not all of them equally. Whether or not discrimination is intended, the racial housing-appreciation gap represents part of the price of being black in America. When housing prices tripled in the 1970s, white homeowners who had been able to take advantage of discriminatory Federal Housing Authority financing policies received vastly increased equity in their homes, while those excluded by the same policies found themselves facing higher costs of entry into the market. Gregory Squires points out, moreover, in *Capital and Communities in Black and White* (1994), that the depressed value of their homes also adversely affects the ability of blacks to obtain home equity loans or loans for business start-ups or education. The harm of residential segregation goes far beyond financial punishment: restricting blacks to inner-city ghettoes and a few isolated metropolitan pockets also denies them information about and access to jobs and better-quality school systems. Indeed, several studies demonstrate that when businesses, plants, and factories relocate or expand, they move away from metropolitan centers and locate in suburban growth zones. This tendency creates a spatial mismatch between where the jobs are and where most minorities live.

This section on institutional and policy discrimination in housing supplies a rough method of tabulating the projected costs of being black in the housing market, as shown in Figure 2.[5] Discrimination in housing markets costs the current generation of blacks about $82 billion. If these biases continue unabated, they will cost the next generation of black homeowners $93 billion. On the basis of our logic, one could take the $93 billion figure as the minimal target of public and private initiatives to help create housing assets in the black community.

We argue in *Black Wealth/White Wealth* that a plethora of state policies from slavery through the mid-20th century blocked and crippled the ability of blacks to gain a foothold in American society. Owing to their severely restricted ability to accumulate wealth, combined with massive discrimination in the private sector and general white hostility, black parents over several generations were unable to pass any appreciable assets on to their kin. We now turn to a closer examination of this process and its legacy for current racial inequality.

INHERITANCE AND RACE

Thus far, our presentation has focused on contemporary aspects of inequality. To the explanation of racial wealth differences already elaborated, we can now contribute tangible evidence suggesting the degree to which inequality is transmitted from one generation to another. We note that the baby-boom generation will inherit close to $7 trillion over the next 25 years, more than has ever been received by earlier generations.

However important they are in the lives of white Americans, and however much money they involve, inheritances are not likely to concern many African Americans. The historical reasons for this state of affairs are crystal clear. Segregation blocked access to education, decent jobs, and livable wages among the grandparents and parents of blacks born before the late 1960s, effectively preventing them from building up much wealth. Until the late 1960s few older black Americans had accrued any savings to speak of, as they likely had working-class jobs. Without savings no wealth could be built up.

Inheritance takes many shapes and forms. In our interviews, people mentioned three kinds of material inheritances that had been or would be very important in determining their financial well-being. The first, which plays its role during a child's formative years, consists of his or her education, experiences, friendships, and contacts. Wealth used to enhance a child's "cultural capital" helps provide a good start in life and can lay a solid groundwork for financial success and independence later on. People often told us about the schooling, weeks at camp, after-school classes and sports, trips, and other experiences that they had enjoyed as kids and wanted to provide for their children. All parents pass along cultural capital to their off-

29

spring. Of the common enrichment that parents can provide, education is the most expensive, and it is where we found the most differences.

Black parents used their financial resources to provide broader educational experiences for their children than those available in public schools. For example, Camille, the owner and director of several preschools, had taught in public schools and knew the value of being able to offer a private-school education to her children. She realized that the advantages provided by private schooling are not only academic but social. While Carol has now fallen from middle-class status, she and her husband had managed to put all three of her children through Catholic school. And even the Dobbs, whose financial condition corresponds most closely to the average in our quantitative data, sacrifice to send their children to a private religious-affiliated school that reflects their beliefs. Their sacrifice has paid off, for their oldest son will be attending a university.

The second kind of inheritance, most often bestowed on young adults, involves milestone life events such as going to college, getting married, buying a first house, and beginning to raise a family. Many of the college graduates we interviewed did not pay their own expenses, especially among white respondents. While a free college education is not often thought of as part of one's inheritance, the difference between having it paid for and borrowing for it is the difference between starting a career with a clean slate or with a financial burden on one's shoulders.

Marriage and buying a first home are other milestones that often lead to wealth transfer. Our interviewees often mentioned getting cash as a wedding present, usually in the $1,000 to $5,000 range, to help them get a start in life. More important, though, is the wealth transferred when a couple buys a home. Other than death, a first-home purchase is the event that triggers the largest asset transfer between generations. Of the home-owning white families we interviewed, all received substantial assistance from their parents in the form of down-payment money. All of the black families we interviewed also had obtained their homes with their parents' help—help that was often quite meager.

Assets bequeathed at death are, of course, the third and most direct form of inheritance. Among the whites we interviewed, the largest sum came to more than $500,000. Among our white interviewees with living parents, most had an idea of what they would inherit. The smallest sum was expected to be $12,000 or probably more. Most anticipated inheritances of between $50,000 and $100,000.

Among black respondents we interviewed, only two expected large inheritances. Camille's parents will leave about $100,000 worth of assets for her and her children. Mary Ellen will inherit substantially more: the family business, valued at $500,000, and real estate investments approaching $2 million will be divided among Mary Ellen and her five siblings. Since she works for the family business, it is not something she thinks about often.

CLOSING THE ASSET GAP

The accumulation of assets has the potential to improve the well-being of disadvantaged families, to enable them to plan for their own social mobility and that of their children, and eventually to launch families out of poverty, thereby promoting, a more equitable society in the long run.

The political exhaustion of the welfare state places antipoverty efforts and social assistance at a crossroads. The time—indeed perhaps, the necessity—for new and bold policy directions is both pressing and opportune.

The concept of asset building as a mechanism for change centers on the proposition that families can escape poverty and achieve social mobility through savings and investment, not through spending and consuming which is characteristic of current welfare policies in the United States. While programs providing income for consumption are essential, programs for accumulating assets invest in the ability of families to become self-reliant and to support their communities by stimulating education, job mobility, home ownership, entrepreneurship, and equity.

The premises underlying asset building also suppose that wealth is not an end in itself; rather, the goal is to provide a host of other positive outcomes resulting from asset accumulation. Such outcomes include positive effects on personal well-being, the well-being of children, economic security, civic and community involvement, and the status of women . Current research (Page-Adams and Sherraden, 1996) indicates positive outcomes in all of these areas, as well as reduced domestic violence; greater house-

31

hold stability; improved long-term thinking and planning; greater development of human capital; a firmer foundation for risk taking; increased personal efficacy, social status, and influence; heightened community involvement and political participation; and greater investment in children's education. While these studies are not definitive, they suggest that the benefits of asset accumulation are very encouraging and promising.

Asset-based policy is not new in the United States. From the Homestead Acts and the Federal Housing Authority (FHA) to the GI Bill and current tax policies, an unappreciated part of America's prosperity is the story of government encouraging asset building. A compelling case can be made that federal policies for asset building greatly contributed to the development of a broad middle class in the United States. Over a century ago, the Homestead Acts helped up to 600,000 American families acquire enough land for homesteading to sustain themselves. The GI Bill made higher education accessible to 10 million Americans, and the Veterans Administration (VA) provided loans for homes and housing for 9.8 million.

Today, more than $200 billion is spent in federal expenditures (e.g., through incentives, institutional structures, and subsidies) to facilitate asset building by the non-poor. However, the hundreds of billions of dollars in asset building offered by the government generally have not been available to half of the nation, which is asset poor. As a nation, we encourage, structure, and subsidize asset acquisition for the non-poor, while actively discouraging the poor from building similar resources.

This direction for policy in the United States views asset building among the non-poor as a success story of economic progress. This success story is one significant reason to devote serious consideration to asset building among the poor and the near poor. It is now both possible and desirable to create new asset-building policies that-unlike the past and present policies—do not discriminate against minorities and the poor. In particular, assets used for improving of human capital (e.g., education), home ownership, and business development have the potential to facilitate social mobility.

One such instrument, Individual Development Accounts (IDAs), has been suggested as a policy initiative that may help promote asset accumulation among low-income and other disadvantaged groups, thus disproportionately benefiting African Americans (Sherraden, 1991). IDAs are dedicated savings accounts, similar in structure to Individual Retirement Accounts (IRAs), that can only be used for purchasing a first home, paying education or job-training expenses, or capitalizing a small business. Contributions for low-income participants are matched, using both private and public sources. Fully funded by the federal government, the program would provide for the first time opportunities for the income and asset poor to accumulate wealth. While these accounts would generate modest levels of assets, only a few assets are necessary to help stabilize families and communities. Even a few thousand dollars can make a big difference:

- The average down payment on a house purchased by low- and moderate- income families is less than $3,000.
- The average annual tuition at a community college is less than $1,200.
- Half of all businesses in the United States are started with less than $5,000.

Small savings, then, can generate big changes in the lives of many Americans. We should consider very seriously the mechanisms and policies that have worked for poor and near-poor people in the past so that we can craft the policies that will work effectively in the future. To do less may consign African Americans to remain at the economic margins of American life well into the next millennium.

THE COST OF BEING BLACK

Percentage not explained by differences between similar white and black households.

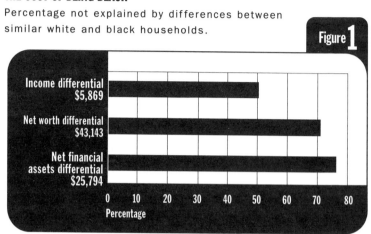

Source: SIPP, 1987 Panel, Wave 4

THE PRICE OF BEING BLACK IN HOUSING AND MORTGAGE MARKETS

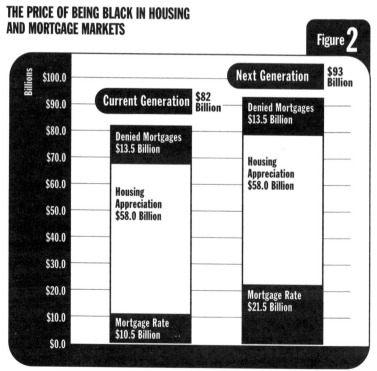

Source: SIPP, 1987 Panel, Wave 4

34

REFERENCES

Cose, Ellis. 1993. *The Rage of the Privileged Class.* New York: HarperCollins.

Massey, Douglas S. and Nancy A. Denton. 1993. *American Apartheid: Segregation and the Making of the Underclass.* Cambridge: Harvard University Press.

Munnell, Alicia H., Lynn E. Browne, James McEneaney, and Geoffrey M.B. Tootel. 1993. "Mortgage Lending in Boston: Interpreting HMDA Data." *Boston: Federal Reserve* Bank of Boston.

Oliver, Melvin L. and Thomas M. Shapiro. 1995. *Black Wealth/White Wealth: A New Perspective on Racial Inequality.* New York: Routledge.

Sherraden, Michael. 1991. *Assets and the Poor: A New American Welfare Policy.* Armonk, New York: M.E. Sharpe.

Squires, Gregory D. 1994. *Capital and Communities in Black and White.* Albany: State University of New York Press.

Terrell, Henry S. 1971. "Wealth Accumulation of Black and White Families: The Empirical Evidence." *Journal of Finance* 26: 363:-77.

NOTES

[1] The interested reader will find the complete set of variables and the full regression equations in *Black Wealth/White Wealth* (Oliver and Shapiro, 1995). They are omitted here for space considerations.

[2] The actual denial rate for minorities was 28 percent, but the Federal Reserve analysis indicates that the denial rate for minority applicants would have been 20 percent if the race of the applicant had not been a factor.

[3] A Home's current market value minus its purchase price provides a rough estimate of the degree to which its value has risen or fallen. We use the amount of a house's first mortgage as a proxy for its purchase price.

[4] To refine our understanding of the housing-appreciation gap, we need to take into account the major factors that influence a home's increased valuation, namely, purchase price and date of purchase. A reliable comparison of black and white housing-appreciation

rates therefore must include several checks to ensure comparability with regard to these factors. We have thus examined homes purchased during two broad time periods, those bought between 1967 and 1977 and those bought between 1978 and 1988. These periods were chosen to highlight the importance of housing inflation, which took off in the late 1970s and kept rising through the 1980s. Within these two periods we used median mortgage figures to distinguish more expensive homes (above the median) from less expensive (below the median) ones.

[5] Among the current generation of black homeowners, to the $10.5 billion paid to banks in extra interest, one must add another $58 billion in lost home equity. Finally, if black home mortgage approval rates were the same as those of similarly qualified whites, 8 percent of the blacks who are annually denied mortgages would be homeowners today. Hence, approximately 14,200 more blacks per year would own homes (8 percent of 177,501 applications in 1992). Thus projecting current institutional bias in residential lending over a twenty-five-year period denies 355,000 qualified blacks home ownership and the opportunity of equity accumulation. Those 355,000 black homeowners would then receive $38,000 in increased home value, a figure that represents the median white housing-appreciation rate, thus acquiring another $13.5 billion.

*The opinions expressed in this article are solely those of the authors and are not the official policies of the Ford Foundation or the universities with which the authors are affiliated.

Building Community

By   L i s b e t h   B .   S c h o r r

Not long before he was killed, Robert F. Kennedy called attention to the destruction of "the thousand invisible strands of common experience and purpose, affection and respect, which tie men to their fellows." He believed that the world beyond the neighborhood had become "impersonal and abstract ... beyond the reach of individual control or even understanding." In his 1968 campaign for the Democratic presidential nomination, he called for the restoration of community as "a place where people can see and know each other, where children can play and adults work together and join in the pleasures and responsibilities of the place where they live."

The loss of community, like most contemporary ills, has hit the poor and persons of color the hardest. The decline of manufacturing, the disappearance of well-paid jobs for the unskilled, racial discrimination in both hiring and housing, and the decreasing value of income supports. The inferior and overwhelmed schools and public services, the flight of the middle class to the suburbs, the easy availability of crack and the crack trade—all have combined to form the inner-city deserts, inhospitable to healthy human development.

But in the last few years, new neighborhood transformation projects emerging in cities around the country, with support from public and philanthropic funds, are rekindling long-dormant hope. These projects may also contain clues to reversing the decline of America's inner cities. These initiatives recognize that no single strand of intervention can produce significant results for populations in high-risk circumstances. They represent the determination of citizens from all walks of life to overcome enormous obstacles to make their neighborhoods into decent places to live and bring up children. They are grounded in a new synthesis that rejects addressing poverty, welfare, employment, education, child development, housing, and crime problems one at a time. The new synthesis posits that the multiple and inter-related problems of poor neighborhoods require multiple and inter-related solutions. It insists on combining physical and economic development with service and education reform, and blends all of these with a commitment to building community institutions and social networks.

Not all of the community initiatives that label themselves as comprehensive neighborhood transformation efforts have been able to implement the ambitious agenda that the new synthesis implies, but, as we will see, the new synthesis is the belief system on which most of the new generation of initiatives is being built.

While there has been a lot of trial and error, a lot of groping in the dark, and much unjustified optimism about how much can be accomplished with severely constrained resources in very little time, a great deal of useful experience is being accumulated that justifies the hope that many attach to the new initiatives.

Two neighborhood change efforts, one in the South Bronx and one in Savannah, Georgia, will serve to illustrate the current surge of community rebuilding.

CCRP, VENTURE CAPITAL, AND THE SOUTH BRONX

Since the 1950s, the South Bronx's claim to fame has been its devastation.

The Bronx had been a fine place to live, with the access it provided to good jobs in Manhattan, until after World War II. Then industries, in search of workers willing to work for lower wages, started to leave. Thousands of job seekers from the rural South and the Caribbean arrived in the 1950s and 1960s, just as the jobs were going the other way.

As drugs, crime, and violence took over in the 1960s and early 1970s, the residents of the Bronx who had a choice, left. So did landlords, banks and insurance companies. That was when the South Bronx really became famous. The New York Times called it "the nation's most infamous symbol of urban blight ... a bombed out relic and a synonym for hopelessness and decay." It became the premier symbol of all that had gone wrong in America's inner cities.

Then came the South Bronx miracle.

"In a city full of surprises, few are as striking as the contrast between the 20-year-old image of the burned out South Bronx, and the reality after what officials call the nation's largest urban rebuilding effort," wrote the New York Times in its news columns. "Take a Sunday drive," the Times editorialized, "and you will be surprised to see that the burned-out Bronx is largely gone."

Burnt out buildings have been replaced by apartment houses with curtains on the windows. And—on the spring day when I was visiting—parents were pushing baby carriages and children were playing on the sidewalks. There are streets with new two-story houses with lawns and gardens and window boxes filled with flowers.

Joe Santiago, a heating and air-conditioning engineer, grows pears, peaches and apples in his backyard. "It's like a piece of the country inside the city," he says.

"The kids love it. They can play in the yard, and I don't have to worry," says Alexandra Immanuel, a nurse who came to New York from St. Lucia as a teen-ager. "The neighbors are good," she says, "everybody looks out for each other here."

The resurrection of the South Bronx has been going on since 1986. Abandoned buildings are rare, and 19,000 apartments have been rehabilitated. More than 2,500 new houses have been built for working-class home buyers, and 2,000 more are under construction.

The heroes of this story, editorialized *The New York Times* in 1995, are "the not-for-profit community development corporations that build and rehabilitate the buildings and who counsel the first-time home buyers who make up just about all of the new owners." Most of the construction was performed not by conventional for-profit developers but by the community development corporations (CDCs) described earlier. Supported by sophisticated national intermediary organizations and aided in recent years by federal tax credits for low-income housing, several CDCs became a particularly potent force in the South Bronx.

But the housing revival was not, initially, matched in other spheres. The public schools were still as bad as they ever were; one-third of adults didn't have a high school degree; one-quarter couldn't read at a fourth-grade level; one half had no history of labor-force participation; and crime was rampant.

If there was one person in New York who was in a position to recognize the paradox of a miraculous physical renaissance occurring in the midst of woefully inadequate human supports, it was Anita Miller.

A one-time banker (she had been CEO of a New Jersey Savings Bank and Acting Chairman of the Federal Home Loan Bank Board in the Carter Administration), Miller had been intimately involved with South Bronx CDCs as a program officer at the Ford Foundation and later as program director at the Local Initiatives Support Corporation. Well-connected to all the relevant people and institutions in both the public and private sectors, Anita Miller not only recognized the paradox, but was bursting to do something about it.

The opportunity came from Edward Skloot, executive director of the New York-based Surdna Foundation. Surdna had been supporting a lot of community development, and Skloot had been wanting to explore a broadened conception of community revitalization. Miller and Skloot together began to puzzle out how Surdna and other foundations might be able to help CDCs to build on their successes, and to move beyond housing to become effective agents for comprehensive revitalization of their neighborhoods. Early in 1991, Skloot asked Miller to do a feasibility study.

Miller not only recognized the opportunity and the need, she also recognized the difficulty. She and Skloot were convinced you had to start with a solid base in the community, and that the CDCs could provide that in a way that no other entity could. CDCs that had run large-scale housing programs had the community ties and the experience that gave them credibility in the neighborhood. And that put them in a unique position to take on a far-reaching revitalization strategy.

But Miller also thought very carefully about what supports these CDCs would need to enable them to take on the broader agenda when there were no readily available sources of flexible money with which to attract and knit together many categorical and hard-to-use programs. She also knew that it would be difficult, if not impossible, for each CDC, operating in isolation, "to create a program with sufficient substance to satisfy funders at the same time leaving participants with sufficient latitude to design their own efforts."

In accordance with this line of thinking, the Surdna Foundation, together with other funders, launched the Comprehensive Community Revitalization Program (CCRP) to help selected CDCs develop their capacity to take on a substantially expanded role and to act as an intermediary—and to make up for the defects in the existing arrangements—to provide funding, technical assistance, time, and expertise.

Anita Miller and colleagues agreed that the key to achieving an ambitious community agenda was to provide socially entrepreneurial organizations that were well-rooted in their communities with a source of what was essentially venture capital. Through CCRP, the South Bronx CDCs would have ready access to funds that could be used flexibly and quickly to leverage additional funds and to support the core activities that were so difficult to fund from other sources. Through CCRP, the South Bronx CDCs could choose from a wider selection of experts, and good ideas, and best practices than they could identify on their own.

By 1996, a total of 12 foundations and two banks had contributed more than $8 million to support the initiatives with flexible money.

In choosing its CDC partners, CCRP decided to "start with the strong and make them stronger." The partnership began in 1992, with teams of residents, local agencies and business interests coming together to plan the physical space in their neighborhoods. No one else was doing this kind of planning. The city was filling every open space with housing projects, and no one else was making sure that vital neighborhoods would emerge from the ashes of the South Bronx. It also seemed important to engage people who lived and worked in the CCRP neighborhoods in a concrete task that required real, big decisions, rather than trying to work out a collaborative process in the abstract. These activities were also an opportunity to establish a precedent in how residents and CDCs could work together with local government and outside experts.

Through months of intensive planning and outreach, CDC-led groups considered where parks, playgrounds, and health- and child-care facilities should be located, what kind of housing should be built on remaining vacant sites; what stores and banking services would be needed; and how physical improvement and resident-police collaboration could deter crime. In involving professional urban planners, Miller made sure that the experts saw themselves—and were seen by the neighborhood people as expert helpers, not as the people who would be calling the shots.

Participating CDCs have attracted more than $3 million—largely in public monies—for 12 different projects to rehabilitate old parks and playgrounds and to create new ones. Vacant lots have been turned into community gardens and residents have removed tons of debris and cleaned up sections of the Bronx River. Three more open-space projects are receiving over $600,000 in grants and technical assistance from the Federal Urban Resources Partnership Program. With start-up money from CCRP, the CDCs were able to begin work on supermarkets and shopping centers expected to bring jobs into the community and significantly improve access to affordable goods for area residents.

The CDCs continued to move beyond their traditional roles to bring disparate elements of their communities together to identify and address common needs. Through CCRP-funded outreach workers, each CDC has expanded its community organizing efforts—spending more time talking and listening to local citizens, and engaging them both to plan and partic-ipate in new programs.

When public safety emerged as a major CDC concern, CCRP organized a workshop with law enforcement officials, and contracted with neigh-borhood security experts from the Citizens Committee for New York City to work with the CDCs. Today CDC staff, resident councils and tenant associations are collaborating with local police and the District Attorney's office to improve police accountability and communications, and to involve residents in strategies aimed at reducing crime and increasing their sense of security.

CCRP has helped the CDCs to build the kind of management capacity that enables them to make a series of separate programs and projects add up to more than the sum of their parts. A cadre of consultants based in established agencies—but committed to providing specialized assistance to CDCs on high-priority issues—help with job training and placement, recreation, and maintaining a sophisticated management information system.

Most recently, the South Bronx CDCs have been moving toward an ever-increasing focus on jobs. The Federated Employment Guidance Services (FEGS), a respected job training and mental health agency, is working with the CDCs to develop employment programs that take into account the many different kinds of supports that would be needed, including English-as-a-Second-Language training, GED classes, training social service personnel in employment-oriented and assessment skills, developing new models for the transition from welfare to work, and putting together a comprehensive online database listing 2,500 educational, vocational and job training/placement programs throughout New York City.

By creating neighborhood-based employment services within each CDC that can engage the hard-to-reach and help them to prepare for, acquire and retain suitable jobs; and by providing intensive post-placement support to newly employed residents, the CDCs have been able to fill yet one more void in their neighborhoods.

THE SAVANNAH YOUTH FUTURES AUTHORITY: A LONG JOURNEY WITHOUT A ROADMAP

The Savannah story begins as a tale of service integration. Ten years later, the story is far from ended, but now contains compelling evidence that the combination of service reforms with community building is proving to be very powerful.

Otis Johnson, founder and director of Youth Futures Authority, dates the beginning of the journey as October 8, 1986, when Savannah city manager, Don Mendonsa, spoke to an upper-middle-class Savannah church audience about the city's "invisible population." He proposed to make it visible. He told of the 35,000 citizens who live in Savannah's inner city, suffering from racial discrimination, from the indifference of the majority community, and from the lack of any community initiative to improve the quality of their lives. He reported that the predominantly African-American residents of the inner city are victims in 90 percent of the city's homicides, almost 90 percent of the rapes, and nearly 80 percent of the assaults. And he warned that unless the entire community worked together for fundamental change, "we must be prepared to accept and live with the injury that is done to the quality of our lives as a consequence of the conditions of their lives."

When Mendonsa took his message to the City Council three weeks later, it struck Council member Otis Johnson as welcome, if overdue. A professor of social work with a Ph.D. in social welfare from Brandeis University, and onetime organizer for the Savannah Model Cities and Community Action programs, Johnson had just been re-elected to his second term as alderman, and was intensely interested in stimulating action on Mendonsa's proposals. In discussions over the next several months, the two worried together about the difficulty of mobilizing community leaders on these issues. Not long after, as if in direct response to their concern, they each received from the mayor copies of a letter that had just come from the Annie E. Casey Foundation, inviting Savannah to become one of 10 cities to receive a planning grant to compete for a much larger sum as part of the foundation's New Futures initiative. They were particularly pleased because, in order to participate, Savannah would be required to make a high-level leadership commitment to make the fundamental changes necessary to improve outcomes for high-risk middle-school youth.

Mendonsa has since retired as city manager, but he and Johnson are still working together today. From the outset, they agreed that the Casey Foundations financial and other support aimed at making schools and service agencies more responsive to the needs of Savannah's at-risk youth could be put to excellent use in Savannah.

However, after two-and-a-half years of effort, very little seemed to be changing-for individual youngsters, for families, or among service agencies. Leaders of the initiative slowly became convinced that the problems they were trying to deal with didn't begin in middle school. If a significant proportion of black children is already two years behind in sixth grade, and if, each year, 90 black boys are suspended from school while they are still in first grade, surely any effective intervention would have to start much earlier—perhaps with prenatal care for the mother. And the object of intervention would have to be not just the individual child, but the whole family—and even the whole school.

These insights shifted the focus of the intervention, from efforts to remediate past failures to preventing youths from acquiring multiple risk factors. "Because of the difficulties we encountered, we had to keep evolving," explains Johnson. "The goal and the vision remain the same: improving outcomes for children and families. But to get there, we had to take on much more, which is how—even though we started by doing services reform—we evolved into a comprehensive community initiative."

They became convinced that "physical, economic, social, and human capital strategies had to be integrated," and that had to be done at the neighborhood level. The work was gradually achieving a much sharper focus, with a series of family resource centers as the physical manifestation of the community building concept. The first of these, the St. Pius X Family Resource Center, in an airy and inviting renovated one-time school building, opened on April 18, 1994. A multitude of services are located at the center, including health, mental health, nutrition, eligibility for income support, and the Uhuru family advocates. Just as important, the center is also home to a collection of activities that welcome participants from throughout the neighborhood, without their having to define a problem to participate. These include a soccer league, the Girl Scouts, Boys and Girls clubs, conflict resolution classes, information and referral services, and a day-care child development/Head Start center for infants, toddlers, and young preschool children. The hope is that the family resource center will become part of the everyday life of the neighborhood, and that it will be powerful enough to create a new culture in which workers feel their primary responsibility is to the community, not their agency.

The center takes seriously the role of clients themselves in defining their needs. It is governed largely by community representatives, most of whom are involved in other neighborhood activities, and have status in the community. Many see the center as evolving to become a cornerstone of the community, showcasing local talent, and sponsoring cultural programs such as African dance and arts.

A theme that runs increasingly through current YFA planning is an

Afrocentric emphasis on the integrity of the community, family, and individual. Community leaders contend that middle-American values of self-reliance, self-discipline, good work habits, healthy ambition—and the reinforcement of family and community ties—are made more accessible to the children and families of the neighborhood within an Afrocentric framework.

YFA leaders believe that if they can show that the existence of the Family Resource Center, with its reoriented and enhanced services and supports and its community-building activities, actually changes outcomes among its participants, then they could get the depth of support needed to change life outcomes among all children at risk in Savannah. If they could document a clear reduction in infant mortality or crime, in the number of new offenders, or in the disparities between black and white children's health or school readiness, they are convinced they could change Savannah.

Promising data are beginning to come in. Black infant mortality has dropped by nearly 45 percent since 1992. Births to black teens have dropped 12 percent. Foster care placements are down almost 25 percent over the last two years.

Why do Johnson and his colleagues believe that they will be able to expand their efforts once they have documented impressive outcomes, when so many wonderful interventions remain, at best, an oasis? That's where the power of the Young Futures Authority comes in, they say. Earlier models didn't have the structure of a ready-made public/private organization that could take what they had developed in the hothouse into the real world.

The Authority is so important, Johnson says, because the present structure doesn't work. He adds: "If the representatives on the school board from my community were doing what they were supposed to do, and were raising the issues that they should be raising, we wouldn't need a special school committee in my neighborhood. If the representatives on the City Council from my community were raising the zoning issues which would keep outsiders from doing whatever they want in Area C, we wouldn't need a special housing and zoning committee in that neighborhood. The structure that is in place, the legitimate structure, is the problem. Because it is not representing the interests of the people."

Johnson has also thought deeply about the mix of people that should constitute a governing entity like the Authority. "To improve life in these communities you can't have an either/or philosophy: it either has to be dominated by the people in the communities or by the power brokers connected to the government. Neighborhood people, because they've been disempowered, don't have the wherewithal to move a comprehensive social-change agenda by themselves, and need other stakeholders in government, in the business sector, and in the service sector as partners. There are too many outside factors impinging on neighborhoods for them to totally change their physical, social, and economic conditions by themselves, without enlisting significant other stakeholders."

Mendonsa concurs and adds that the other difficulty with existing governmental structures is that they are set up categorically, and not set up to accomplish common goals. "We have to figure out a better design, so that on issues of housing, public order, crime and economic development, government could deal with neighborhoods much more coherently."

If they succeed in changing lives in Savannah, and if they can prove that they had done so, would the nation have the capacity to do it everywhere? Johnson has thought about that, too. "If the will were there to make these [inner city] communities livable, then a lot of this discussion about capacity wouldn't be necessary. When the Russians sent up Sputnik, this country didn't have the capacity to match that feat. But the will was there. And the competition between Russia and the U.S. provided an opportunity to exert that will, and to agree on the expectation that in X number of years we will have a man on the moon. We built that capacity, and we did it. If this country ever develops the will, if we agree that we are not going to allow these conditions in any neighborhood, then I think we will build the capacity to do it."

EMPOWERMENT ZONES: A NEWCOMER WITH MOMENTOUS POTENTIAL

Deborah Wright, CEO of the Upper Manhattan Empowerment Zone, says that the federal Empowerment Zone initiative is a statement that inner cities matter to the future of this country.

Authorized by Congress in 1993, the Empowerment Zones (Ezs) are the government's most comprehensive effort in 30 years to rebuild areas

of persistent poverty. EZs are indeed remarkable, both for their symbol-
ism and their potential.

Significantly, the design of the federal program makes use of the
lessons of past experience. Cities are not told what to do, but asked what
they could and would do to revive their most distressed neighborhoods,
with a pledge of federal help in getting it done. The legislation foresees a
long-term (10-year) scope, legitimizes the neighborhood as a locus of
change, and mandates simultaneous investments in economic and human
development, community-building, and service reform. It encourages the
use of EZ funds to leverage money from other sources, and requires
involvement of community residents, businesses and local institutions—
a much broader array of participants than the initiatives of the War on
Poverty included. And it targets the bulk of its funds on just eight cities
and three rural areas.

In addition to tax benefits and tax credits, the staples of past efforts to
regenerate depressed areas, each of the distressed communities designated an Empowerment Zone is entitled to $100 million in social services
funds. (A designation as an Enterprise Community went to 60 urban and
33 rural communities, as a sort of consolation prize with fewer benefits.)
The designers of the legislation had learned from the past that communities would need help in making federal funding easier to use. They made
it possible for federal agencies to waive specific program requirements,
so that funds from different programs could be combined and reallocat-
ed. Communities were encouraged to identify bureaucratic impediments
to better program design and service delivery. To help local communities
negotiate their way through the maze of federal programs, President
Clinton created a high-level interagency structure, the Community
Empowerment Board (chaired by Vice President Al Gore, it includes the
heads of 17 federal agencies). States and local governments were encouraged to take analogous steps.

If this process achieves its promise, it will shatter precedent and enable
communities to use federal resources more coherently—and therefore
more effectively—than in the past. Policies of economic uplift for inner
city neighborhoods—from housing to business development, from public

safety to service reform—have traditionally been, according to former Philadelphia Councilman Ed Schwarz, "a bureaucratic nightmare." Getting the federal act together would go far toward making this initiative succeed where past efforts have failed.

Perhaps reflecting confidence that this could indeed happen, the Department of HUD designed an unusually promising approach to evaluation. The criteria for assessing success are based on the local vision for the community's transformation. But they also include "key dimensions of community transformation that are common to all sites, or that are so important to national objectives that they shall be documented consistently for all ... communities."

The communities that would receive EZ awards were chosen in December, 1994. Some encountered early snags, due primarily to disagreements about the composition and powers of governing boards. There were also some hopeful early signs. In October 1994, anticipating formal designation of the Harlem-South Bronx area as an EZ, Fleet Bank announced $70 million in low-interest loans for the area. Fleet Bank's James Murphy said, "Harlem's coming back, and the EZ deserves a lot of credit."

A month after the EZs were designated, urban affairs columnist Neal Pierce reported that the competition had "already sparked a wave of local partnerships and commitments that's worth many times any federal cash or tax benefit."

By early 1996, the private sector in Detroit had already pledged $2 billion to the EZ, including a $750 million investment from the Chrysler Corporation in a new engine plant, and a $200 million investment from General Motors to expand and improve an existing assembly plant in the zone. Local universities and colleges also responded with targeted plans for job training, work readiness, and education programs.

In Philadelphia, a commercial glass-making company that had left for the suburbs seven years ago is returning bringing all 48 jobs back with it. A soldering business based in Malaysia will expand into the U.S. , with the Philadelphia Zone as its base. At least one Pathmark supermarket, and possibly two, will be moving into the Philadelphia Zone, with jobs for several hundred people who live there.

By mid-1996, the Harlem EZ reported being "flooded" with applications to share in the more than $250 million to be distributed over 10 years to businesses and not-for-profit social agencies that were prepared to contribute to the revitalization of the area. The applicants include the Gap ("We think Harlem is retailing's best kept secret"); a marina that would build 105 new boat slips at the northern tip of Manhattan; a restauranteur hoping to resurrect the jazz club where bebop was born; Greyhound Bus Lines, which proposed to build an employee training center; and the Sony Corporation, seeking a partnership with Magic Johnson to build a multiplex cinema, a health club, a rooftop skating rink, and other stores that would make it the largest retail complex in Harlem, and, with 500 workers, its largest commercial employer.

The potential of the Empowerment Zones, whose realization depends on developments that cannot yet be foreseen, is enormous because its enabling legislation incorporated past lessons learned: structured to attract a massive infusion of investment to inner cities, EZs appeal to both conservatives and liberals.

CONCLUSION

Community rebuilding efforts under both public and private auspices, of which I have described only three examples, add up to an extraordinary social development with stunning implications for the future. "While the nation has been looking away," says the Committee on Economic Development, "residents and grass-roots institutions in many decaying neighborhoods have quietly begun to turn their communities around ... offering new hope that the complex problems of the inner cities can be solved. Something is working."

Both research and experience suggest that these developments deserve far more attention than they have been getting. The evidence suggests that we know enough about what works in putting together effective interventions in targeted neighborhoods, and that comprehensive place-based interventions could become the key to responding to some of the deepest problems of America's inner cities. In the longterm comprehensive community building could—alongside new macro-economic policies and other measures to restore opportunity to people now stuck at the bottom—become a major national strategy to combat poverty, rebuild the inner city, and make sure that all the nation's children will come into adulthood sharing in the American dream.

The Future of Work and Who Will Get It

By Julianne Malveaux, Ph.D

For the past five years President Clinton has been privileged to preside over an economy that has been expanding relentlessly. Growth has averaged about three percent in the past several years, unemployment rates have dropped below 5 percent, and the Dow Jones Industrial Average has increased by more than a third. Millions of new jobs have been "created" by the current economic expansion, and assumptions of continued prosperity have driven nearly every aspect of public policy—from the blueprint for budget balancing in the year 2002 to predictions about the number of jobs that are available for people who are being moved off welfare rolls. The euphoria accompanying the current economic expansion has been so consuming that an array of related economic issues has been knocked off page one except when a crisis , such as the August 1997 UPS strike, forces us to examine the current economic expansion in the context of worker well-being. For many reasons, however, policy-makers seem more interested in macroeconomic expansion than in the microeconomic angst that many workers are experiencing.

Thus, a newspaper reader might be forgiven for her confusion if the front page announces a layoff or downsizing in a community, while the business page highlights low unemployment rates. An observer might also be forgiven her confusion if she attempts to reconcile Federal Reserve Board Chairman Alan Greenspan's periodic comments about the economy "overheating" with the number of people who are seeking work. And the average worker, who saw wages rise by a paltry 3 percent in 1996, might be forgiven if he is skeptical about the economic expansion that pushed up stock prices by 24 percent in the same year.

While issues of worker well-being do not often make the headlines, they are important to that overwhelming majority of Americans—75 percent over age 15—who have wage income and rely on their wages for survival. As Jeremy Rifkin has noted in his book, *The End of Work: The Decline of the Global Labor Force and the Dawn of the Post Market Era*, the labor market has changed. People are less likely to work at the same job for 30 or 40 years (and be rewarded with a gold watch) than they are to hold multiple jobs during their work life and to collide, at least once, with a pink slip. As corporations emphasize short-term profits, instead of making long-term investments, people are less likely to find employers loyal to them and, thus, are less likely to be loyal to employers.

These workplace changes have implications for the way we live, and they have particular implications for African Americans. Thus, this essay will explore the future of work and who will get it, with special attention to the likely future status of African-American workers. My discussion begins with an exploration of the relationship between economic expansion and worker well-being, and continues by focusing on some of the influences that will shape the labor market of the future. The legislative climate and its impact of the work place are considered, and a set of recommendations for the future empowerment of African-American workers is offered.

I. THE UNEVEN ECONOMIC EXPANSION

"The American economy today is the healthiest it has been in three decades," boasts the opening sentence of Chapter One of the *1997 Economic Report of the President*. The report details impressive economic accomplishments since 1993, such as the reduction of the unemployment rate by a third, the reduction of the federal deficit, the low inflation rate, the stabilization of prices, and a reduction in poverty. The economic good news has crowded out an examination of the unevenness of the economic expansion, and ignored the fact that a rising tide does not necessarily lift all boats.

The 1996 unemployment rate of 5.4 percent, for example, translated into an unemployment rate of 10.8 percent for African Americans.

Further, many economists have been skeptical that the unemployment rate is an accurate measure of economic well-being for workers, given the way the rate is defined and the fact that many, especially in inner cities, are not counted at all among the unemployed because they have dropped out of the labor force since they think they cannot find work.

Preoccupation with the unemployment rate is also problematic when the terms and conditions of work are considered. Average hourly earnings rose from $11.44 in 1995 to $11.82 in 1996, an increase of a scant 38 cents, or 3.3 percent. Anecdotal evidence suggests that many workers are working longer hours and are reluctant to ask for pay increases because they are insecure about the stability of their employment.

During economic good times, it is often possible to address issues of economic inequality, but when macroeconomic expansion is coupled with microeconomic angst, there is such a focus on maintaining employment that there is little energy for closing pay gaps that exist by race, gender, or location. Thus, "urban policy" is rarely addressed. Concepts like "pay equity" and "racial discrimination" are frequently ignored. Although surveys of workers indicate that these are areas of concern, little attention has been focused on them.

Indeed, popular focus has been more on business news than on labor market news. Although more people work than invest in the stock market, the news media is more likely to focus on stock market trends than on labor-market trends. None of the nation's major newspapers has a reporter covering a labor beat full time, although many economics reporters also cover labor issues. While work rules are evolving, less attention is being paid to this set of key issues.

The media's focus on business news has also included a focus on the lives, lifestyles, and earnings of the upper fifth of our nation's workers. From the work-related content of prime-time television programs to the headlines that dominate the news, it is interesting to note the near-preoccupation with well-paid professionals that crowds out news about more typical workers. It is instructive, then, to realize that of our nation's 90 million full-time, full-year workers, just 3.2 million (or 3.5 percent) earned more than $100,000 per year. This point is not made to engender "class envy" or divisiveness, but to indicate the imbalance of attention given to a small group of workers by the press and policy makers. In contrast, there is much less focus on those full-time workers who earn less than $25,000. In some cases, especially when women workers are considered, those at the low end of the earnings scale represent the majority of workers in that race-sex group (see Table Two).

The data suggest that there have been some productivity increases in the labor market, but these gains have sometimes led to job losses. The Federal Reserve Bank's June, 1997 nationwide survey indicated that there were not enough skilled workers to meet industry demand in some parts of the country. The same survey indicated that technology and productivity advances in some areas of the country were the direct cause of layoffs. Whatever macroeconomic benefits derived from productivity increases may well be canceled out by the cost that layoffs impose on our society.

Some of the "productivity increases" have layoff consequences that are both frustrating and amusing. Late-night comedians love to parody telephone answering systems that lead one to a "voice mail limbo," a limbo that is less amusing when one realizes that the people who used to answer telephones may now not have jobs. Their layoffs fatten corporate profits, but at what cost? Their lack of pay will ultimately mean less demand for goods and services, something that those planning layoffs have failed to consider.

There has been another source of job losses that has been ignored because of macroeconomic expansion. Proponents of free trade have relentlessly argued that trade agreements, such as NAFTA, benefit workers in the United States, asserting that trade spurs job growth and that it creates higher-paying export jobs. There is evidence to the contrary, though. Economic Policy Institute researchers Robert E. Scott, Thea Lee and John Schmitt argue that, between 1979 and 1994, some 2.4 million job opportunities were eliminated by an increase in our trade deficit. Most of the job losses were in manufacturing. While the EPI researchers say some jobs were created by trade, they indicate that there were net job losses because of it. While it is clear that trade does boost the nation's macroeconomic growth, it is not clear that this growth is a net good when job losses are balanced against it, especially given the concentration of those experiencing job losses, particularly among manufacturing workers and non-college graduates.

A critical economic relationship has been severed. Once, economic expansion meant an increase in worker well-being. Now, economic expansion means an increase in the well being of some, but not all, workers. Once, hard work was a sufficient condition for individual economic prosperity. Now, those who are located in the wrong industries, or in the wrong areas, will find that their hard work is not enough to get them out of poverty. In today's economy, economic expansion coexists with worker malaise, job insecurity, and the constant threat of layoffs. Too many people have not benefited from the economic good news.

II. WORKERS AT THE PERIPHERY

The August 1997 strike of United Parcel Service workers perhaps best illustrates the uneven distribution of prosperity and security in our economy. A company with more than a 7 percent profit rate used part-time workers to keep labor costs down and to maintain its profit level. Nearly half of its work force is employed part time; the company said it could not afford to bring workers into its full-time work force as quickly as they wanted. The company also indicated that many workers preferred part-time jobs for reasons of flexibility. But many adult workers who held part-time jobs with UPS said they desperately needed full-time employment. Their bills, appetites, and obligations were full-time, not part-time. The company's argument that some workers wanted part-time was true for students and moonlighters, but many workers' part-time jobs were their only ones.

There were 103 million full-time workers and 23 million part-time workers in the labor market in 1996. Three million part-time workers say they worked part time for "economic reasons" (which means they would choose full-time work if they could find it), while 18 million worked part-time "voluntarily." The word "voluntarily" is subjective, though: many women who work part-time would work full time if they could make child-care or transportation arrangements. The number of workers (7.8 million) who hold multiple part-time jobs indicate the need some workers have for full-time employment with flexible arrangements.

Employers, however, require workers to give something up, such as benefits or overtime pay, to get flexibility.

In addition to those who hold multiple part-time jobs, 250,000 workers have more than one full-time job. The data do not indicate these workers' pay, but it is possible to speculate that their pay must be very low for them to endure the strain of two full-time jobs! Clearly, the number of workers who are sorting out employment arrangements is incompatible with the notion of a robust economy with worker shortages.

Self-employment is now the fastest growing segment of our economy; nearly 9 million are self-employed. Many pursue self-employment because they say they want to be independent, but many others pursue self-employment because they have no choice. The peculiar nature of contemporary downsizing sometimes means that a worker's job is "contracted out." In that case, a worker can hold her former job at a fraction of her old pay—without her former benefits.

Between part-time work, temporary work, and self-employment, there are millions of workers who survive at the periphery of the traditional labor market. Some of them are at the bottom of the wage and occupational ladder, working as cleaning service workers, clerical temps, and in other low-paying jobs. Economic insecurity is not restricted to those with the lowest , though. Those at the top—consultants, executive temporaries, and others earn better paychecks, have as much uncertainty and as little security.

The peripheral work force is likely to grow as the Temporary Aid to Needy Families (TANF) legislation—the welfare reform legislation—is implemented. As many as 3.5 million women who receive public assistance will have between 15 months and 2 years to leave the welfare rolls. Since training opportunities have been streamlined and truncated to short-term programs, most of those on public assistance are likely to move into low-paying, temporary and part-time jobs. Indeed, in some cases, low-wage workers compete directly with public-assistance recipients for employment—sometimes in the same workplace, and sometimes existing workers' hours (and pay) cut to provide opportunities for welfare recipients.

There are many grounds on which to criticize the nation's new welfare policies. In this context, though, the most important criticism is that the government's projected pace of transition from welfare to work assumes continuous economic expansion and provides no contingency plans for a downturn. In terms of the future shape of the workplace, the placement of millions of women workers at the bottom of the wage distribution ladder is likely to further erode their already weak economic security. Education and training are not emphasized as much as employment. That suggests many recipients will be pushed into the "quick fix" of low-wage jobs instead of being offered training for a set of expanded employment options.

The growing size of the peripheral work force sets up two tiers of employees; one that benefits from a workplace based social policy and another that does not. When government attempts to implement social policy by mandating that employers provide a certain set of employee benefits, it unwittingly widens the gap between those in the traditional labor force and those at the periphery. Those who work for large employers have access to medical insurance, vacation pay, pensions, family and medical leave, and other benefits. Those who are temporary or part-time workers, or are self-employed must provide such benefits for themselves or forego them. Policy makers, accustomed to social benefits being delivered by the workplace will have to develop new ways of providing benefits-or accept the gap between the growing group of peripheral workers and the shrinking group of those who hold traditional jobs.

While high unemployment rates and low levels of income and earnings for African Americans indicate that they experience more economic insecurity than others, data on part-time employment and self-employment do not suggest that African Americans are more likely to be represented in these categories. In the case of low levels of black employment, one might posit that African Americans are more risk-averse and face more barriers to self-employment and business ownership than others. One wonders whether the gap in part-time employment can be explained by the representation of African Americans in the legal, but peripheral, underground economy.

III. THE NEW EMPLOYERS

In 1979, Fortune 500 companies had about 18 million employees, representing nearly 20 percent of the labor market at that time. Now the Fortune 500 have about 11 million employees, a little more than 10 percent of the total labor market. This is fascinating for two reasons. First, the Fortune 500 have a disproportionate amount of influence on public policy in our society. Consider, for example, a congressional hearing that features a large corporation CEO discussing the labor market. One has to be struck with the irony that this executive, who may have downsized or will downsize a portion of her labor force, is hardly in a position to offer an unbiased perspective. Changing employment patterns, therefore, require us to reevaluate the role that Fortune 500 executives have in making and shaping public policies.

If Fortune 500 companies are employing fewer people, then what kinds of firms are now employing workers? The answer is clear—small and medium-sized companies in emerging industries are the new employers. Indeed, leaders of NAWBO (National Association of Women Business Owners) have estimated that their members employ more people than Fortune 500 companies! Massachusetts Institute of Technology professor David Birch has focused attention on companies he calls "gazelles"— companies that have doubled in profit and size in the last five years. Most of them, despite their growth, still have fewer than 100 employees. Their rapid expansion sometimes means that their workplaces are less structured, and that they pose special challenges to their employees. Harriet Michel, president of the Minority Development Supplier Council, has noted that new black-owned businesses fall heavily into this gazelle category. She estimates that these businesses will hire 80 percent of new black workers in the next decade.

The smaller the firm, the less likely it is to be regulated by current employment standards and civil rights laws that, depending on the statute, exempt firms with fewer than 15, 25, or 50 workers from complying with regulations on overtime, discrimination, health and safety, and a range of other matters.

Temporary and part-time workers at the periphery of the traditional labor market are now joined by a growing number of employees whose small and medium-sized companies do not provide the same array of benefits as larger employers. Small companies are less likely to provide pensions, health care, vacation time, and the whole range of other benefits that have become part of workers' benefits package. Companies with fewer than 100 workers are only one third as likely to offer pension benefits as Fortune 500 companies. This has long-term implications for people's well-being, especially given the aging of America.

IV. THE MIXED BLESSING OF TECHNOLOGY

The reconfiguration of the labor market has been hastened by the mixed blessings of technology, especially the proliferation of personal computers in the home and workplace. Several workplace innovations—including increased telecommuting and distributed information networks, are clearly made possible by computer technology.

I have described technology as a mixed blessing because, while technological mastery is a necessary condition for career success, especially at the upper end of the occupational spectrum, the misuse of technology can have a deleterious impact on the terms and conditions of work for some. There has been a tendency, in the latter half of the 20th century to worship technology's possibilities, to focus on access to the Internet and on the communications potential of computers—but not to consider the content of the Internet and ways technology can be misused.

This discussion is complicated by the fact that African Americans are behind the technological curve, being less likely than their white counterparts to own computers and less likely to have access to computers in the workplace. Additionally, while many elementary and secondary schools have had their curricula enhanced by the availability of computers, inner city schools are less than a third as likely as suburban schools to be wired for the Internet. There is a technology gap between African Americans and the rest of the population in the classroom, in the workplace, and in the home. This gap has significant implications for the future workplace.

At the same time, technology can be misused both in the workplace

61

and in the classroom. In the workplace, although computers can increase efficiency, they may also increase the amount of monitoring that workers are subjected to. Computers can track the length of time a customer-service representative spends on telephone calls and the amount of time that she spends away from her computer or making personal telephone calls. In such cases, do computers increase the level of efficiency or the level of intrusiveness?

Technology's efficiencies have not been cost-free. According to Cecelia Conrad, more than 100,000 bank jobs have been lost since the introduction of the Automatic Teller Machine (ATM). To be sure, the number computer sales jobs have simultaneously increased. But this job shift also represents a demographic shift—from jobs that were dominated by women of color, to jobs more likely to be held by men. This type of employment shift typifies the African American experience with technology, as summarized by Jeremy Rifkin, who wrote, "Unskilled and unneeded, the commodity value of (black) labor has been rendered virtually useless by the automated technologies that have come to displace them in the new high-tech global economy."

If the current trajectory is not altered, African Americans may be displaced in a number of labor markets, as well. I was recently told by a bank lobbyist that "everybody" would bank by computer by the year 2000. What a fascinating projection, given that in 1997 only a third of all white families and 10 percent of all African-American households had personal computers. How will "everybody" get computer access by 2000, short of a massive giveaway program? Or does the "everybody" term really mean "everybody with access."

It is possible to separate people on the basis of their access to technology. Is technology being used to, not bring more people into the information age, but, instead, to separate them from information? The Congressional Black Caucus, concerned about just such a development, has talked of providing access to technology as a way of achieving community empowerment. Consider, for example, the increased access, for example, that a homeless person would have if he had an e-mail address!

African-American workers must master technology in order to ensure their ability to compete in the workplace of the future. We must also concern ourselves with issues of access, especially for those in areas not yet wired for the Internet. In addition to mastery, however, we must consider the broader questions about the appropriate use of technology, and the unevenly borne costs in our society of introducing technology to some industries.

VI. FREELANCE EMPLOYEES INSIDE AND OUTSIDE THE CORPORATION

Technology, peripheral employment, and labor-market trends have contributed to increases in the number of free lance employees, both inside and outside large companies. Outside the corporation, the "contracting out" phenomenon has affected everything in the entire realm of procurement. Some of these services are procured in neighborhoods, but some are also provided by prison labor, suggesting that the prison-industrial complex is something more than a rhetorical construct. Internationally, it has contributed to offshore offices in the Caribbean Basin, computer microchip manufacturing in Ireland, and auto parts manufacturing in Japan and Germany.

Inside the corporation, the freelance concept is not as visible or dynamic. But to some extent the free-lance employment concept is demonstrated through the increasing self-reliance of employees defining their own jobs and taking on diverse functions, being forced to prove themselves, while concepts like seniority are being rendered obsolete. What does all this mean to an organization and to its employees' sense of stability and well-being? For many workers it means increased uncertainty, which is why—even during this period of economic expansion people are expressing great concern about their labor-market and economic futures.

From a broader labor-market perspective, the notion that every worker can make their own way in the labor-market is a re-assertion of the "yellow dog contract" of the early 20th century. In other words, the current climate, as typified by the Republican Party's "Contract On America," pushes the rights of individuals over those of groups. That would enable an employer to bargain with individuals, as opposed to members of groups—thus denying workers the collective power they have as groups in processes like collective bargaining. But in most work, individual attributes are not valued. The person working behind a cash register does not need to possess unique abilities, and if she does, they aren't applicable to her job. Employees are empowered as groups that can bargain collectively; employers benefit financially when they erode collective bargaining and deal with individuals.

Legislation emerging from Congress, however, has attempted to both weaken unions and employment standards, and to focus individuals at the expense of the group. Opposition to affirmative action stresses individual accomplishment over group status, although it is arguable that barriers to workplace entry are often group-based (employment ads don't say "no Julianne Malveaux," but "no women" or "men only"). Legislation that would relax employment standards to conform to individual needs—such as the statutes that would require workers to work 80 hours before collecting overtime in the name of "flexibility"—seem to take individual scheduling variations into account. But they would actually give employers extraordinary control over hours worked while freeing them of the obligation to pay overtime.

The assumptions underlying legislation that weakens groups are that individuals can create better deals for themselves in dynamic labor markets. This may be true for those with unique skills in markets that value those skills. But for workers at the bottom and in the middle of the skill distribution, this is not often the case, and protections like tenure or seniority, employment standards and minimum wages, provide workers with some measure of security.

The power of groups to improve wages is best illustrated by viewing the relative situation of unionized and non-unionized workers, by race-sex groups. Those workers who tend to be concentrated in the lowest paying jobs by race-sex group have their wages most enhanced by actions of unions they belong to. Legislative attempts to erode the power of unions adversely affect those with the lowest wages, especially Hispanic and African-American men and women.

Collective bargaining, then, has been able to produce benefits for people of color that they haven't been able to get from the system by bargaining individually. It makes sense, then, to consider organizing public-assistance recipients when they are forced into the labor market, since they are not likely to be able to influence the terms and conditions of their employment without collective bargaining. In that regard, it's worth noting that public-assistance recipients now being pushed into workforce jobs are very much being treated as a group; their individual circumstances are rarely being taken into account. Thus, the notion that these low-wage workers can individually bargain favorable working conditions is ludicrous. Instead, the requirement that they must find and keep jobs may well encourage employers to exploit them with low wages and substandard working conditions.

VII. EMPLOYMENT AND ECONOMIC POWER

The snapshot I have developed of the labor market and the trends that will determine the future of work suggest a less hierarchical labor market with fewer guarantees than in the past. For some, this dynamic, transitional situation provides opportunities. But for many, the situation poses challenges and erodes employment security and well-being.

Even if some worker protections are maintained through legislation and enforcement of existing regulations, the dominance of "gazelles" and other small employers suggests that workers must take more responsibility for being fully prepared and competitive. Absent employer benefits, workers will be charged with providing their own pensions and health insurance. A new set of inequities, not based on race or gender, but on employer size and access to technology, will exist and will likely grow wider.

The Urban League concern is economic power as a key part of the civil rights agenda. This article makes it clear that economic power will not be gained solely through employment. People do not have enough control, enough power, enough negotiating strength to create new wealth solely on the basis of work. While stable employment is a foundation of economic power for most people, it is a necessary, not a sufficient condition, for economic development for the African-American community.

As long as employment is a necessary condition for economic survival, the civil rights movement cannot ignore issues of employment protection, issues of the terms and conditions of work, and issues of pay. As central a part of the civil rights agenda as employment is, however, issues of entrepreneurship become equally important. Thus, the whole matter of minority business set asides and investigations of bias in the contracting process are important for African American's economic development. Also, ways that supposedly "race neutral" legislation (such as the Telecommunications Act of 1996) have had a negative effect on African-American ownership (radio station ownership has dropped by 10 percent since the passage of the Telecommunications Act) and must be part of the civil rights agenda. It is not sufficient to simply use race as a consideration in dealing with entrepreneurial issues. The presumption of race neutrality must also be challenged when the outcome of neutral legislation stifle African-American economic development.

From a broader perspective, we must look at the impact that African-American entrepreneurship has on the larger community. What role does distribution and fairness play in the issues of entrepreneurship? In other words, it makes no sense to create several black millionaires if all they do is hire people under the same terms and conditions of work as exploiters do. If black owned businesses pay low wages and have poor employment standards, is the community better off? When we talk about African-American entrepreneurship and developing economic power, we must also talk about distribution and about class.

If we do not, we run the risk of damaging the notion of "community" among African Americans. Consider, for example, the passage of Proposition 209 in California. Many African-American working-class people didn't vote against 209 or for it, they just didn't vote. They didn't see their stake in affirmative action because they consider it a middle class issue. They needed to be reminded that affirmative action opened doors not only for African-American professors, but also for African-American bus drivers. Increasingly, though, African Americans will have to pay attention to issues of class.

In terms of economic power, it seems to me that the civil rights movement needs to look at a set of emerging trends—including the rediscovery of the worth of service work (as the economy grows more complex) and individuals who are bargaining on their own. The African-American community has essentially moved away from service. But there may be some very lucrative opportunities in service worth considering; and indeed, some potential monopolies may exist in such areas of service as elder care, transportation, and child care. Furthermore, as the health industry restructures, there may well be opportunities for African Americans that are being ignored.

Albert Camus, the noted French author, wrote, "without work all life is rotten." He meant that human beings work not only for survival, but for purpose. Work will be as important for African Americans in the future as it has been in the past. But the transformed labor market may offer less to African Americans if we are not prepared to take advantage of emerging trends, and if we are unable to move beyond work to deal with the broader issues of economic empowerment.

THE COST OF BEING BLACK

Percentage not explained by differences between similar white and black households.

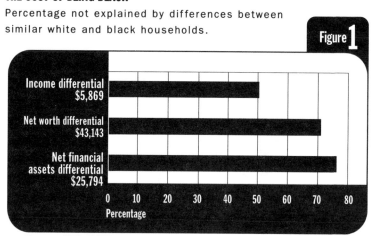

Source: SIPP, 1987 Panel, Wave 4

THE PRICE OF BEING BLACK IN HOUSING AND MORTGAGE MARKETS

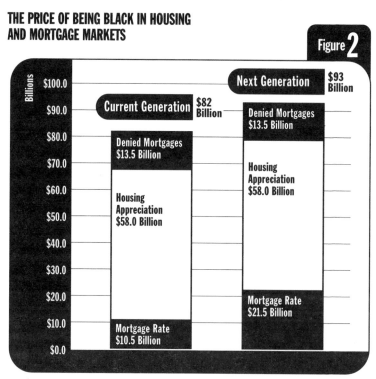

Source: SIPP, 1987 Panel, Wave 4

FULL-TIME, YEAR-ROUND WORKERS
WITH EARNINGS OVER $100,000 PER YEAR – 1996
Numbers in thousands

Table 1

	Worker Type	Number in thousands	Percentage of Total
White	Male	2,554	79.3
	Female	383	11.9
Black	Male	70	2.2
	Female	29	0.9
Hispanic	Male	68	2.1
	Female	17	0.5
	TOTAL	3,221	—

FULL-TIME, YEAR-ROUND WORKERS
WITH EARNINGS UNDER $25,000 PER YEAR – 1996
Numbers in thousands

Table 2

	Worker Type	Full-time workers	Full-time workers	Percentage of Total
Male	TOTAL	53,801	17,881	33.2%
	White	46,663	14,684	31.9
	Black	4,799	2,185	45.5
	Hispanic	5,542	3,353	60.5
Female	TOTAL	36,457	19,379	53.2%
	White	29,612	15,430	52.1
	Black	5,098	3,053	59.9
	Hispanic	2,954	2,067	70.0

Source: Money Income in the United States, 1996
(US Department of Commerce), Table 10.

Black Philanthropy in the New Millennium

By Emmett D. Carson

INTRODUCTION

Black Philanthropy is one of the least understood, yet most important, forces responsible for the socioeconomic survival and advancement of African Americans. The lack of understanding about the role of Black Philanthropy has led many—both within and outside the African-American community—to persist in promoting dangerous misperceptions about the willingness and capacity of African Americans to contribute money and time to support their individual and collective interests. The myths contribute to existing negative racial stereotypes by suggesting that African Americans lack the motivation for self-sufficiency and self-help, and are more likely to be recipients than givers of charity. In general, these myths have lead people to one of two erroneous beliefs: either African Americans don't give at all or affluent African Americans don't give enough.

Among many who are unaware of the history of Black Philanthropy, the term is thought to be an oxymoron contradiction in terms. There is a persistent belief that African Americans have no philanthropic traditions of their own. Such a belief ignores the obvious historical reality: If African Americans were not active in efforts to help themselves when they had no legal rights as citizens, who should receive credit for their survival? The belief also overlook the fact that, in today's context, African Americans have no legal or moral obligation—beyond paying taxes—to direct their philanthropy in ways that support poor African Americans, although overwhelming evidence demonstrates they do.

The other popular myth—that affluent African Americans don't give enough—is also wrong. Despite the well-publicized charitable contributions of affluent entertainers, athletes and business people— such as Oprah Winfrey, Bill and Camille Cosby, Michael Jackson and the late Reginald Lewis—these impressive public displays of Black Philanthropy are often distorted in ways as to question rather than affirm African-American generosity. In addition, many have suggested that middle-class African Americans have been negligent in their efforts to assist the poor. There is no evidence to indicate that these individuals are somehow less generous than their Euro-American counterparts. It is important to note that the use of Black Philanthropy to help poor African Americans does not lessen the obligation of the larger society to assist all impoverished Americans. After all, the argument is never advanced that affluent Euro-Americans have a unique obligation or responsibility to direct their philanthropy in support of poor Euro-Americans.

Unfortunately, neither belief expressed above—that Black Philanthropy doesn't exist or that it is only relevant in connection with the insufficient charitable giving of affluent African Americans—adequately or accurately describes the 200-year old tradition of Black Philanthropy. Such views also provide an inadequate context for assessing the current opportunities and challenges to the evolution of Black Philanthropy. While the gifts made by wealthy African Americans certainly build on the earlier philanthropic traditions of Paul Cuffe (1759-1817) and Madame C. J. Walker (1869-1919), narrowly defining Black Philanthropy by focusing only on the charitable giving of these individuals ignores the communal nature of Black Philanthropy and grossly overstates the historical importance of wealthy individuals in supporting group interests. It is of enormous importance to recognize that the only difference between the charitable giving of affluent African Americans and those with more moderate incomes is the size of the contribution; all are philanthropists. Until this view of Black Philanthropy is broadly accepted, African Americans will continue to believe and promulgate false myths about their willingness and propensity to give.

The purpose of this article is to examine the unprecedented opportunities and challenges that exist to further focus Black Philanthropy on African American interests. At no other time in American history have

African Americans, in nearly every area of human endeavor, achieved so much economic success. At the same time, African Americans continue to be disproportionately incarcerated, subjected to violent crimes and burdened with poorer health than other Americans. In addition, the broader public's weakening commitment to affirmative action to provide equal access and opportunity (as evidenced by California's proposition 209, which eliminates consideration of race and gender in hiring and contracting), its increasing emphasis on long-term incarceration (through programs such as "three strikes and you're out"), and its support of new federal devolution (which puts a lifetime time limit of five years on financial assistance to help needy families to survive) will likely have disastrous consequences for the African-American community.

The central issue about the future of Black Philanthropy is whether, given these developments, African Americans will either continue directing their philanthropic resources in ways that will, at least in part, focus on uplifting their community—or will they become "Americanized Africans" whose philanthropy largely reflects individual interests rather than group concerns.

This article is divided into six sections. The first section compares the distinguishing characteristics of Black Philanthropy and Euro-American Philanthropy. The second section describes how Black Philanthropy has evolved over the decades in response to the changing citizenship status of African Americans in American society. The third section explores the societal forces that will help shape Black Philanthropy in the new millennium. The next two sections review how Black Philanthropy is again evolving—to respond to the challenges and opportunities—by establishing new vehicles for individual and institutional charitable giving. And concluding observations are provided in the last section.

Before continuing, it is important to note several limitations of this article. There is only limited statistical information on Black Philanthropy, and many basic questions remain unanswered. For example, there is no firm estimate of the number of foundations that have been established by African Americans or the total amount that is donated to charitable organizations by them. While Black Philanthropy encompasses giving money, volunteering time, donating goods and services, and soliciting these gifts, this article will focus only on the giving of financial contributions. Finally, this article defines all giving by African Americans as Black Philanthropy regardless of whether donations are made to a charitable institution that exclusively focuses on African-American issues. Such an approach is warranted, given the multi-faceted interests and experiences of African-Americans as well as the complexities and value judgments in deciding what constitutes an African American interest or concern and what does not.

DISTINGUISHING BLACK PHILANTHROPY

The evolution of Black Philanthropy is embedded in the history of African Americans. Black Philanthropy has served as a collective survival mechanism for African Americans, providing for their basic needs, and supporting advocacy efforts—when blacks could not rely on the vast array of public, private and non-profit institutions that served the larger, predominantly Euro-American society. There are at least three important aspects to the unique character and evolution of Black Philanthropy that have to be understood: its communal rather than hierarchical character, its historic relationship to the Black Church, and its adaptability to the changing legal status and rights of African Americans. Each of these aspects of Black Philanthropy are discussed below.

Unlike the hierarchical, noblesse oblige character of European and Euro-American philanthropy—in which the wealthy believed that they had an obligation to assist the poor—Black Philanthropy evolved from the communal traditions of Africa, coupled with the hard economic realities of second-class citizenship. It has been only since the 1970s that cumulative civil rights victories provided opportunities for African Americans in large numbers to earn higher incomes and accumulate wealth. Before then, African Americans recognized that theirs was a group experience based not on individual achievements but rather the color of their skin. As a result, African Americans accepted the necessity of pooling their limited resources for mutual aid in a hostile environment. And, in the process, they created a communitywide expectation that mutual survival required individuals to support common group interests. The motivation to support group interests was stronger and more enforceable when most African Americans endured the same hardships, lived in the same segregated neighborhoods, and could identify a visible common denominator to many of their problems—legalized denial of equal rights. As will be discussed, a key question is, to what extent will Black Philanthropy continue to reflect its communal origins in the absence of mutual adversity, overt daily humiliations, and the visible common barrier of racism?

The second distinguishing feature of Black Philanthropy is its relationship to the Black Church. In the not so distant past, the Black Church (a catch-all phrase used to characterize over 65,000 largely independent institutions) was the only institution controlled and operated by African Americans. As a result, the church provided enormous leadership on behalf of the African-American community, and collected and directed the charitable contributions that flowed through it. In many ways, the Black Church was required to operate like a community foundation or United Way. The church served as the collection point for relatively small individual contributions that were then used to support the basic needs and advocacy interests of the congregation and the African-American community. No other group in American society has so heavily relied on its religious institutions to provide the range of secular services that are commonly offered by the Black Church.

Over the years, Black Philanthropy directed through the church has provided support for the abolition movement, the first African-American schools, banks, mutual aid organizations, and the civil rights movement. Today, black churches continue to harness and leverage the power of Black Philanthropy to support large-scale economic development projects, homeless shelters, feeding programs, day and after-school care programs and educational scholarships, a growing number of international aid projects, and other activities.

The third distinguishing feature of Black Philanthropy is that—as the status and rights of African Americans changed over the years—it has evolved to reflect those changes. As each generation harnessed and directed its philanthropic efforts to provide its basic needs and help it inch its way toward full equality and citizenship, Black Philanthropy moved out of the shadows to develop new institutions that took advantage of blacks' changing citizenship status. The evolution of Black Philanthropy can be divided into four major periods: slavery, Jim Crow, civil rights, and post-civil rights. The current post-civil rights period is examined separately in the subsequent sections.

During slavery, free African Americans directed their philanthropy through their churches and mutual-aid associations to provide for their basic needs—food, shelter and education, and to help free those who were enslaved. A major activity was supporting the Underground Railroad, which is believed to have helped over 100,000 people escape from slavery. Unfortunately, there are no firm estimates on the number of mutual-aid societies that existed at that time. One reason for this lack of information is that many of these activities were carried out in secret because they were illegal; those caught or even accused of involvement faced imprisonment or death.

Several states including Maryland, Virginia and North Carolina—had laws that prevented African Americans from establishing organizations to help themselves.[1] Despite these dangers, mutual-aid organizations—such as the Grand Order of Odd Fellows, the Independent Order of Good Samaritans, the International Order of Twelve Knights and the Daughters of Tabor—operated in several states and were active in antislavery efforts.[2]

The Jim Crow period legitimized in separate—but—equal treatment for African Americans that, in practice, was almost always separate and seldom equal. During this time, African Americans began to create and support their own charitable institutions because they were denied access to similar organizations that served Euro-Americans. African Americans continued to focus primarily on self-improvement and educational advancement, which was considered critically important for the newly freed slaves. One institution that stands out is the AME church. Between 1800 and 1900, it raised and spent over $1 million to support its 20 colleges and universities.[3]

By the early 1900s, African Americans had started to use their philanthropic resources to establish and support the organizations that would—along with Black churches—help spearhead the civil rights movement.

Premier organizations—such as the National Urban League (then the National League on Urban Coalition) and the National Association for the Advancement of Colored People—came into existence. While both institutions received support from African Americans, they also received financial support and leadership from like-minded Euro-Americans. The effectiveness of these organizations is perhaps best demonstrated by the fact that other racial and ethnic communities have also created and supported similar charitable organizations to advance their groups' interests. During this period, W.E.B Du Bois' call for a "talented tenth" was heard; it helped lead to the creation of the first Black college fraternities and sororities. These groups saw their mission as providing assistance to the entire African American community, and they continue that commitment to community service, in varying degrees, today.

An early forerunner of organizations to come was the United Negro College Fund, founded in 1944. The UNCF established a national fundraising federation to provide financial support to historically Black colleges. By the 1970s, African Americans began to benefit from new laws that had been established to promote equal access and opportunity. As in the past, new charitable organizations were created to respond to the emerging geographic mobility and decreasing housing discrimination encountered by African Americans. These organizations, which marked an important development in the evolution of Black Philanthropy, provided the impetus for changes that eventually would impact the entire nonprofit sector. An important characteristic of these new institutions is that they relied heavily on the willingness of others, unlike the philanthropic organizations of prior decades, which often involved friends and neighbors helping each other.

The National Black United Fund, which traces its roots to the Los Angeles riot of 1965, was founded in 1972 to focus and direct the charitable contributions of African Americans. A key motivating factor was the founders' belief that the African-American community should be more strategic in the methods and approaches it used to collect and distribute money from African Americans to support African-American organizations and causes.

One of the most important fund-raising methods available is the payroll deduction plan, which allows employees to have a given amount of money automatically deducted from their paychecks to support a charitable cause. Small contributions regularly deducted over the course of a year, coupled with an employer's encouragement to increase participation, result in a large cumulative gift at year-end. The federal payroll system, with its high percentage of African-American employees, at one time allowed employees to designate only charitable contributions that would be used by the United Way. The Black United Fund's successful Supreme Court challenges to allow other fund-raising federations to participate in this monopoly system marked a new period in the development of Black Philanthropy. Access to the federal payroll deduction system— and later to the payroll deduction plans of private companies—enabled the Black United Fund to receive charitable contributions for its member organizations and it paved the way for the formation of other charitable federations—representing women, the environment and other groups—to gain similar access.[4]

A NEW ERA FOR BLACK PHILANTHROPY

The widening economic and social gap between affluent and poor African Americans, the changing demographics of American society, and the largest transfer of wealth in history are converging to create a new era for Black Philanthropy. African Americans find themselves confronting a difficult and perplexing dilemma. Never before have so many African Americans been able to enjoy the opportunities afforded by full citizenship and participation in the American economic system. Notwithstanding the tangible negative impact of declining past and current discrimination, African Americans are more successful today than at any other time in American history. As a result, the potential for charitable giving by individual African Americans has never been greater. At the same time, new research studies continue to show that African Americans are disproportionately poor, more likely to be incarcerated and experience poorer health. Moreover, the videotaped beating of Rodney King by the Los Angeles police and the alleged beating and sodomizing of a Haitian immigrant, Abner Louima, by New York City police reinforce the belief that overt racial discrimination is not simply a feature of the distant past. There is still an important role for civil rights advocacy groups in challenging systems that continue to exhibit racial bias in carrying out their duties.

At the same time that African Americans have a greater potential to give, non-profit organizations are increasingly interested in soliciting charitable contributions from diverse ethnic communities. The American Association of Fund Raising Counsel estimates that $143 billion was contributed to charitable organizations in 1995.[5] Of this amount, a total of 87 percent was contributed by individuals, including bequests.

As people of color become tomorrow's demographic majority, it will become increasingly important for charitable organizations to successfully solicit charitable contributions from the growing populations of African Americans and other people of color if they are to maintain their current operations. Based on these trends, a broad range of charitable organizations have begun intensive efforts to diversify their governing boards, staffs and participating clients in an effort to become more responsive to the concerns of people of color who donate. This has meant that, in addition to deciding how to respond to the continuing needs in the African-American community, African Americans must consider how to respond to the growing number of appeals from non-profit organizations that do not exclusively focus on issues that concern their communities.

In addition to dealing with economic pressures exerted by changing demographics, charitable organizations have intensified their efforts to solicit African-American donors because of the magnitude of the impending wealth transfer. Over the next decade, it is estimated that $10 trillion will be transferred from one generation to the next—the largest transfer of wealth in American history. While African-American wealth is seldom discussed, the reality is that they, too, will have significant assets to transfer. The changing demographics and impending wealth transfer are reshaping how non-profit organizations view African-American donors. After all, money is green and what institution wouldn't want to receive a charitable contribution from basketball great Michael Jordan or other affluent African Americans?

It has been only since the 1980s that scholars have begun to study the history, scope and patterns of Black Philanthropy. As discussed below, this research has confirmed three consistent findings about African-American giving traditions, with regard to the level of contributions, patterns of giving, and likelihood of being solicited for a charitable gift.

African Americans and Euro-Americans with the same incomes have been found to contribute comparable amounts to charities.[6] This finding is significant for at least two reasons. First, it firmly refutes the recurring and erroneous suggestion that African Americans are somehow less charitable than Euro-Americans. Second, given that African Americans have significantly fewer assets than Euro-Americans, their charitable contributions from disposable incomes create a greater financial hardship because they do not have similar resources, (financial investments and property) that could be liquidated for cash in emergencies. The median net worth of the average Euro-American household ($48,000) is 12 times greater than that of the average African-American household ($3,700). [7]

It is worth noting that the independent sector has found that fewer African American households (53 percent) made a charitable contribution compared with Euro-American households (73 percent).[8] The magnitude of this difference is often used to support claims that African Americans are less likely to give than Euro-Americans—an interpretation that is incorrect for several reasons. First, there are more African Americans who are poor than Euro-Americans, so the fact that significantly fewer African Americans made no contribution to charity is to be expected. Moreover, as previously stated, when African Americans and Euro-Americans with the same incomes are compared, the percentage differences in contributions are not statistically significant.

Second, African Americans have different charitable interests than Euro-Americans. African American, consistent with their traditions, continue to contribute largely directed through the church. It is estimated that a little more than 60 percent of all African-American giving is directed through the Black Church.[9] African Americans also are likely to be interested more in poverty alleviation and education and less on the arts, culture, and international affairs. These interests likely reflect the reality that many African

Americans are only one generation removed from poverty, and continue to have memories of being poor, and of relatives who remain so.

The third finding, which is in the process of changing, is that African Americans and other groups are asked to contribute to charitable organizations far less frequently than Euro-Americans. But these same groups are asked to contribute, they are more likely than Euro-Americans to do so.[10] This finding may be, in part, responsible for the continuing misperceptions that African Americans are not generous. If African Americans—or other groups—are not asked to contribute, then it becomes more likely they will give very little, if anything.

Nevertheless, the current economic and demographic trends are helping to create a new renaissance for Black Philanthropy that has both individual and institutional dimensions.

THE NEW BLACK PHILANTHROPISTS

There is growing anecdotal evidence that the current generation of African Americans has, in large measure, decided to continue and further the legacy of Black Philanthropy. They remain committed to directing a significant part of their philanthropy to non-profit organizations and causes that focus on the myriad concerns in the African-American community. As mentioned earlier, a growing number of wealthy African Americans are active in making large contributions, lending their names to causes and starting foundations to further their charitable interests.

In addition to the more widely known philanthropic activities of celebrities, ordinary people are exhibiting extraordinary generosity. For example, consider the stories of Oseola McCarty and Thomas Cannon, who have helped to reinspire and redefine Black Philanthropy. McCarty, an 89-year old woman from Mississippi who washed clothes most of her life to support herself, had incredibly managed to save $150,000. She donated her nest egg, earned one dollar at a time, to the University of Southern Mississippi to start the Oseola McCarty Scholarship Fund. Her unselfish gift has helped to inspire the nation and challenges those with greater economic means to reconsider whether they are doing all that they can or should.

When asked how she was able to accumulate her savings, she said, "The secret to building a fortune is compounding interest." McCarty decided to make the gift when asked about her estate plans by her banker. The never-married woman, who quit school in the sixth grade to work and care for her grandmother, decided that she wanted to donate her money while she was still living. Perhaps the most important lesson to be learned from McCarty's example is the importance of estate planning. She was fortunate enough to have a banker that prompted her to think about what she wanted to do with her assets while she was alive.[11]

Too many people, especially African Americans, are reluctant to confront their mortality and assume what little they have will simply be inherited by their children and divided and disposed of as they see fit. Unfortunately, such assumptions will often leave children with more anguish and less money. Death is inevitable. Die with a will and your family and your charitable interests benefit. But without a will, and the state and federal governments are likely to be the biggest beneficiaries. The proper use of estate planning by African Americans has the potential to provide millions of dollars to charitable organizations. A national education campaign is warranted—a campaign in which African-American attorneys and estate planners should be enlisted to provide pro bono seminars at churches and other gatherings to inform African Americans about the importance of estate planning.

Thomas Cannon, a retired postal worker, lives in Richmond, Virginia. Over the last 23 years, he has contributed over $85,000 to individuals and non-profit organizations through $1,000 gifts. During his career, his annual salary never exceeded $32,000, and he and his bed-ridden wife survive on a retirement income of $1,400 a month. Cannon's generosity to support a wide range of ethnicities that interest him is another powerful example of the unselfish spirit that exists within the African-American community.[12]

What makes Oseola McCarty and Thomas Cannon unique is not that they gave to charity, but rather the size of their contributions, given their modest annual earnings. The U.S. Census Bureau found that in 1995, a total of 259,000 African-American households had incomes in excess of $100,000.[13] This total, which represents an enormous growth from the late 1960s, can be directly attributed to the success of the civil rights movement (however, one should note that 6.5 million Euro-American households have incomes of more than $100,000). Although many of these individuals are still in their primary earning years, examples abound of their philanthropic commitment.

Willie Gary, a successful Florida attorney and entrepreneur, made national news when he contributed $10 million to Shaw University in Raleigh, North Carolina. The son of sharecroppers who has childhood memories of picking sugar cane in Florida, Gary wanted to give something back to his alma mater and his community.[14] Similarly, William Mays, an Indianapolis businessman, annually contributes $250,000 to support his multiple charitable interests. He gives $50,000 from his income and $200,000 from his business pretax business profits.[15] Similar acts of individual philanthropy occur every day by people who seek no recognition for doing their part to support both the African-American and larger communities. The same energy to give back can be seen in the new institutions that are being created to further the legacy of Black Philanthropy.

ACCESS TO NEW INSTITUTIONAL VEHICLES

In this new era of Black Philanthropy, African Americans are displaying increasing comfort in using mainstream institutions to further their philanthropic interests. Rather than responding to emergencies by making one-time gifts that are quickly depleted, more African Americans are establishing endowment funds that will invest the principal gift and only spend a small percentage of the interest earned for the charitable cause. The remaining interest is used to offset inflation and increase the principal of the fund. Studies show that through prudent investment management, an endowment will provide an organization with more income over time—more than than if it received the charitable gift in one lump sum.

A growing number of affluent African Americans have established their own foundations. For example, Jackie Robinson, Dionne Warwick, Oprah Winfrey, Allan Page, Magic Johnson and David Winfield, among others, have established foundations to further their charitable interests. While the assets of these institutions are modest, compared with some of the older, more established foundations, they are expected to grow larger over time through compound interest. Since endowed institutions are likely to exist in perpetuity, they will provide lasting benefits to the African-American broader communities.

Another important development: The nation's 450 community foundations have launched consistent outreach efforts to attract donors from the African-American community. Community foundations are public charities that allow individuals to create charitable funds (accounts) through which they can recommend grants to support their charitable interests. Donors receive a charitable tax deduction for establishing a fund. Despite existing since 1914, community foundations have only recently begun efforts to reach out to the African-American community.[16] Unlike private foundations—in which donors need to have $20 million or more to operate effectively—a fund can be established at most community foundations for about $10,000. Numerous African-American philanthropists have established funds at community foundations to support their charitable interests.

Consistent with the communal nature of Black Philanthropy, African Americans have come together in several cities to contribute jointly to establish funds that support the local African-American community. Such African-American funds have been created, for example, at the Dayton Foundation (Ohio); Community Foundation of Greater Lorain County (Ohio); the Saint Paul Foundation (Minnesota); the Foundation for the Carolinas (North Carolina). The existence of these funds has enabled a new generation of African Americans to direct their charitable giving to address community concerns.

Black churches have also begun to establish endowment funds at community foundations. For example, The Mother Bethel AME church has a fund at The Philadelphia Foundation. Black churches have established similar funds at The Cleveland Foundation and the Community Foundation of Southeastern Michigan. These endowments allow churches to better focus and structure their philanthropic activities and operating support while benefiting from steady investment growth. In addition to establishing funds at community foundations, Black churches and Black college sororities and fraternities have also begun to establish and manage their own endowments to support the church's community missions. One such well-known fund, belonging to the Concord Baptist Church in New York, has an endowment that exceeds $1 million. It is apparent that, during the millennium, there will continue to be a growth in new philanthropic vehicles that increase the effectiveness of black giving.

CONCLUSION

This article has strongly suggested that Black Philanthropy is experiencing a renaissance. After 200 years, African Americans have begun to recognize and celebrate their unique charitable traditions—and to make more strategic choices about how to better harness and direct their philanthropic resources to serve the interests of their communities. The First National Conference on Black Philanthropy, held in Philadelphia, Pennsylvania, in March 1997, was the most recent tangible sign of the growing national interest in Black Philanthropy. The conferees—consisting of clergy, business people, foundation executives, fund-raisers and community non-profit leaders—concluded that new opportunities and institutional vehicles would enable Black Philanthropy to address the continuing needs of the African-American community.

This is important because recent statistics from the Foundation Center indicate that African Americans received only 2.4 percent of all Foundation giving—and of grants made to specific areas, civil rights groups received only 1.2 percent of all foundation giving.[17] These statistics confirm that African Americans must continue to rely, in large part, on their own self-help efforts.

A key concern of many is how to inform the broader African-American community about opportunities that exist for individual African Americans and their families to engage in meaningful philanthropy. Five suggestions seem especially appropriate for strengthening Black Philanthropy.

1. Create a will and, as part of your estate planning, consider what charitable organizations you would like to support.

2. At the start of every year, establish how much of your income you want to use for giving, and actively investigate charitable organizations you want to receive that support.

3. Start a charitable club with your family and friends, to make contributions to non-profit organizations the club selects. Such clubs are wonderful activities to conduct at family gatherings during Thanksgiving, Christmas, Kwanzaa or Juneteenth. One club in Indianapolis, known as the "Minority Key Club," has raised over $420,000.[18]

4. Have your church or a non-profit organization you are involved with consider whether it should establish an endowment. Even small endowments grow over time, and they help ensure that the needs of the community will be served in perpetuity.

5. Consider whether you and your family should start a fund at a local community foundation. Such funds can often be started with a relatively modest initial amount that can be added to over time.

Regardless of the approaches African Americans select to further their philanthropy, it is essential that they demand that any charitable organizations they support adhere to at least two standards. First, donors should expect non-profit organizations they support to have flawless accounting methods and annual audits and reports that detail and confirm that monies received were properly spent. Second, each organization's governing board, staff and clientele should be assessed in terms of the extent to which they appropriately represent the interests of African Americans. Having an African American on the board or staff of a charitable organization certainly does not guarantee that the institution is interested in or responsive to the heterogeneous concerns of the African American community. But having no such representation is a clear signal that it would be more difficult for the institution to ascertain the views of African Americans were the need to arise. While such litmus tests are not foolproof, they do help assure that limited resources are properly spent and that organizations, regardless of their purpose, reflect the interests and concerns of the African-American community.

The problem of the 20th century, for African Americans, was that access to opportunities was decided based on color. But the problem of the 21st century will be how African Americans respond to group concerns, in light of individual economic success and increasing economic disparities between African-American haves and have nots. The available evidence suggests that, notwithstanding the wherewithal and varied cultural experiences, African Americans will continue a legacy of Black Philanthropy that recognizes the importance of mutual self-help while accommodating the diversity of individual philanthropic interests.

NOTES

[1] Emmett D. Carson, *A Hand Up: Black Philanthropy and Self-Help in America*, (Washington, DC: Joint Center for Political and Economic Studies Press, 1993), p. 11.

[2] [N1] Ibid, p. 13.

[3] Ibid, p. 17.

[4] Emmett D. Carson, "The National Black United Fund: From Movement for Social Change to Social Change Organization," *New Directions for Philanthropic Fundraising*, No. 1, Fall 1993, pp. 53-71.

[5] AAFRC Trust for Philanthropy, *Giving USA*, 1996 Edition, New York: American Association for Fundraising Counsel, p. 12.

[6] Emmett D. Carson, "The Evolution of Black Philanthropy: Patterns of Giving and Voluntarism," *Philanthropic Giving*, ed. Richard Magat, (New York: Oxford University Press, 1989), pp. 92-102.

[7] Melvin Oliver and Thomas M. Shapiro, *Black Wealth/White Wealth*, (New York: Routledge, 1995), p. 86.

[8] Virginia A. Hodgkinson and Murray S. Weitzman, *Giving and Volunteering in the United States*, (Washington, DC: Independent Sector, 1996), p. 3.

[9] Emmett D. Carson, *The Charitable Appeals Fact Book* (Washington, DC: Joint Center for Political Studies Press, 1989), p. 9.

[10] Virginia A. Hodgkinson and Murray S. Weitzman, *Giving and Volunteering in the United States*, (Washington, DC: Independent Sector, 1992), p. 210.

[11] Rick Bragg, "Selfless Gift Has Transformed Her Isolated Life," *Star Tribune*, November 17, 1996, p. A22.

[12]Donald P. Baker, "From His Meager Means, A Wealth of Giving," *The Washington Post*, July 1, 1996, p. D3 and Will Jones, "Philanthropist Comes Through for Native Vietnamese Student," *The Richmond Times Dispatch*, July 4, 1996, p. B6.

[13]U.S. Department of Commerce, Bureau of the Census, Current Population Reports, *Consumer Income*, P 60-193, September 1996, p. 5.

[14]Joseph A. Kirby, "Prosperous Blacks Called on to Give More to Good Causes," *Chicago Tribune*, March 9, 1997, p. 4.

[15]Lori Sharn, "Black Philanthropy is Growing," *USA Today*, March 6, 1997, p. 3A.

[16]Emmett D. Carson, "Community Foundations, Racial Diversity, and Institutional Change," *New Directions for Philanthropic Fundraising*, No. 5, Fall 1994, pp. 33-43.

[17]Loren Renz, *Foundation Giving*, (New York: Foundation Center, 1996), pp. 77 and 86.

[18]Kirby, p. 4.

Jobless Ghettos: The Impact of the Disappearance of Work in Segregated Neighborhoods

By   William   Julius   Wilson

JOBLESS GHETTOS

In 1950, a substantial portion of the urban black population was poor but they were working. Urban poverty was quite extensive but people held jobs. However, as we entered the 1990s, most adults in many inner-city ghetto neighborhoods were not working in a typical week. For example, in 1950, a significant majority of adults held jobs in a typical week in the three neighborhoods that represent the historic core of the Black Belt in Chicago—Douglas, Grand Boulevard and Washington Park. But by 1990, only 4 in 10 in Douglas worked in a typical week, 1 in 3 in Washington Park, and 1 in 4 in Grand Boulevard. In 1950, 69 percent of all males 14 and over who lived in these three neighborhoods worked in a typical week, and in 1960, 64 percent of this group were so employed. However, by 1990, only 37 percent of all males 16 and over held jobs in a typical week in these neighborhoods.

The disappearance of work has had devastating effects not only on individuals and families, but on the social life of neighborhoods as well. Inner-city joblessness is a severe problem that is often overlooked or obscured when the focus is mainly on poverty and its consequences. Despite increases in the concentration of poverty since 1970, inner cities have always featured high levels of poverty, but the levels of inner-city joblessness reached during the first half of the 1990s were unprecedented.

I should note that when I refer to *joblessness* I am not solely referring to official unemployment. The unemployment rate represents only the percentage of workers in the *official* labor-force—that is, those who are *actively* looking for work. It does not include those who are outside or have dropped out of the labor market, including the nearly 6 million males, 25 to 60, who appeared in the census statistics but were not recorded in the labor market statistics (Thurow 1995) in 1990.

These uncounted males who are outside the labor market are disproportionately represented in the inner-city ghettos. Accordingly, in my book *When Work Disappears* (1996) I use a more appropriate measure of joblessness that takes into account both official unemployment and non-labor-force participation. That measure is the employment-to-population ratio, which corresponds to the percentage of adults, 16 and older, who are working. Using the ratio we find, for example, that in 1990 only one in three adults, 16 and older, held a job in the ghetto poverty areas of Chicago, areas representing roughly 425,000 men, women, and children. And in the ghetto tracts of the nation's 100 largest cities, for every 10 adults who did not hold a job in a typical week in 1990 there were only 6 employed persons (Kasarda 1993).

The consequences of high neighborhood joblessness are more devastating than those of high neighborhood poverty. A neighborhood in which people are poor, but employed, is much different from a neighborhood in which people are poor and jobless. In *When Work Disappears* I attempt to show that many of today's problems in the inner-city ghetto neighborhoods— crime, family dissolution, welfare, low levels of social organization and so on—are fundamentally the consequences of the disappearance of work.

When I speak of the disappearance of work, I am referring to the declining involvement in or lack of attachment to the formal labor market. It could be argued that the general sense of the term *joblessness* does not necessarily mean non-work. In other words, to be officially unemployed or officially outside the labor market does not mean that one is totally removed from all form of work activity. Many people who are officially jobless are nonetheless involved in informal kinds of work activity, ranging from unpaid housework to work in the informal or illegal economics that draw income.

Housework is work, baby-sitting is work, even drug dealing is work. However, what contrasts work in the formal economy with work in the informal and illegal economies is that work in the formal economy is characterized by, indeed calls for, greater regularity and consistency in schedules and hours. Work schedules and hours are formalized; the demands for discipline are greater. It is true that some work activities outside the formal economy also call for discipline and regular schedules. Several studies reveal that the social organization of the drug industry is driven by discipline and a work ethic, however perverse.

However, as a general rule, work in the informal and illegal economies is far less governed by norms or expectations that place a premium on discipline and regularity. For all these reason, when I speak of the disappearance of work, I mean work in the formal economy, work that provides a framework for daily behavior because of the discipline and regularity that it imposes.

In the absence of regular employment, a person lacks not only a place in which to work and the receipt of regular income but also a coherent organization of the present—that is, a system of concrete expectations and goals. Regular employment provides the anchor for the spatial and temporal aspects of daily life. It determines where you are going to be and when you are going to be there. In the absence of regular employment, life including family life, becomes less coherent. Persistent unemployment and irregular employment hinder rational planning in daily life, a necessary condition of adaptation to an industrial economy. (Bourdieu 1965).

Thus, a youngster who grows up in a family with a steady breadwinner and in a neighborhood in which most of the adults are employed will tend to develop some of the disciplined habits associated with stable or steady employment—habits that are reflected in the behavior of his or her parents and of other neighborhood adults. These might include attachment to a routine, recognition of the hierarchy found in most work situations, attainment of a sense of personal efficacy through the routine management of financial affairs, endorsement of a system of personal and material rewards associated with dependability and responsibility, and so on. Accordingly, when this youngster enters the labor market, he or she has a distinct advantage over youngsters who grow up in households without a steady breadwinner and in neighborhoods that are not organized around work—in other words, a milieu in which one is more exposed to the less disciplined habits associated with casual or infrequent work.

Our research revealed that many adolescents in poor inner-city neighborhoods of Chicago were anxious to work in summer jobs and were very excited when they found employment. But until they fully comprehended the norms of the workplace, it was not unusual for them to show up for work 15 or 20 minutes late and then express surprise that the employer was upset.

With the recent sharp rise of solo-parent families, black children who live in inner-city households are less likely to socialize in a work environment for two main reasons. Their mothers, saddled with child-care responsibilities, can prevent a slide deeper into poverty by accepting welfare. Their fathers, removed from family responsibilities and obligations, are more likely to become idle as a response to restricted employment opportunities, which further weakens their influence in the household and attenuates their contact with the family. In short, the social and cultural responses to limiting constraints and changing norms are reflected in the organization of family life and patterns of family formation; these have implications for labor-force attachment as well.

Given the current policy debates that assign blame and attribute failure to personal shortcomings, these are the points that have to be re-emphasized in discussions of the responses and adaptations to chronic subordination, including those that have evolved into cultural patterns. The social actions—including behavior, habits, skills, styles, orientations, attitudes—ought not be analyzed as if they are unrelated to the broader structure of opportunities and constraints that have evolved over time. This is not to argue that individuals and groups lack the freedom to make their own choices, engage in certain conduct, and develop certain styles and orientations, but it is to maintain that these decisions and action occur within a context of constraints and opportunities that are drastically different from those in middle-class society.

EXPLANATIONS OF THE GROWTH OF JOBLESS GHETTOS

What accounts for the growing proportion of jobless adults in inner-city communities? An easy explanation would be racial segregation. However, a race-specific argument is not sufficient to explain recent changes in such neighborhoods. After all, these historical black-belt neighborhoods were *just as segregated by skin color in 1950* as they are today, yet the level of employment was much higher then. One has to account for the ways in which racial segregation interacts with other changes in society to produce the recent escalating rates of joblessness. Several factors stand out.

The disappearance of work in many inner-city neighborhoods is in part related to the nationwide decline in the fortunes of low-skilled workers. Over the past two decades, wage inequality has increased sharply, and gaps in labor-market outcomes between the less- and more-skilled workers have risen substantially. Research suggest that these changes are the result of "a substantial decline in the relative demand for the less-educated and those doing more routinized tasks compared to the relative supply of such workers" (Katz 1996). Two factors appear to have shifted the relative demand against the less-skilled workers—the computer revolutions, i.e., skill-based technological change, and the growing internationalization of economic activity (Katz 1996). Inner-city workers face an additional problem—the growing suburbanization of jobs. Most ghetto residents cannot afford an automobile and therefore have to rely on public transit systems that make the connection between inner-city neighborhoods and suburban job locations difficult and time consuming.

Although the relative importance of the different underlying causes in the growing job problems of the less-skilled, including those in the inner city, continue to be debated, there is little disagreement about the underlying trends. They are unlikely to reverse themselves. In short, over a sustained period, the labor market in the United States has twisted against disadvantaged workers—those with limited skills or education, and/or from poor families and neighborhoods—and therefore greatly diminished their actual and potential earnings (Katz 1996).

Changes in the class, racial, and demographic composition of inner-city neighborhoods have also contributed to the high percentage of jobless adults in these neighborhoods. Because of the steady out-migration of more advantaged families, the proportion of non-poor families and prime-age working adults has decreased sharply in the typical inner-city ghetto since 1970 (Wilson 1987). In the face of increasing and prolong joblessness, the declining proportion of non-poor families and the overall depopulation has made it increasingly more difficult to sustain basic neighborhood institutions or to achieve adequate levels of social organization. The declining presence of working-and middle-class blacks has also deprived ghetto neighborhoods of key resources, including structural resources such as residents with incomes to sustain neighborhood services, and cultural resources such as conventional role models for neighborhood children.

On the basis of our research in Chicago, it appears that what many high jobless neighborhoods have in common is a relatively high degree of social integration (high levels of local neighboring while being relatively isolated from contacts in the broader mainstream society) and low levels of informal social control (feelings that they have little control over their immediate environment, including the environment's negative influences on their children). In such areas, children are not only at risk because of the lack of informal social controls but also disadvantaged because the social interactions among neighbors tends to be confined to those whose skills, styles, orientations, and habits are not as conducive to promoting positive social outcomes (academic success, pro-social behavior, employment in the formal labor market, etc.) as are those in more stable neighborhoods. Although the close interactions among neighbors in such areas may be useful in devising strategies, disseminating information, and developing styles of behavior that are helpful in a ghetto milieu (teaching children to avoid eye-to-eye contact with strangers and to develop a tough demeanor in the public sphere for self-protection), they may be less effective in promoting the welfare of children in the society at large.

Despite being socially integrated, the residents in Chicago's ghetto neighborhoods shared a feeling that they had little informal social control over the children in their environment. A primary reason was the absence of a strong organizational capacity or an institutional resource that would provide an extra layer of social support in their neighborhoods. It is easier for parents to control the behavior of children in their neighborhoods when a strong institutional resource base exists, and when the links between community institutions—such as churches, schools, political organizations, businesses, and civic clubs—are strong or secure. The higher the density and stability of formal organizations, the less illicit activities—such as drug trafficking, crime, prostitution, and the formation of gangs—can take root in the neighborhood.

A weak institutional resource base is what distinguishes high-jobless inner-city neighborhoods from stable middle-class and working-class areas. As one resident of a high-jobless neighborhood on the South side of Chicago put it, "Our children, you know, seem to be more at risk than any other children there, because there's no library for them to go to. There's not a center they can go to, there's no field house that they can go into. There's nothing. There's nothing at all." Parents in high-jobless neighborhoods have a much more difficult task of controlling the behavior of their adolescents, or preventing them from getting involved in activities detrimental to pro-social development. Given the lack of organizational capacity and a weak institutional base, some parents choose to protect their children by isolating them from activities in the neighborhood, including the avoiding contact and interacting with neighborhood families. Wherever possible, and often with great difficulty when one considers the problems of transportation and limited financial resources, parents attempt to establish contacts and cultivate relations with individuals, families and institutions outside their neighborhood such as church groups, schools, and community recreation programs.

It is just as indefensible to treat inner-city residents as superheroes who overcome racist oppression as it is to view them as helpless victims. We should, however, appreciate the range of choices, including choices representing cultural influences, that are available to inner-city residents who live under constraints that most people in the larger society do not experience.

In short, the social and cultural responses to limiting constraints and changing norms are reflected in the organization of family life and patterns of family formation; these also have implications for labor-force attachments.

It is within this context that public-policy discussions on welfare reform and family values should be couched. The research we have conducted in Chicago suggest that as employment prospects recede, the foundation for stable relationships becomes weaker over time. More permanent relationships such as marriage give way to temporary liaisons that result in broken unions, out-of-wedlock pregnancies and birth, and, to a lesser extent, separation and divorce. The changing norms concerning marriage in the larger society reinforce the movement toward temporary liaisons in the inner city; therefore economic considerations in marital decisions take on even greater weight. The evolving cultural patterns are seen in the sharing of negative outlooks toward marriage and toward the relationships between males and females in the inner city—outlooks that are developed in and influenced by an environment featuring persistent joblessness. This combination of factors has increased out-of-wedlock births, weakened the family structure, expanded the welfare rolls, and, as a result, caused poor inner-city blacks to be even more disconnected from the job market and discouraged about their role in the labor force. The economic marginality of the ghetto poor is cruelly reinforced, therefore, by conditions in the neighborhoods in which they live.

In the eyes of employers in metropolitan Chicago, social conditions in the ghetto render inner-city blacks less desirable as workers; therefore many are reluctant to hire them. One of the three studies that provided the empirical foundation *When Work Disappears* included a representative sample of employers in the greater Chicago area who provided entry-level jobs. An overwhelming majority of them, both white and black, expressed negative views about inner-city ghetto workers, and many stated that they were reluctant to hire them. For example, a president of an inner-city manufacturing firm expressed a concern about employing residents from certain inner-city neighborhoods.

Interviewer: "If somebody gave me their address, uh, Cabrini Green, I might unavoidably have some concerns." Interviewer: "What would your concerns be?"

Respondent: "That the poor guy probably would be frequently unable to get to work and...I probably would watch him more carefully, even if it wasn't fair, than I would with somebody else. I know what I should do though, is recognize that here's a guy that is trying to get out of his situation and probably will work harder than somebody else who's already out of there, and he might be the best one around here. But I think I would have to struggle accepting that premise at the beginning."

In addition to qualms about the neighborhood milieu of inner-city residents, employers frequently mentioned concerns about applicants' language skills and educational training. An employer from a computer software firm in Chicago expressed the view that "in many businesses, the ability to meet the public is paramount, and you do not talk street talk to the buying public. Almost all your black welfare people talk street talk. And who's going to sit them down and change their speech patterns?"

A Chicago real estate broker made a similar point: A lot of times I will interview applicants who are black, who are sort of lower class. ... They'll come to me and I cannot hire them because their language skills are so poor. Their speaking voice for one thing is poor... they have no verbal facility with the language... and these...you know, they just don't know how to speak, and they'll say "salesmens" instead of "salesmen," and that's a problem.... They don't know punctuation, they don't know how to use correct grammar, and they cannot spell. And I can't hire them. And I feel bad about that, and I think they're being very disadvantaged by the Chicago Public School system.

Another respondent defended his method of screening out most job applicants on the telephone on the basis of their use of "grammar and English." I have every right to say that that's a requirement for this job. I don't care if you're pink, black, green, yellow or orange. I demand someone who speaks well. You want to tell me that I'm a bigot, fine, call me a bigot. I know blacks, you don't even know they're black. So do you.

Finally, an inner-city banker claimed that many blacks in the ghetto "simply cannot read. When you're talking our type of business, that disqualifies them immediately. We don't have a job here that doesn't require that somebody have minimum reading and writing skills."

How should we interpret the negative attitudes and actions of employers? To what extent do they represent an aversion to blacks per se, and to what degree do they reflect judgments based on the job-related skills and training of inner-city blacks in a changing labor market? I should point out that the statements made by the African-American employers concerning the qualifications of inner-city black workers do not differ significantly from those of the white employers. Whereas 74 percent of all the white employers who responded to the open-ended questions expressed negative views of the job-related traits of inner-city blacks, 80 percent of the black employers did so as well.

This raises a question about the meaning and significance of race in certain situations—in other words, how race intersects with other factors. A key hypothesis in this connection is that given the recent shifts in the economy, employers are looking for workers with a broad range of abilities: "hard" skills (literacy, mathematical, basic mechanical and other testable attributes), and "soft" skills (demeanor suitable to the work environment, good grooming, group-oriented work behavior, etc.). While hard skills are the product of education and training—benefits that are apparently in short supply in inner-city schools—soft skills, strongly tied to culture, are therefore shaped by the harsh environment of the inner-city ghetto. For example, our research revealed that many parents in the inner-city neighborhoods of Chicago wanted their children to avoid eye-to-eye contact with strangers and to exhibit a tough demeanor when interacting with people on the streets. While such behavior is helpful for survival in the ghetto, it hinders successful interaction in mainstream society.

If employers are indeed reacting to differences in skills between white and black applicants, it becomes increasingly difficult to discuss the motives of employers: are they rejecting inner-city black applicants out of overt racial discrimination or on the basis of qualifications?

Nonetheless, many of the recruitment practices do represent what economists call "statistical discrimination:" employers make assumptions about inner-city black workers *in general,* and reach decisions based on those assumptions before they systematically review the qualifications of an applicant. The net effect: many black inner-city applicants are never given a chance to prove they're qualified because they are systematically screened out by the selective recruitment process. Statistical discrimination, although representing elements of class bias against poor workers in inner cities, is clearly a matter of race. The selective recruitment patterns effectively screen out far more black applicants from inner cities than Hispanics or whites from the same types of backgrounds. But race is also a Hispanic or white factor, even in those decisions to deny employment to inner-city black workers on the basis of objective and thorough evaluations of their qualifications. The hard and soft skills among inner-city blacks that do not match the current needs of the labor market are products of racially segregated communities, communities that have historically featured widespread social constraints and restricted opportunities.

Thus the job prospects of inner-city workers have diminished not only because of the decreasing relative demand for low-skilled labor in the United States economy, the suburbanization of jobs, and the social deterioration in ghetto neighborhoods, but also because of negative employer attitudes. This combination of factors presents a real challenge to policymakers. Indeed, considering the narrow range of social policy options in the "balance-the-budget" political climate, how can we immediately alleviate the inner-city jobs problem—a problem that will undoubtedly grow when the new welfare reform bill takes full effect and creates a situation that will be even more harmful to inner-city children and teenagers.

PUBLIC POLICY DILEMMAS

If firms in the private sector cannot use or refuse to hire low-skilled adults who are willing to take minimum-wage jobs, then the jobs problem for inner-city workers cannot be adequately addressed without considering a policy of public-sector employment of last resort. Indeed, until current trends in the labor market are reversed or until the skills of the next generation can be upgraded before it enters the labor market, many future applicants, especially those who are not in the official labor force, will not be able to find jobs unless the government becomes the employer of last resort (Danziger and Gottschalk, 1995). This argument applies especially to low-skilled inner-city blacks. It is bad enough that they face the problems of shifts in labor-market demand shared by all low-skilled workers; it is even worse that they confront negative employer perceptions about their work-related skills and attitudes.

For all these reasons, the passage of the recent welfare reform bill, which did not include a program of job creation, could have very negative social consequences in inner cities. Unless something is done to enhance the employment opportunities of inner-city welfare recipients who reach the two-year time limit for receiving welfare, they will flood a pool already filled with low-skilled jobless workers.

New research in urban labor markets by the economist Harry Holzer (1996) of Michigan State University reveals the magnitude of the problem. Surveying 3,000 employers in Atlanta, Boston, and Los Angeles, Holzer found that only 5 percent to 10 percent of the jobs in central-city areas for workers who are *non-college graduates* require very few work credentials or cognitive skills. This means that most inner-city workers today need not only to have basic skills in reading, writing, and performing arithmetic calculations, but also to know how to operate a computer. Also, most employers require a high school degree, particular kinds of previous work experiences, and job references. Because of the large oversupply of low-skilled workers relative to the number of low-skilled jobs, many low-educated and poorly trained individuals have difficulty finding jobs, even when the local labor market is strong (Holzer, 1996, and Center on Budget and Policy Priorities, 1996).

The problem is that in recent years tight labor markets have been of relatively short duration, frequently followed by a recession that either wipes out previous gains for many workers or does not allow others to fully recover from a previous period of economic stagnation. It would take sustained tight labor markets over many years to draw back those discouraged inner-city workers who have dropped out of the labor market altogether, some for very long periods. We are currently in one of the longest economic expansions in the last half century, one that has lasted six years, generated 13 million net new jobs, and produced the lowest official unemployment rate in 23 years. This sustained recovery is beginning to have some positive effects on the hard-core unemployed. The black teenage unemployment rate has declined to levels not seen since the late 1960s. How long this period of economic growth will last is anybody's guess. Given our recent economic history, we should not be surprised if it soon comes to an end, and we are faced with a new recession.

Concerned about these issues, I sent President Clinton a memorandum shortly before the Democratic Convention in August 1996. I pointed out that he has long realized the crucial relationship between welfare reform and job creation. His initial welfare plan emphasized job creation. However, the welfare bill that he signed included no such provision. I pointed out that to remedy the most glaring defects of the bill, a mechanism for state and local governments to respond to widespread joblessness in inner cities is essential. When I wrote this memorandum, I was aware that the president was giving some thought to the idea of tax credits and wage subsidies to encourage businesses to hire welfare recipients. I pointed out that while giving subsidies and tax credits to private employers to hire welfare recipients and other disadvantaged individuals may help, research suggests that subsidies and credits are hardly sufficient by themselves to accomplish this goal.

The track record of private employers is not especially encouraging. Past efforts to subsidize employers to hire welfare recipients and other disadvantaged individuals have generally failed to work on a large scale. For example, during the late 1960s and early 1970s, the federal government funded a program by the National Alliance of Business (NAB), whereby employers received a $3,200 subsidy for each disadvantaged worker, including welfare recipients, they hired (an amount that would be much higher in inflation-adjusted terms today). That effort resulted in a very low hiring rate among employers (Center on Budget and Policy Priorities, 1996). Why? Simply because not enough employers have been willing to hire people whom they view as troublesome or "damaged goods." Indeed, a study by the economist Gary Burtless (1985) revealed that low-income individuals who were supposed to be aided were *less* likely to be hired as a result of a targeted wage subsidy. Employers evidently thought that if the government was willing to subsidize the hiring of these individuals so heavily, they must have serious work-related problems.

Studies also show that when employers do receive a subsidy for hiring such individuals—whether through a tax credit or a direct subsidy—the subsidy often rewards an employer for a hire he or she would have made anyway.

101

When that occurs, it costs the government money, but the number of jobs for this disadvantaged population does not increase (Center on Budget and Policy Priorities, 1996). Thus, studies conducted over the past two decades suggest that a single approach involving tax credits or wage subsidies will fail to move a significant number of welfare recipients into employment.

On the other hand, as pointed out by Michael Katz (1996), empirical research does support the idea that public-sector job creation and a program involving a mix of employer subsidies, training and education can have significant positive effects in moving disadvantaged workers, including welfare recipients, into jobs. For example, The Youth Incentive Entitlement Pilot Project (YIEPP), conducted in selected communities from late 1978 to early 1981, guaranteed part-time, school-year jobs and full-time summer jobs to disadvantaged youths aged 16 to 19 at the minimum wage if they stayed in school (Parkas *et al*, 1982 and 1984; U.S. Department of Labor, 1995). The project not only created jobs in the public and non-profit sectors, but also offered 100 percent wage subsidies to private sector for-profit firms to entice them to hire disadvantaged in-school youth. Representing a saturation job-creation program for in-school youths from impoverished neighborhoods, it attempted to involve both public- and private-sector employers. Indeed, private, for-profit employers, especially those representing retail trades, provided 29 percent of the jobs in the program.

The project substantially increased the employment rates and earnings of those in the programs, compared with those in four "comparable" areas that were selected as control sites (Farkas et 4, 1982, 1984). The program sites were Baltimore, Denver, Cincinnati, and Mississippi (Eight rural counties); the comparison sites were Cleveland, Phoenix, Louisville, and Mississippi (Six neighboring rural counties). As Judith Gueron (1984, p. 12) pointed out, "to assure, to the maximum extent possible, that differences in the behavior of youths reflected program effects rather than site differences, the comparison areas were chosen to match program sites over a wide variety of dimensions.

The employment rates of minorities in the program were raised to the levels of whites in the same areas. Black male employment increased from two-thirds of the white male rate to parity with the employment levels of white males. "Black female employment increased even more, from two-thirds of the white rate to one-third above it" (Farkas *et al*, 1984). For the 15- to 16-year-old cohort, the employment rates during the school year "increased by 115 percent over what it would have been in the absence of the program" (Farkas *et al*, p. xvi). During different years of the project, earnings during the school year were estimated to have increased from 46 percent to 161 percent. Summer earnings jumped by approximately 50 percent. Since the program only funded jobs at the minimum wage, most of the gains in earnings were due to increases in employment rates and hours worked per week, instead of higher wages. The youth employment in the private sector increased by an average of 18 percent during the program (Katz, 1996).

Although the private-sector employer hiring rate was low, efforts by intermediaries (i.e., community-based agencies) to place youths in jobs, combined with substantial wage subsidies, substantially expanded private-sector employment for disadvantaged youths who are normally difficult to employ. In other words, the probable reasons for the relatively large private-sector component was the full (100 percent) wage subsidy to employers and the intensive outreach efforts by community agencies to find youths jobs. Nonetheless, in spite of these initiatives, only 20 percent of the employers contacted agreed to hire a disadvantage youth.

In my memorandum to the president, I therefore urged caution in not placing too many of his "eggs" in the private-sector job-placement basket. I pointed out that we will need a mix of both private- and public-sector initiatives to enhance employment. In inner cities, where the number of very low-skilled individuals vastly exceeds the number of low-skilled jobs even before welfare reform adds tens of thousands more people to the low-skilled labor pool, a healthy dose of public-sector job creation will be needed. Public jobs can help people, whom private employers will not touch, to learn acceptable work habits and build an employment record from which they may be able to graduate to private-sector positions.

In order to make my point really clear, I pointed out to President Clinton that I am not suggesting that he call for a new federal public-works program, because I understand the difficulties in getting such a program approved in today's political climate. I am only recommending that he enable governors and mayors to use a mix of private-sector and public-sector approaches, as they see fit, based on local conditions. I pointed out that he could not be criticized for a "big government" approach if he allows state and local officials, so many of whom are now Republicans, to make this choice. Indeed, Governor Thompson's welfare plan in Wisconsin includes significant public-sector employment along with private-sector employment.

The president responded to my memorandum by indicating that several of my recommendations were already under consideration by his administration. He later proposed to Congress two initiatives, which were subsequently included in the budget and tax bills recently signed into law: 1) a $3 billion welfare-to-work jobs challenge, to help cities and states create employment opportunities for the hardest to hire welfare recipients by the year 2000, and 2) an enhanced and targeted work opportunity tax credit, to increase financial incentives to create jobs in the private sector for long-term welfare recipients. Although the second initiative emphasizes tax credits, the former allows for the creation and administration of community service work. Nonetheless, when I reread the description of the budget for fiscal year 1998, it was clear that the emphasis in the first initiative was on the use of these funds "to provide subsidies and other incentives to private businesses."

The conclusion I draw from the current evidence is that the president and Congress, as they take future steps to address the jobs problem for welfare recipients and other disadvantaged workers, ought not to rely heavily on the strategy of employer subsidies—either tax credits or wage subsidies. Instead they ought to consider a mixed strategy that places major emphasis on job creation in the public- and non-profit private sectors (Katz 1996).

At the same time that the new welfare law has generated a greater need for work opportunities, high-jobless urban and rural areas will experience more difficulty in placing individuals in private-sector jobs. To create work opportunities for welfare recipients, these areas will therefore have to "rely more heavily upon job creation strategies in the public and private non-profit sectors" (Center on Budget and Policy Priorities, 1996). Although the placement of disadvantaged workers in private-sector jobs can help contain the overall costs, in some communities, including many jobless ghetto areas and depressed rural areas, a mainly private-sector initiative will not be sufficient to generate enough jobs to accommodate the large oversupply of low-skilled individuals.

West Virginia, a state that has been plagued with a severe shortage of work opportunities, has provided community-service jobs to recipients of welfare for several years. In Wisconsin, Governor Thompson's welfare reform plan envisions community-service jobs for many parents in the more depressed areas of state. And the New Hope program in Milwaukee provides community-service jobs for those unable to find employment in the private sector (Center on Budget and Policy Priorities, 1996). It is especially important that this mixed strategy includes a plan to make *adequate* monies available to localities or communities with high-jobless and welfare dependency rates. Three billion dollars for this purpose is hardly sufficient.

Obviously as more people become employed and gain work experiences, they will have a better chance of finding jobs in the private sector when they become available. The attitudes of employers toward inner-city workers could undergo change, in part because they would be dealing with job applicants who have steady work experiences and who could furnish references from their previous supervisors. Children are more likely to be socialized in a work-oriented environment and to develop the job-readiness skills that are seen as important, even for entry-level jobs.

Thus, given the recent welfare reform legislation, *adequate* strategies to enhance the employment opportunities of inner-city residents are more important now than ever. In the absence of such programs, welfare recipients who reach the time limit will aggravate a severe jobless problem that persists, even during this period of economic growth. We could be facing a real catastrophe in many urban areas—including a sharp increase in the number of homeless families with children—if steps are not taken soon to enhance the job prospects of hundreds of thousands of inner-city youths and adults.

REFERENCES

Bloch, Farrell. 1994. *Antidiscrimination Law and Minority Employment: Recruitment Practices and Regulatory Constraints.* Chicago: University of Chicago Press.

Bourdieu, Pierre. 1965. *Travail et travailleurs en Algerie.* Paris: Editions Mouton.

Bourgois, Philippe. 1995. *In Search of Respect: Selling Crack in El Barrio.* New York: Cambridge University Press.

Burtless, Gary. 1985. "Are Targeted Wage Subsidies Harmful? Evidence from a Wage Voucher Experiment." *Industrial and Labor Relations Review 39* (October).

Caraley, Demetrios. 1992. "Washington Abandons the Cities," *Political Science Quarterly 107* (Spring): 1-30.

Center on Budget and Policy Priorities. 1995. "The Earned Income Tax Credit Reductions in the Senate Budget Resolution." Washington, D.C. June 5.

Center on Budget and Policy Priorities. 1996. "The Administration's $3 Billion Jobs Proposal." Washington, D.C.

Danziger, Sheldon H. and Peter Gottschalk. 1995. *America Unequal.* Cambridge: Harvard University Press.

Gueron, Judith. President, Manpower Demonstration Research Corporation. Private Communication, 1996.

Hamermesh, Daniel S. "Subsidies for Jobs in the Private Sector," in J. Palmer, ed, *Creating Jobs Washington, D.C:* The Brookings Institution, 1978, pp. 87 - 122.

Farkas, George, U. Alton Smith, Ernst W. Stromsdofer, Gail Trask, and Robert Jerreft, III. 1982. *Impacts of the Youth Incentive Entitlement Pilot Projects:* New York: Manpower Demonstration Research Corporation.

Parkas, George, Randall Olsen, Ernst W. Stromsdofer, Linda C. Sharpe, Felicity Skidmore, U. Alton Smith, and Sally Merrill. 1984. *Post Program Impacts of the Youth Incentive Entitlement Pilot Projects.* NewYork: Manpower Demonstration Research Corporation.

Gueron, Judith M. 1984. *Lessons From a Job Guarantee: The Youth Incentive Entitlement Pilot Projects.* New York: Manpower Demonstration Research Corporation.

Holzer, Harry. 1996. *What Employers Want: Job Prospects for Less-Educated Workers.* New York: Russell Sage Foundation.

Kasarda, John U. 1993. "Inner-City Concentrated Poverty and Neighborhood Distress: 1970-1990." *Housing Policy Debate* 4(3): pp. 253-302.

Katz, Lawrence. 1996. "Wage Subsidies for the Disadvantaged." National Bureau of Economic Research, Inc. Cambridge, MA, Working Paper 5679.

Local Community Fact Book for Chicago-1950.1953. Chicago Community Inventory, University of Chicago.

Local Community Fact Book for Chicago-Chicago Area. 1960. 1953. Chicago Community Inventory, University of Chicago.

Massey, Douglas S., and Nancy A. Denton. 1993. *Amencan Apartheid: Segregation and the Making of the Underclass.* Cambridge, MA: Harvard University Press.

Newman, Katherine and Chauncy Lennon. 1995. "Finding Work in the Inner City: How Hard is it Now? How Hard will it be for AFUC Recipients?" Russell Sage Foundation, Working Paper #76, October.

Thurow, Lester. "The Crusade That's Killing Prosperity." *American Prospect*, March-April, pp. 54 - 59.

Venkatesh, Sudhir. 1996. *Private Lives. Public Housing: An Ethnography of the Robert Taylor Homes Ph.D. dissertation*, University of Chicago.

William, Robin M. Jr. 1947. "The Reduction of Intergroup Tensions," *Social Science Research Council Bulletin 57.*

Wilson, William Julius. 1987. *The Truly Disadvantaged: The Inner City. The Underclass and Public Policy.* Chicago: University of Chicago Press.

Wilson, William Julius. 1996. *When Work Disappears: The World of the New Urban Poor.* New York: Alfred A. Knopf.

New Standards, Old Inequalities: The Current Challenge for African-American Education

By Linda Darling-Hammond

The education reform movement in the United States has begun to focus increasingly on the development of new standards for students: virtually all states have begun the process of creating standards for graduation, new curriculum frameworks to guide instruction, and new assessments to test students' knowledge. President Clinton has proposed a new national test, and many school districts across the country are weighing in with their own versions of standards-based reform, including new curricula, testing systems, accountability mechanisms, and promotion or graduation requirements.

The rhetoric of these reforms is appealing. Students cannot succeed in meeting the demands of the new economy if they do riot encounter much more challenging work in school, many argue, and schools cannot be stimulated to improve, unless the real accomplishments—or deficits—of their students are brought to public attention. There is certainly merit to these arguments. But standards and tests alone will not improve schools or create educational opportunities where they do not now exist. The implications for students who have not received an adequate education are suggested by such back-to-school headlines as this one in the Raleigh, North Carolina News and Observer: "20% of Wake Forest University Seniors Could Fail Competency Test." The article states: "Among this year's ninth graders, 40 percent of black students have met the eighth-grade competency requirement; among 12th graders, 66 percent have" (September 11, 1997).

The bottom line for students, especially African-American and other students of color, is whether investments in better teaching, curriculum,

109

and schooling will follow the press for new standards, or whether standards built on a foundation of continued inequality in education will simply support tests that more effectively certify student failure and reduce access to future education and employment.

In this article, I review the current educational attainment of African-American students, the relationship of educational achievement to school inputs, the existence of continued inequalities in access to key educational resources, and the implications for developing policies that can improve children's chances for school and life success.

THE SOCIAL AND ECONOMIC CHALLENGE

The requirements for success in today's knowledge-based economy are indeed changing. By the first decade of the 21st century, nearly 50 percent of all jobs will require the high levels of knowledge and skills once reserved for educating the few. Only about 10 percent of all jobs will offer the kind of routine work factories once provided for low-skilled workers, and these will pay far less than what such jobs offered only 20 years ago (Drucker, 1994). As Figure 1 shows, only college-educated workers have come close to holding their own economically over the last two decades, while those with a high school education or less have steadily lost real income, as previously well-paid factory jobs have become automated or moved overseas.

Peter Drucker (1994) notes that the rise and fall of the blue-collar class between 1950 and 2000 is the most rapid of any class in the history of the world. From half of all U.S. jobs at mid-century, blue-collar employment will constitute only about 10 percent of the total by the end of this decade. People once able to earn high wages for routine forms of work are often unable to move into the more intellectually and interpersonally demanding jobs the new economy has to offer—jobs that require greater capacity to take initiative, to organize work with others, to deal with novel problems, and to use technologies as well as higher levels of basic literacy and mathematical skills.

The great majority of the new jobs require qualifications the industrial worker does not possess and is poorly equipped to acquire. They require a good deal of formal education and the ability to acquire and to apply theoretical and analytical knowledge. They require a different approach to work and a different mind-set. Above all, they require a habit of continuous learning. Displaced industrial workers thus cannot simply move into knowledge work or services the way displaced farmers and domestic workers moved into industrial work (Drucker, 1986, p. 62).

The attainment of these skills is rapidly becoming the major predictor of employment and wages, and demand for these skills has created growing disparities in wages between high school and college graduates. Longitudinal studies of high school graduates show that even among individuals with the same degrees, those with higher levels of skill increasingly have greater earning capacity. Surveys of employers indicate that even entry-level jobs require workers who have mastered higher levels of basic skills, are technologically literate, and can plan and monitor much of their own work (Murnane and Levy, 1996).

More than ever before in our nation's history, education is not only the ticket to economic success but to basic survival. Whereas a high school dropout had two chances out of three of getting a job 20 years ago, today he has less than one chance out of three, and the job he can get pays less than half of what he would once have earned (WT Grant Foundation, 1988). The effects of dropping out are much worse for African-American young people than for whites. In 1993, a recent school dropout who was black had only a one in four chance of being employed, whereas the odds for his white counterpart were about one in two (NCES, 1995, p. 88). Even recent graduates from high school struggle to find jobs. Among African-American high school graduates not enrolled in college, only 42 percent were employed in 1993, as compared with 72 percent of white graduates (Figure 2). Those who do not succeed in school are becoming part of a growing underclass, cut off from productive engagement in society. And working-class young people and adults who were prepared for the disappearing jobs of the past teeter on the brink of downward social mobility.

Because the economy can no longer absorb many unskilled workers at decent wages, lack of education is increasingly linked to crime and welfare dependency. Women who have not finished high school are much

111

more likely than others to be on welfare (Figure 3), while men are much more likely to be incarcerated. National investments in the last decade have tipped heavily toward imprisonment rather than empowerment through education. While schools in California have experienced continuous cutbacks over the last decade, for example, the prison population there has increased by more than 600 percent.

Nationwide, during the 1980s, federal, state, and local expenditures for corrections grew by over 900 percent, and for prosecution and legal services by over 1,000 percent (Miller, 1997), while prison populations more than doubled (U.S. Department of Commerce, 1996, 219). During the same decade, per pupil expenditures for schools grew by only about 26 percent in real dollar terms, and much less in cities (NCES, 1994).

In 1993, there were more African-American citizens on probation, in jail, in prison, or on parole (1,985,000) than there were in college (1,412,000) (U.S. Department of Commerce, table numbers 281 and 354, pp. 181 and 221). Increased incarceration, and its disproportionate effects on the African-American community, are a function of new criminal justice policies, ongoing police discrimination (see, e.g., Miller, 1997), and a lack of access to education that could lead to employment. More than half the adult prison population has literacy skills below those required by the labor market (Barton & Coley, 1996), and nearly 40 percent of adjudicated juvenile delinquents have treatable learning disabilities that went undiagnosed and untreated in the schools (Gemignani, 1994).

Meanwhile, schools have changed slowly. Most are still organized to prepare only about 20 percent of their students for "thinking work"—those students who are tracked very early into gifted and talented, "advanced," or honors courses. These opportunities are least available to African-American, Latino and Native-American students. Furthermore, schools that serve large numbers of African-American students are least likely to offer the kind of curriculum and teaching needed to meet the new standards. They are typically funded at lower levels than schools serving a white and more affluent population, and they often lack the courses, materials, equipment, and qualified teachers needed to give students access to the education they will need to participate in today's and tomorrow's economy.

As a consequence of structural inequalities in access to knowledge and resources, students from racial and ethnic "minority" groups in the United States face persistent and profound barriers to educational opportunities. Serious policy attention to these ongoing, systematic inequalities is critical for improving educational quality and outcomes. If Americans do not recognize that students experience very different educational realities, policies will continue to be based on the presumption that it is students, not their schools or classroom circumstances, that are the sources of unequal educational attainment.

CLOSING THE GAP: CHANGES IN EDUCATIONAL ACHIEVEMENT

The struggle to close the gap in educational achievement between African-American and white students has been a tortuous one featuring both progress and pitfalls over the last 20 years. The good news is that overall educational attainment for black Americans has increased sharply and fairly steadily since 1960 (see Figure 4) in terms of the proportion completing both high school and college. By 1995, nearly three-quarters (74 percent) of black Americans had completed four or more years of high school—up from only 20 percent in 1960—a trajectory that has closed much of the gap with white Americans in this regard. However, the 13 percent of black Americans who had completed four or more years of college by 1995 represented just over half the proportion of white Americans attaining a college degree—a critical differential, given the declining returns to high school education and the growing demands for higher levels of education and skills (Table 1).

That black citizens want more education is witnessed by the fact that there are more African Americans of all ages who are enrolled in schools and colleges than ever before. In fact, for the first time ever, the proportion of blacks enrolled in school exceeds the proportion of whites in every age group—from preschoolers to adults—with the exception of 18- to 24-year-olds (Table 2). These trends suggest the passion with which most black Americans pursue learning as an avenue to greater opportunity. Rates of participation in preschool education, however, vary sharply by income, with high-income families more than twice as likely as low-

113

income families to have 3- and 4-year-olds enrolled (NCES, 1995, p. 28). The lower rates of attendance for African American 18- to 21- year-olds, particularly in comparison with others in their peer group, also suggest a problem that requires serious attention.

One source of concern is the fact that dropout rates have been increasing for black male students since 1990, reaching 17.5 percent in 1994, following steady declines between 1975 and 1990 (Table 3). This undercuts the good news regarding recent improvements in college-going rates of black high school graduates, which had declined during the 1980s, but have climbed in the last few years to reach 50 percent (Table 4), as compared with 63 percent for white graduates. The increase in college-going rates appears to be at least partly a function of improvements in financial aid and in the overall economy, which may be putting a college education within reach for a greater number of young students. As Figure 5 indicates, while family income is still an important determinant of college enrollment, opportunities for low-income students have improved since 1991. With college dropout rates also hovering around 50 percent, however, and African-American students still concentrated in two-year colleges where attrition rates are high, the question remains: How well will students be able to capitalize on these opportunities to graduate with the skills needed to compete in the current labor market?

Questions about the adequacy of black students' skill levels remain serious. On national assessments in reading, writing, mathematics, and science, black students' performance continues to lag behind that of white students, with uneven progress in closing the gap. In reading, large gains in black students' performance throughout the 1970s and '80s have actually reversed. Since 1988, with scores registering declines at all age levels (see Figure 6). There are several possible reasons for these recent trends, ranging from increased family and community stresses (poverty, poor health, family difficulties, and community violence) to lower rates of in-school or out-of-school reading among children, and to declining school quality in the central cities where most black students are enrolled. The situation in many urban schools has deteriorated, as drops in per pupil expenditures have been accompanied by tax cuts and growing immigration and enrollments; by increased numbers of students requiring special educational services; and by growing numbers of unqualified teachers who have been hired since the late 1980s, a trend which I discuss below.

Another possibility is that the curriculum in central-city schools is proving increasingly inadequate to the demands of new curricula and assessments (including the revised National Assessment of Educational Progress, which is the source of these data). Many urban systems have focused their curricula more on rote learning of "basic" skills than on thoughtful examination of serious literature or assignments requiring frequent and extended writing (Cooper & Sherk, 1989; Darling-Hammond, 1997). As new tests focus more on reading for meaning and ask students to construct written responses that demonstrate their ability to analyze and interpret text, they diverge from the low-level skills taught in many texts and tested by multiple choice examinations. Students whose education is guided mostly by the basal readers and workbooks compatible with older kinds of tests find themselves at a growing disadvantage when they confront the more challenging expectations of new standards and assessments, as I describe further below.

In writing, both white students' and African-American students' scores declined between 1984 and 1990, but increased between 1990 and 1992, except for those of black 11th graders. Huge increases for black 8th graders and smaller ones for 4th graders may signal a shift in schools' attention to the teaching of writing once again, and to the use of assessments that go beyond multiple choice and short-answer responses. Even with these strides, however, black 4th graders have still not reached the level of performance their age-mates had achieved in 1984, and they lag further behind their white peers than they did then.

Although black students' scores have increased significantly in mathematics and science over the years, the gap has widened since the late 1980s, as white students' scores have improved even faster (Figure 7). In 1992, the average black 17-year-old did about as well as the average white 13-year-old in mathematics and about as well as the average white 9-year-old in science. As I discuss below, black students' lack of access to quali-

115

fied teachers, challenging curriculum, high-quality materials, equipment, and laboratories are serious impediments to progress in these subjects.

INEQUALITY AND ACHIEVEMENT

Despite the rhetoric of American equality and the efforts of many involved in school desegregation and finance reform, the school experiences of African-American and other "minority" students in the United States continue to be substantially separate and unequal. Nearly two-thirds of "minority" students attend predominantly minority schools, and one-third of black students attend intensely segregated schools (90 percent or more minority enrollment) (Garfield, Monfort, and Aaron, 1989, cited in Schofield, 1992, p. 336), most of which are in central cities.

As of 1993, 55 percent of all students in central-city schools were black or Hispanic (NCES, 1995, p.121). This concentration facilitates inequality. Not only do funding systems and tax policies leave most urban districts with fewer resources than their suburban neighbors, but schools with high concentrations of "minority" students receive fewer resources than other schools within these districts. And tracking systems exacerbate these inequalities by segregating many "minority" students within schools, allocating still fewer educational opportunities to them at the classroom level.

In their review of resource allocation studies, Macphail-Wilcox and King (1986) summarize the resulting situation as follows:

School expenditure levels correlate positively with student socioeconomic status and negatively with educational need when school size and grade level are controlled statistically.... Teachers with higher salaries are concentrated in high income and low minority schools. Furthermore, pupil-teacher ratios are higher in schools with larger minority and low-income student populations.... Educational units with higher proportions of low-income and minority students are allocated fewer fiscal and educational resources than are more affluent educational units, despite the probability that these students have substantially greater need for both (p. 425).

Although some progress has been made since Brown v. Board of Education, dramatic disparities persist. Jonathan Kozol's 1991 *Savage*

Inequalities describes the striking differences between public schools in urban settings—schools whose population is between 95 percent and 99 percent non-white (Kozol, 1991, p. 3)—and their suburban counterparts. While Chicago public schools spent just over $5,000 per student in 1989, nearby Niles Township High School spent $9,371 per student. While central city Camden, New Jersey, schools spent $3,500 that year, affluent suburban Princeton spent $7,725 per student. Schools in New York City spent $7,300 per student in 1990, while those in nearby suburbs like Manhasset and Great Neck spent over $15,000 per student for a population with many fewer special needs (Kozol, 1991, pp. 236-237).

Savage Inequalities is replete with familiar yet poignant stories: MacKenzie High School in Detroit where word processing courses are taught without word processors because the school cannot afford them (Kozol, 1991, p. 198); public School 261 in New York City, which has no windows in many classrooms and where recess is not possible because there is no playground (Kozol, 1991, pp. 85-87); and East St. Louis Senior High School whose biology lab has no laboratory tables or usable dissecting kits (Kozol, 1991, p. 28). Meanwhile, children in neighboring suburban schools enjoy features like a 27-acre campus (Kozol, 1991, p. 65), an athletic program featuring golf, fencing, ice hockey, and lacrosse (Kozol, 1991, p.157), and a computer hookup to Dow Jones to study stock transactions (Kazol, 1991, p.158).

The students notice. As one New York City 16-year-old notes of his school, where holes in ceilings expose rusty pipes and water pours in on rainy days:

"You can understand things better when you go among the wealthy. You look around you at their school, although it's impolite to do that, and you take a deep breath at the sight of all those beautiful surroundings. Then you come back home and see that these are things you do not have. You think of the difference (Kozol, 1991, p. 104)."

A classmate adds:

If you ... put white children in this building in our place, this school would start to shine. No question. The parents would say: 'This building sucks. It's ugly. Fix it up.' They'd fix it fast—no question .... People on the outside may think that we don't know what it is like for other students, but we visit other schools and we have eyes and we have brains. You cannot hide the differences. You see it and compare ..." (Kozol, 1991, p.104)

The disparities in physical facilities are just the tip of the iceberg. Shortages of funds make it difficult for urban and poor rural schools to compete in the marketplace for qualified teachers and to provide the equipment and learning materials students need. When districts do not find qualified teachers, they assign the least able individuals to the students with the least political clout. In 1990, for example, the Los Angeles City School District was sued by students in predominantly minority schools because their schools were not only overcrowded and less well-funded than other schools, they were also disproportionately staffed by inexperienced and unprepared teachers hired on emergency credentials. Unequal assignment of teachers creates ongoing differentials in expenditures and access to educational resources, including the knowledge that well-prepared teachers rely on in offering high-quality instruction. (Rodriguez *et al* v. Los Angeles Unified School District, Superior Court of the County of Los Angeles #C611358. Consent decree filed August 12, 1992).

Recent studies of resource allocations in New York found similar patterns. By virtually any resource measure—state and local dollars per pupil, student-teacher ratios and student-staff ratios, class sizes, teacher experience, and teacher qualifications—districts with greater proportions of poor and minority students receive fewer resources than others (Berne, 1995; NY Study Group, 1993).

Such disparities in resources are a function of how public education in the United States is funded. In most cases, education costs are supported by a system of general taxes—primarily local property taxes—along with state grants-in-aid. Because these funds are typically raised and spent locally, districts with higher property values have greater resources with which to fund their schools, even when poorer districts tax themselves at proportionally higher rates. In Texas, for instance, the 100 wealthiest districts taxed their local property at an average rate of 47 cents per $100 of assessed worth in 1989; at that level of taxes, they were able to spend over

$7,000 per student. Meanwhile, the 100 poorest districts, taxing themselves at a rate of over 70 cents per $100, were able to raise only enough to spend some $3,000 per student (Kozol, 1991, p.225).

These disparities translate into real differences in the services provided in schools: higher spending districts have smaller classes, higher paid and more experienced teachers, and greater instructional resources (Hartman, 1988); They also have better facilities, more up-to-date equipment, and a wider range of course offerings (ETS, 1991). Districts serving large proportions of poor children generally have the fewest resources. Thus, those students least likely to encounter a wide array of educational resources at home are also least likely to encounter them at school (ETS, 1991). As Taylor and Piche (1991) demonstrate:

Inequitable systems of school finance inflict disproportionate harm on minority and economically disadvantaged students. On an inter-state basis, such students are concentrated in states, primarily in the South, that have the lowest capacities to finance public education. On an intra-state basis, many of the states with the widest disparities in educational expenditures are large industrial states. In these states, many minorities and economically disadvantaged students are located in property-poor urban districts which fare the worst in educational expenditures. In addition, in several states economically disadvantaged students, white and black, are concentrated in rural districts, which suffer from fiscal inequity (pp. xi-xii).

Furthermore, this connection between inadequate funding and the race and social status of students exacerbates the difficulties of creating either integrated schools or adequately funded ones. The vicious cycle was described early on in the fight for school funding reform:

School inequality between suburbia and central city crucially reinforces racial isolation in housing; and the resulting racial segregation of the schools constantly inhibits progress toward funding a therapeutic answer for the elimination of school inequality. If we are to exercise the evils of separateness and inequality, we must view them together, for each dimension of the problem renders the other more difficult to solve—racially separate schools inhibit elimination of school inequality, and unequal schools retard eradication of school segregation (Silard & Goldstein, 1974, p. 324).

In total, courts in ten of the thirty-one states where suits have been filed have found their state's school finance scheme to be unconstitutional on one of three grounds: the federal Constitution's fourteenth amendment, the state constitution's equal opportunity clause, or the state constitution's education article (Mcusic, 1991, p. 307). A series of state challenges in the 1970s was followed by a decade of little activity. During this time there has remained substantial variation in the share of school funding provided by different states, with less activism aimed at equalization in states where judicial pressure has been absent (Wong, 1989). The issue was rejoined in the late 1980s, when successful finance suits were brought in New Jersey, Texas, Montana, Kentucky, and Tennessee (ETS, 1991).

Although the legal intricacies by which the courts have made their decisions are beyond the scope of this article, some of the conceptual grounds on which opponents of such decisions rest their arguments are not. In particular, opponents of school finance reform often argue that differences in per-pupil expenditures are irrelevant to issues of equity, since financial input does not affect the quality of education a district offers. They argue that no definitive correlation has been shown between money spent and educational quality.

The relationship between educational funding and educational achievement was placed in question in 1966, when James Coleman (1966) and a team of researchers issued *Equality of Educational Opportunity*, which later came to be known as the Coleman Report. Although the report pointed out sources of inequality that, it argued, should be remedied, its assertion that "[s]chools bring little influence to bear on a child's achievement that is independent of his background and general social context" (cited in Ferguson, 1991, p. 468) became widely viewed asserting that school funding does not affect school achievement. As later analyses pointed out, it is in part the high correlation between students' backgrounds and their schools' resources that makes it difficult in macroanalytic studies to identify an independent effect of schooling on achievement (see e.g., Macphail-Wilcox & King, 1986). The "no effect" finding in the Coleman Report was also a predictable result of the use of gross measures of inputs and outcomes aggregated to the school level, a shortcoming of the data also noted by the report's authors.

Recent studies, however, have provided solid evidence that money does make a difference, especially for African-American children. Analyzing a data set covering 900 Texas school districts, with data more extensive than that available to Coleman and his team of researchers, Ronald Ferguson (1991) found that the single most important measurable cause of increased student learning was teacher expertise, measured by teacher performance on a statewide recertification exam, as well as teacher experience and possession of a master's degree. Together, these variables accounted for 40 percent of the variance in student test scores. Holding socioeconomic status constant, the wide variation in teachers' qualifications in Texas accounted almost entirely for the variation in black and white students' test scores.

Ferguson also found that class size, at the critical point of a teacher/student ratio of 1:18, was a statistically significant determinant of student outcomes (Ferguson, 1991), as was small school size. Other data also indicate that black students are more likely to attend large schools than white students (Paterson Institute, 1996) with much larger than average class sizes (NCES, 1997a, p. A-119), and confirm that smaller schools and classes make a difference for student achievement (for a review, see Darling-Hammond, 1997).

Ferguson repeated this analysis with a less well-developed data set in Alabama, and still found sizable influences of teacher expertise and smaller class sizes on student achievement; gains in reading and mathematics (Ferguson and Ladd, 1996). They found that 31 percent of the predicted difference in mathematics achievement between districts in the top and bottom quartiles was explained by teacher qualifications and class sizes, while 29.5 percent was explained by poverty, race, and parent education.

Both of these findings are confirmed elsewhere. For example, when Eleanor Armour-Thomas and her colleagues (1989) compared a group of exceptionally effective elementary schools to a group of low-achieving schools with similar demographic characteristics in New York City, they

found that differences in teacher qualifications and experience accounted for roughly 90 percent of the variance in student reading and mathematics scores at grades 3, 6, and 8. Far more than any other factor, teacher
expertise made the difference in what children learned. And unequal
access to well-qualified teachers, a major side effect of unequal expenditures, is one of the most critical factors in the underachievement of
African-American students.

WHAT MATTERS IN TEACHING?

Over the last 20 years, educational research has exploded the myths
that any teaching is as effective as any other and that unequally trained
and experienced teachers are equally advantageous to students. In a
study documenting the positive effects of teaching experience on teaching effectiveness, Murnane and Phillips (1981, pp. 453-454) note:

The question of whether teachers become more productive as they
gain teaching experience has been of interest to policymakers for many
years. One reason is that schools serving children from low-income families have typically been staffed with less experienced teachers than
schools serving middle-class children. This has led to court tests of
whether the uneven distribution of teaching experience constitutes discrimination against low-income children.

Studies consistently find that new teachers—those with fewer than
three years of experience—tend to be less effective than more experienced teachers (Murnane & Phillips, 1981; Moskowitz & Hayman, 1974;
Rottenberg & Berliner, 1990). Especially in the unsupported environment most encounter, beginning teachers experience a wide range of
problems in learning to teach: problems with classroom management,
motivating students, being aware of and dealing appropriately with individual learning needs and differences, and developing a diverse repertoire of instructional strategies (Veenman, 1984; Johnston & Ryan, 1983;
Rottenberg & Berliner, 1990).

Researchers are now identifying what it is that expert veterans do in the
classroom that distinguishes their teaching from that of novices (see, e.g.,
Berliner, 1986; Shulman, 1987; Grossman, 1990). Among other things,

expert teachers are much more sensitive to students' needs and individual differences; they are more skilled at engaging and motivating students; and they have a wider repertoire of instructional strategies to call upon for addressing student needs. Much of this research also demonstrates the importance of educating teachers with the knowledge and skills that, when used in the classroom, improve the caliber of instruction and the success of students' learning (Berliner, 1984; Darling-Hammond, 1992).

This is particularly important in light of the fact that policy-makers have nearly always been willing to fill teaching vacancies by lowering standards, so that people who have had little or no preparation for teaching can be hired, especially if their clients are minority and low-income students. Although this practice is often excused on the presumption that virtually anyone can figure out how to teach, various reviews of research summarizing the results of more than 200 studies have concluded that fully prepared and certified teachers are more highly rated and more successful with students than teachers without full preparation (Darling-Hammond, 1992; Evertson, Hawley, & Zlotnik, 1985; Ashton & Crocker, 1986; Ashton & Crocker, 1987; Greenberg, 1983; Druva & Anderson, 1983). Thus, policies that resolve shortages in poor districts by supporting the hiring of unprepared teachers serve only to exacerbate the inequalities low-income and minority children experience.

The extent and kind of teacher preparation are especially important in determining the effectiveness of teachers in "school-based" subjects (those that students tend to learn primarily in school rather than through informal learning outside of school), such as mathematics, science, and early reading (Hice, 1970; Lupone 1961; Mcneil, 1974). Teacher education is also related to the use of teaching strategies that encourage higher order learning and the use of strategies responsive to students' needs and learning styles.

A number of studies have found that teachers who enter without full preparation are less able to plan and redirect instruction to meet students' needs (and less aware of the need to do so), less skilled in implementing instruction, less able to anticipate students' knowledge and potential difficulties, and less likely to see it as their job to do so, often blaming students if their teaching is not successful (Bledsoe, Cox, & Burnham, 1967; Copley, 1974; Rottenberg & Berliner, Bents & Bents, 1990; Grossman, 1989; 1990).

These findings are reflected in Gomez and Grobe's (1990) study of the performance of alternate-route candidates hired in Dallas with only a few weeks of prior training. The performance of these candidates was much more uneven than that of trained beginners, with markedly lower ratings on their knowledge of instructional techniques and models, and with a much greater proportion of them (from 2 to 16 times as many) likely to be rated "poor" on each of the teaching factors evaluated. The proportions rated "poor" ranged from 8 percent on reading instruction to 17 percent on classroom management. The effects of this unevenness showed up most strongly on students' achievement in language arts, where students of the alternate route teachers scored significantly lower than students of fully prepared beginning teachers after adjusting for initial achievement levels.

The reasons for this are no mystery. Dorothy Strickland (1985) stresses that, for early literacy development, teachers must be able to develop programs that accommodate a variety of cognitive styles and learning rates, with activities that broaden rather than reduce the range of possibilities for learning. Teachers must receive preparation that allows them to understand the nature of language and language development, as well as the nature of child growth and development. These understandings undergird knowledge of appropriate procedures for fostering language growth at various stages of development. Recent data from the National Assessment of Educational Progress show that the kinds of classroom practices associated with higher reading scores—using trade books and literature rather than basal readers and workbooks, frequent discussions and writing, group projects and oral presentations—are also more frequently found in the classrooms of teachers with more training in education and in teaching reading (NAEP, 1994). Unfortunately, the same report shows that these practices and better-trained teachers are less likely to be available to urban and minority students.

James Comer (1988) similarly emphasizes the importance of preparing teachers with a strong background in child development, as a key to the kind of teaching that has been so successful in his School

Development Program. Although the evidence clearly indicates that such preparation makes a difference in what children learn, few teachers have had access to such preparation and even fewer of them are teaching in high-poverty schools.

Furthermore, it seems that appropriate preparation in planning and classroom management is one of the factors that allows teachers to focus on the kind of complex teaching that is needed to develop higher order skills. Since the novel tasks required for complex problem-solving are more difficult to manage than the routine tasks associated with learning simple skills, lack of classroom management ability can lead teachers to "dumb down" the curriculum to more easily control student work (Carter & Doyle, 1987; Doyle, 1986).

Access to Good Teaching. In *Closing the Divide*, Robert Dreeben (1987) describes the results of his study of reading instruction and outcomes for 300 black and white first-graders across seven schools in the Chicago area. He found that differences in reading outcomes among students were almost entirely explained, not by socioeconomic status or race, but by the quality of instruction the students received:

Our evidence shows that the level of learning responds strongly to the quality of instruction: having and using enough time, covering a substantial amount of rich curricular material, and matching instruction appropriately to the ability levels of groups .... When black and white children of comparable ability experience the same instruction, they do about equally well, and this is true when the instruction is excellent in quality and when it is inadequate (p. 34).

However, the study also found that the quality of instruction received by African-American students was, on average, much lower than that received by white students, thus creating a racial gap in aggregate achievement at the end of first grade. In fact, the highest ability group in Dreeben's sample was in a school in a low-income African-American neighborhood. These students, though, learned less during first grade than their lower-aptitude white counterparts. Why? Because their teacher was unable to provide the kind of appropriate and challenging instruction this highly talented group deserved.

Another study of African-American high school youths randomly placed in public housing in the Chicago suburbs rather than in the city found similar results. Compared with their comparable city-placed peers, who were of equivalent income and initial academic attainment, the students who were enabled to attend largely white and better-funded suburban schools had better educational outcomes across many dimensions: They were substantially more likely to have the opportunity to take challenging courses, receive additional academic help, graduate on time, attend college, and secure good jobs (Kaufman & Rosenbaum, 1992).

These examples are drawn from carefully controlled studies that confirm what many other studies have suggested: Much of the difference in school achievement found between African-American students and others is due to the effects of substantially different school opportunities—in particular, greatly disparate access to high-quality teachers and teaching (see, e.g., Barr & Dreeben, 1983; Dreeben & Gamoran, 1986; Dreeben & Barr, 1987; College Board, 1985; Oakes, 1990; Darling-Hammond & Snyder, 1992)

The Unequal Distribution of Teachers. Minority and low-income students in urban settings are most likely to find themselves in classrooms staffed by inadequately prepared, inexperienced, and ill-qualified teachers. That's because funding inequities, distributions of local power, labor-market conditions, and dysfunctional hiring practices conspire to produce teacher shortages of which these students bear the brunt. The data confirm that these difficulties continue to be structural conditions of urban schooling.

● In 1994, shortages of teachers—as measured by difficulty in filling vacancies—were two to three times greater in central cities than in suburbs in fields ranging from elementary education to mathematics, biology, bilingual education, music, and industrial arts (NCES, 1996, pp. 142-143).

● By every measure of qualifications—certification, major or minor in the field taught, or preparation for secondary assignment field—unqualified and underprepared teachers continue to be found disproportionately in schools serving greater numbers of low-income or minority students (NCES, 1997a).

● In 1994, just over 20 percent of newly hired public school teachers were hired without having met regular certification requirements (NCTAF, 1997). The vast majority of these teachers were assigned to the most disadvantaged schools in central city and poor rural school districts.

All of this means that districts with the greatest concentrations of poor children, minority children, and children of immigrants are also those where incoming teachers are least likely to have learned about up-to-date teaching methods or about how children grow, learn, and develop—and what to do if they are having difficulties.

Teacher shortages subvert the quality of education in a number of ways. They make it hard for districts to be selective in the quality of teachers they hire, and they often result in the hiring of teachers who have not completed (or sometimes even begun) their pedagogical training. In addition, when faced with shortages, districts often hire substitutes, assign teachers outside their fields of qualification, expand class sizes, or cancel course offerings. As Figure 8 illustrates, all of these strategies are used most frequently in schools serving large numbers of minority students. No matter what strategies are adopted, the quality of instruction suffers.

The vast majority of underprepared teachers are assigned to the most disadvantaged central-city schools where working conditions are least attractive and turnover rates are highest (Darling-Hammond, 1990a; 1992). As Figures 9 and 10 show, students in schools serving large numbers of low-income and minority students are least likely to have the best-qualified teachers (those with certification and a degree in the field they teach) and most likely to have totally unqualified or underqualified teachers (those that lack a regular certificate for their jobs). This situation is partly a function of real shortages, but is mostly due to urban district hiring practices that are often cumbersome, poorly managed, insensitive to teacher qualifications, and slowed down by both seniority transfer rules and a variety of other self-inflicted procedures (National Commission on Teaching and America's Future, 1996).

Furthermore, since many of the more expert and experienced teachers transfer to more desirable schools and districts, when they are able to, new teachers are typically given assignments in the most disadvantaged schools that offer the fewest supports (Wise, Darling-Hammond, & Berry, 1987; Murnane *et al*, 1991). Because they confront challenging assignments without mentoring or other help, attrition rates for new teachers, especially in cities, average 30 percent or more over the first five years of teaching (Wise, Darling-Hammond, & Berry, 1987; Grissmer & Kirby, 1987; NCES, 1997b).

This adds more problems, from staff instability to the already difficult circumstances in which central-city youths attend school. Where these practices persist, many children in central-city schools are taught by a parade of short-term substitute teachers, inexperienced teachers without support, and underqualified teachers who know neither their subject matter nor effective teaching methods well. The California Commission on Teaching (1985) concluded that disproportionate numbers of minority and poor students are taught throughout their entire school careers by the least qualified teachers. This sets up the school failure that society predicts for low-income and minority children—a failure that it helps to create for them by its ineffectiveness in dealing with the issues of teacher supply and quality.

Oakes' (1990) nationwide study of the distribution of mathematics and science opportunities confirmed these pervasive patterns. Based on teacher experience, certification status, preparation in his discipline, degrees, self-confidence, and teacher's and principal's perceptions of children's competence, it is clear that low-income and minority students have less contact with the best-qualified science and mathematics teachers. Principals of high-minority and low-income schools report that they have high levels of teaching vacancies and great difficulties filling them with qualified teachers. Students in such schools have only a 50-percent chance of being taught by a math or science teacher who is certified at all, and an even less chance of being taught by one who is fully qualified for his teaching assignment by virtue of the subject area(s) he prepared to teach. Oakes concludes:

Our evidence lends considerable support to the argument that low-income, minority, and inner-city students have fewer opportunities. ...

They have considerably less access to science and mathematics knowledge at school, fewer material resources, less-engaging learning activities in their classrooms, and less-qualified teachers .... The differences we have observed are likely to reflect more general patterns of educational inequality (pp. *x-xi*).

Just as Dreeben found in his study of early reading teaching, Oakes discovered that "high-ability students at low-socioeconomic status, high-minority schools may actually have fewer opportunities than low-ability students who attend more advantaged schools" (p. *vii*). The pattern of systematic underexposure to good teaching tends to put all children in high-minority schools at risk.

Access to High Quality Curriculum. In addition to being taught by less-qualified teachers than their white and suburban counterparts, urban and minority students face dramatic differences in courses, curriculum materials, and equipment. One easily measured resource important to work in the modern world is computer availability. A number of studies demonstrates that access to and uses of computers differ significantly for minority and white students, both at home and at school. Although the situation is improving, only about 11 percent of African-American and Hispanic students compared with 33 percent of white students, had access to computers at home in 1993; schools did not equalize access. About 52 percent of African-American and Hispanic students used computers at school, compared with 62 percent of white students (see Table 5).

Within schools, students in classrooms with greater numbers of minority students have less access to computers both in terms of numbers per student and time available; their schools have far fewer teachers trained in the uses of computers (Becker, 1983; 1986; Oakes, 1990; Sutton, 1991). Furthermore, in predominantly minority schools and classrooms, personal computers are much more frequently used for drill-and-practice and much less frequently used to teach students to program, access data, and solve problems, with the computer serving as a tool rather than a master (Becker, 1983; Winkler *et al*, 1984; Sutton, 1991).

Lack of access to materials and equipment is a comparatively minor part of the problem. But unequal access to high-level courses and chal-

129

lenging curriculum explains much of the difference in achievement between minority and white students. For example, analyses of data from the High School and Beyond surveys demonstrate dramatic differences among students of various racial and ethnic groups in course-taking, in such areas as mathematics, science, and foreign languages (Pelavin & Kane, 1990). These data also demonstrate that, for students of all racial and ethnic groups, course-taking is strongly related to achievement: For students with similar course-taking records, achievement test score differences by race or ethnicity narrow substantially (College Board, 1985, 38; Jones, 1984; Jones et al, 1986; Moore & Smith, 1985).

One source of inequality is the fact that high-minority schools are much less likely to offer advanced and college preparatory courses in mathematics and science than are schools that serve affluent and largely white populations of students (Matthews, 1984; Cakes, 1990). Schools serving predominantly minority and poor populations offer fewer advanced and more remedial courses in academic subjects, and they have smaller academic tracks and larger vocational programs (NCES, 1985; Rock et al, 1985). The size and rigor of college-preparatory programs within its schools vary with the race and socioeconomic status of school populations (California State Department of Education, 1984). As plaintiffs noted in the New Jersey school finance case, wealthy and predominantly white Montclair offers foreign languages at the preschool level, while poor and predominantly black Paterson does not offer any until high school—and then, relatively few. And while 20 percent of 11th and 12th graders in wealthy Moorestown participate in Advanced Placement courses, none are even offered in any school in poor and predominantly Black Camden and East Orange (ETS, 1991, p. 9).

When high-minority, low-income schools offer any advanced or college-preparatory courses, they offer them to only a very tiny fraction of students. Thus, at the high school level, African Americans, Hispanics, and American Indians have traditionally been underrepresented in academic programs and overrepresented in vocational education programs, where they receive fewer courses in areas such as English, mathematics, and science (College Board, 1985). Furthermore, minority students in vocational education programs are enrolled earlier and more extensively in programs that train specifically for low-status occupations than are white students (Oakes, 1983). Even among the college bound, non-Asian minority students take fewer and less demanding mathematics, science, and foreign language courses (Pelavin & Kane, 1990).

The National Educational Longitudinal Survey of 1988 shows that African-American, Latino, Native American and low-income students continue to be much more likely than white or upper-income students to be placed in remedial and low-level courses (NCES, 1991). As Cakes (1992) explains:

The extraordinarily complex connections between tracking and social stratification play out in two ways. First, schools with predominantly low-income and minority student populations tend to be "bottom heavy." That is, they offer smaller academic tracks and larger remedial and vocational programs than do schools serving whiter, more affluent student bodies .... The second link between tracking and students' race and social class is forged in racially mixed schools through the disproportionate assignment of African-American and Latino students to low-track classes (p. 13).

The same forces that produce the flow of good teachers and rich educational resources to advantaged schools, and the ebb of opportunities from disadvantaged schools and students are at work within schools wherever tracking persists. Tracking persists in the face of growing evidence that it does not substantially benefit high achievers and tends to put low achievers at a serious disadvantage (Oakes, 1985; 1986; Hoffer, 1992; Kulik & Kulik, 1982; Slavin, 1990), in part because good teaching, a scarce resource, must be allocated. Scarce resources tend to get allocated to the students whose parents, advocates, or representatives have the most political clout. This results, not entirely but disproportionately, in the most highly qualified teachers teaching the most enriched curricula to the most advantaged students.

Evidence suggests that teachers themselves are tracked, with those judged to be the most competent and experienced—or those with the highest status-assigned to the top tracks (Cakes, 1986; Davis, 1986; Finley, 1984; Rosenbaum, 1976; Talbert, 1990; NCTAF, 1996). Expert, experienced

131

teachers who are in great demand are rewarded with opportunities to teach students who already know a lot. New teachers, unprepared teachers, and those teaching outside their field of preparation are often assigned students and classes that others do not care to teach; such teachers instruct students who would benefit most from the skills of expert, experienced teachers.

Tracking in U.S. schools is much more extensive than in most other countries. Starting in elementary schools as instructional groups and programs based on test scores and recommendations, tracking becomes highly formalized by junior high school. The result of this practice: Challenging curricula are rationed to a very small proportion of students, and far fewer of our students ever encounter the kinds of curricula that students in other countries typically experience (Mcknight *et al*, 1987; Usiskin, 1987; Useem, 1990; Wheelock, 1992).

Tracking exacerbates differential access to knowledge. As Oakes (1986) notes, assignments of poor and minority students to lower tracks are predictable:

One finding about placements is undisputed .... Disproportionate percentages of poor and minority youngsters (principally black and Hispanic) are placed in tracks for low-ability or non-college-bound students (NCES, 1985; Rosenbaum, 1980); further, minority students are consistently underrepresented in programs for the gifted and talented (College Board, 1985).

Though test scores and prior educational opportunities may provide one reason for these differential placements, race and socioeconomic status play a distinct role. Even after test scores are statistically controlled, race and socioeconomic status determine assignments to high school honors courses (Gamoran, 1992). This is true in part because of prior placements of students in upper tracks in earlier grades, in part because of counselors' views that they should advise students in ways that are "realistic" about their futures, and in part because of the greater effectiveness of parent interventions in tracking decisions for higher-SES students.

For similar reasons, race and socioeconomic status also affect students' placements in vocational and academic programs and more or less challenging courses within them (Oakes *et al*, 1992; Useem, 1990; Cicourel & Kitsuse, 1963). The seeds of this tracking are planted in "ability grouping" in elementary schools, and students' placements are well established long before they enter high schools (Moore & Davenport, 1988).

From "gifted and talented" programs at the elementary level through advanced courses in secondary schools, teachers who are generally the most skilled offer rich, challenging curricula to select groups of students, on the theory that only a few students can benefit from them. Yet the distinguishing feature of such programs, particularly at the elementary level, is not their difficulty, but their quality. Students in these programs are given opportunities to integrate ideas across fields of study. They have opportunities to think, write, create, and develop projects. They are challenged to explore. Though virtually all students would benefit from being similarly challenged, the opportunities for this sort of schooling remain acutely restricted.

Curricula differences like those I have described are widespread, and they explain much of the disparity between the achievements of white and minority students and between those of higher- and lower-income levels (Oakes, 1985; Lee & Bryk, 1988). When students of similar backgrounds and initial achievement levels are exposed to either more or less challenging curricula materials, those given richer opportunities outperform those placed in less challenging classes (Alexander & McDill, 1976; Oakes, 1985; Gamoran & Behrends, 1987).

Most studies have estimated the effects statistically, based on natural occurrences of different tracking policies. However, one study that randomly assigned 7th-grade at-risk students to either remedial, average, or honors mathematics classes found that at the end of the year, the at-risk students who took the honors class offering a pre-algebra curriculum outperformed all other students of similar backgrounds (Peterson, 1989).

In many instances, the reasons for restricting access to challenging courses is the scarcity of teachers who can teach in the fashion such curricula demand. In addition, schools continue to believe that few students need or will profit from such demanding instruction. Those beliefs are especially strong with respect to students of color. The disproportionately small enrollment of non-Asian minority students in gifted and talented programs is widespread. In most districts, though there are exceptions that result from different policies, African-American and Hispanic students in such courses are represented at well under half their representation in the population (College Board, 1985, pp. 31-33). Statistical patterns are brought alive by descriptions of sorting, like those offered by Kozol (1991) of a school in New York City:

The school is integrated in the strict sense that the middle and upper-middle-class white children here do occupy a building that contains some Asian and Hispanic and black children; but there is little integration in the classrooms ... (p. 93).

He describes how minority children are disproportionately assigned to special education classes that occupy small, cramped corners and split classrooms, while gifted and talented classes, overwhelmingly white with a few Asian students, occupy the most desirable spaces, filled with books and computers, where they learn, in the children's words, "logical thinking, problem-solving, respect for someone else's logic, and "reasoning." Students are recommended for these classes by their teachers and parents as well as by their test scores. Kozol wrote in his notes:

Six girls, four boys. Nine white, one Chinese. I am glad they have this class. But what about the others? Aren't there ten black children in the school who could enjoy this also? (p. 97)

Meanwhile, students placed in lower tracks are exposed to a limited, rote-oriented curriculum and ultimately achieve less than students of similar aptitude who are placed in academic programs or untracked classes (Gamoran & Mare, 1989; Cakes, 1985, 1990; Gamoran, 1990). Teacher interaction with students in low-track classes is less motivating and less supportive, as well as less demanding of higher order reasoning and responses (Good & Brophy, 1987). These interactions are also less academically oriented, and more likely to focus on behavioral criticisms, especially for minority students (Eckstrom & Villegas, 1991; Oakes, 1985). Presentations are less clear and less focused on higher order cognitive goals (Oakes, 1985).

In addition, many studies have found that students placed in the lowest tracks or in remedial programs—disproportionately low-income and minority students—are most apt to experience instruction geared only to multiple-choice tests, working at a low-cognitive level on test-oriented tasks that are profoundly disconnected from the skills they need to learn. Rarely are they given the opportunity to talk about what they know, to read challenging books, to write, to construct and solve problems in mathematics, science, or other subjects (Oakes, 1985; Cooper & Sherk, 1989; Davis, 1986; Trimble & Sinclair, 1986). Cooper & Sherk (1989) describe how such worksheet-based instruction focuses on the discrete "skill" bits featured on multiple-choice tests impedes students' progress toward literacy:

When hundreds of these worksheets, each of which presents a small, low-level skill related to reading, have been completed, children are said to have completed the "mastery" skills program. Often, these children still cannot read very well, if one defines reading as the ability to discern connected prose for comprehension.

[Furthermore], worksheets are devised in such a way, teachers are told, that the material teaches itself. As a result, the amount of oral communication between pupil and teacher and between pupil and pupil is drastically reduced .... [Yet] if children are to learn language, a part of which is reading, they must interact and communicate. They must have some opportunity to hear words being spoken, to pose questions, to conjecture, and to hypothesize .... (p. 318).

Their discussion—of what teachers should be able to do to support children's literacy development—maps onto what is known about the knowledge base for effective instruction generally. Good teachers construct active learning opportunities involving student collaboration and many uses of oral and written language; help students access prior knowledge that will frame for them the material to be learned; structure learning tasks, so that students have a basis for interpreting the new experiences they encounter; and engage students' higher order thought processes, including their capacities to hypothesize, predict, evaluate, integrate, and synthesize ideas (Cooper & Sherk, 1969; see also Resnick, 1987; Bowman, 1993; Braddock & McPartland, 1993; Garcia, 1993).

POLICY FOR EQUALITY: TOWARD EQUALIZATION OF EDUCATIONAL OPPORTUNITY

The common presumption about educational inequality is that it resides primarily in those students who come to school with inadequate capacities to benefit from what education a school has to offer. The fact that U.S. schools are structured in ways that routinely offer students dramatically unequal learning opportunities, based on their race and social status, is simply not widely recognized. If the academic outcomes for minority and low-income children are to change, aggressive action must be taken to enhance the caliber and quantity of learning opportunities they encounter. These efforts must include equalization of financial resources; changes in curriculum and testing policies; and improvements in the availability of highly qualified teachers for all students.

Resource Equalization. Progress in equalizing resources to students will require attention to inequalities at all levels among states, among districts, among schools within districts, and among students differentially placed in classrooms, courses, and tracks that offer substantially disparate opportunities to learn. As a consequence of systematic inequalities at each of these levels, minority and low-income students not only are frequently at risk from poverty or community factors, but they are placed further at risk by the schools they attend.

Special programs such as compensatory or bilingual education will never be effective at remedying underachievement, so long as these services are layered on a system that, to begin with, so poorly educates minority and low-income children. The presumption that "the schools are fine, it's the children who need help" is flawed. The schools serving large concentrations of low-income and minority students are generally not fine. Many of their problems originate with district and state policies and practices that fund them inadequately, send them incompetent staffs, require inordinate attention to arcane administrative requirements that fragment educational programs and drain resources from classrooms, and preclude the adoption of more promising curricula and teaching strategies.

Current initiatives to create special labels and programs for at-risk children and youths are unlikely to succeed if they do not attend to the structural conditions of schools that place children at risk, not only from their home or community circumstances but also from their school experiences. In the pursuit of equity, our goal should be to develop strategies that improve the core structures and practices of schooling rather than layering additional programs and regulations on foundations that are already faulty. The pressures to respond to special circumstances with special categorical programs are great, and the tradition of succumbing to those pressures in an add-on fashion is well established, in education as in other areas of national life. But special programs, with all their accouterments of new rules and procedures, separate budgets and fragmented, pull-out programs will be counterproductive, as long as the status quo remains unchanged in more significant ways.

As the 1992 interim report of an independent commission on Chapter 1 observes: Given the inequitable distribution of state and local resources, the current notion that Chapter 1 provides supplemental aid to disadvantaged children added to a level playing field is a fiction (Commission on Chapter 1, 1992, p. 4). The commission proposes that each state be held accountable for assuring comparability in "vital services" among all its and in all schools within each district. Among these vital services, perhaps the most important is highly qualified teaching, not just for specific Chapter 1 services but for all classrooms.

Intradistrict suits challenging the unequal distribution of qualified teachers and other curriculum opportunities are being considered in many cities, following an initial success in challenging Los Angeles. These strategies should continue to be pursued. Ferguson's (1991) recommendation that equalization focus on district capacity to hire high-quality teachers is an important one, with empirical support. In addition to the weight of evidence indicating the central importance of qualified teachers to student learning, there is real-world experience with the positive effects of teacher quality and their distribution. When Connecticut raised and equalized beginning teacher salaries under its 1986 Education Enhancement Act, shortages of teachers (including those that had plagued urban areas) evaporated. By 1989, many teaching fields showed surpluses, leading the state to consider ending its alternative certification program, since it appeared no longer necessary to staff schools (Darling-Hammond, 1992; Bliss, 1992). This is a useful beginning point for other policies aimed at equalizing access to good teaching.

The new wave of school finance lawsuits that are challenging resource allocation disparities both within states and within districts are also promising. These suits are increasingly able to demonstrate how access to concrete learning opportunities is impaired by differential access to money, and how these learning opportunities translate into academic achievement for students. As standards are used to articulate clearer conceptions of what students need to learn to function in today's society and what schools need to do to support these levels of learning, lawsuits like one recently won in Alabama may be linked to definitions of the quality of education that is "adequate" to meet the state's expectations for student achievement. Such cases are requiring remedies that link levels of funding to minimum standards of learning and teaching. As suits based on the adequacy theory establish that learning experiences depend on resources and influence outcomes, they establish the principle of "opportunity to learn" that could allow states to define a curriculum entitlement—one that becomes the basis for both funding and reviewing school practices.

Opportunity-to-Learn Standards. The idea of opportunity-to-learn standards was first developed by the National Council on Education Standards and Testing (NCEST). It supported student performance standards but acknowledged that they would result in greater inequality if not accompanied by policies ensuring access to resources, including appropriate instructional materials and well-prepared teachers (NCEST 1992, E12-E13). The Council's Assessment Task Force proposed that states collect evidence on the extent to which schools and districts provide opportunities to learn the curricula implied by standards—a prerequisite to using tests for school graduation or other decisions (NCEST 1992, F17-F18).

Opportunity-to-learn standards would establish, for example, that if a state's curriculum frameworks and assessments outline standards for science learning that require laboratory work and computers, then resources for certain kinds of coursework and knowledgeable teachers must be allocated; and policies must be fashioned to provide these entitlements. Such a strategy would leverage both school improvement and school equity reform, providing a basis for state legislation or for litigation where opportunities to learn were not adequately funded.

Such standards would define a floor of core resources, coupling them with incentives for schools to work toward professional standards of practice that support high-quality learning opportunities. Based on a combination of funding commitments, educational indicators, and school review practices, such standards would provide a basis for:

● Supporting state legislation and, if necessary, litigation that supports greater equity in funding and in the distribution of qualified teachers;

● Accumulating information on the nature of the teaching and learning opportunities made available to students in different districts and schools across the state;

● Offering incentives to states and school districts to create policies that ensure adequate and equitable resources, curriculum opportunities, and teaching to all schools;

● Developing a school review process that helps schools and districts engage in self-assessments and peer reviews of practice in light of standards;

● Identifying schools that need additional support or intervention to achieve adequate opportunities to learn for their students.

CURRICULUM AND ASSESSMENT REFORM

As I have noted, the curriculum offered to many students, and to most African-American students, in U.S. schools is geared primarily toward lower order "rote" skills—memorizing pieces of information and conducting simple operations based on formulas or rules—that are insufficient for the demands of modern life or for the new standards being proposed and enacted by states and national associations. These new standards will require students to be able to independently analyze and solve problems, extensively research and write, use new technologies, and employ various strategies for accessing and using resources in new situations. Major changes in curriculum and resources will be needed to ensure that these kinds of activities are commonplace in the classrooms of black students and others.

These efforts to create a "thinking curriculum" for all students are important for our national welfare. They are unlikely to pay off, however, unless other critical changes are made in curriculum—in the ways students are tracked for instruction, and the ways teachers are prepared and supported. Although mounting evidence indicates that low tracked students are disadvantaged by current practices and that high-ability students do not benefit more from homogeneous classrooms than from heterogeneous grouping (Slavin, 1990) the long-established American tracking system will be difficult to reform until there is an adequate supply of well-trained teachers—teachers who are both prepared to teach the more advanced curriculum that U.S. schools now fail to offer most students and to assume the challenging task of teaching in integrated classroom settings many kinds of students with diverse needs, interests, aptitudes, and learning styles.

Other important changes concern the types and uses of achievement tests in U.S. schools. As a 1990 study of the implementation of California's new mathematics curriculum framework points out, when a curriculum reform—aimed at problem-solving and the development of higher order thinking skills—encounters an already-mandated rote-oriented basic skills testing program, the tests win out (Cohen *et al*, 1990; Darling-Hammond, 1990b). As one teacher put it:

Teaching for understanding is what we are supposed to be doing ... [but] the bottom line here is that all they really want to know is how are these kids doing on the tests? ... They want me to teach in a way that they can't test, except that I'm held accountable to the test. Its' a Catch 22. ... (Wilson, 1990, p. 318).

In schools that organize most of their efforts around the kind of low-level learning represented by commercially developed multiple-choice tests, students will be profoundly disadvantaged when they encounter more rigorous evaluations like those being developed by states, the College Board, and the federal government—evaluations that require greater analysis, writing, and producing elaborate answers. Initiatives in some states and cities to develop

140

richer curricula and more performance-oriented assessments that develop higher order skills may begin to address this problem.

An equally important issue is how tests are used. If new assessments are used, like current tests, primarily for sorting, screening, and tracking, the quality of education for African-American students is unlikely to improve. Qualitatively better education will come only from creating more adaptive approaches to teaching; that means using assessments, not as a sorting and labeling device, but as a tool for identifying students' strengths and needs, and as a basis for adapting instruction more successfully (Glaser, 1981; 1990). Robert Glaser (1990) argues that schools must shift from an approach "characterized by minimal variation in the conditions for learning" in which "a narrow range of instructional options and a limited number of paths to success are available" (p. 16) to one in which "conceptions of learning and modes of teaching are adjusted to individuals—their backgrounds, talents, interests, and the nature of their past performances and experiences" (p. 17).

Thus, the outcomes of the current wave of curriculum and assessment reforms will depend in large measure on the extent to which developers and users of new standards and tests use them to improve teaching and learning, rather than to merely reinforce our tendencies to sort and select those who will get high-quality education from those who will not. They will also need to pursue broader reforms to improve and equalize access to educational resources and to support the professional development of teachers, so new standards and tests are used to inform more skillful and adaptive teaching that enables more successful learning for all students (Darling-Hammond, 1997).

INVESTMENTS IN QUALITY TEACHING

A key corollary to this analysis of inequality is that improved opportunities for minority students will rest, in large part, on policies that professionalize teaching by increasing the knowledge base for teaching and mastery of this knowledge by all teachers permitted to practice. This means providing all teachers with a stronger understanding of how children learn and develop, how a variety of curricular and instructional strategies can address their needs, and how changes in school and class-room practices can support their growth and achievement.

There are two reasons for this approach. First, the professionalization of an occupation raises the level below which no entrants will be admitted to practice. It eliminates practices of substandard or irregular licensure that allow untrained entrants to practice disproportionately on under-served and poorly protected clients. Second, professionalization increases the overall knowledge base for the occupation, thus improving the quality of services for all clients, especially those most in need of high-quality teaching (Darling-Hammond, 1990a; Wise & Darling-Hammond, 1987).

The students who have, in general, the poorest opportunities to learn—those attending the inner-city schools that are compelled by the current incentive structure to hire disproportionate numbers of substitute teach-ers, uncertified teachers, and inexperienced teachers, and that lack resources for mitigating the uneven distribution of good teaching—are the students who will benefit most from measures that raise the standards of practice for all teachers. They will also benefit from targeted policies that provide quality preparation programs and financial aid for highly qualified prospective teachers who will teach in central cities and poor rural areas. Providing equity in the distribution of teacher quality requires changing policies and long-standing incentive structures in education, so that shortages of trained teachers are overcome, and schools serving low-income and minority students are not disadvantaged by lower salaries and poorer working conditions in the bidding war for good teachers.

Building and sustaining a well-prepared teaching force will require local, state, and federal initiatives. To recruit an adequate supply of teach-ers, states and localities will need to upgrade teachers' salaries to levels competitive with those of college graduates in other occupations, who currently earn 25 to 50 percent more, depending on their fields. This should occur as part of a general restructuring effort, which places more resources and decision-making authority at the school level and allocates a greater share of education dollars to classrooms, rather than to large bureaucracies that oversee them (see, e.g., Darling-Hammond, 1997).

Incentive structures also must be reshaped to encourage the provision of highly qualified teachers to low-income and minority students. Some models are emerging. In Rochester, New York, for example, master teachers who have been recognized for their demonstrated expertise can be called upon, as part of their privilege and their obligation, to teach children and create new programs in the schools that currently most lack expert teaching. In New York City, dynamic groups of teachers and principals have developed proposals to launch new schools. More than 100 new small schools have been started in the last five years, with significantly better outcomes for students (Darling-Hammond, 1997). In such experiments, and in the policy changes they incorporate, lie part of the hope for equalizing opportunities to learn.

States must also strengthen teacher education and certification. In almost all states, teacher education is more poorly funded than other university departments (Ebmeier, Twombly, & Teeter, 1990). It has long been used as a revenue producer for programs that train future engineers, accountants, lawyers, and doctors. Rather than bemoaning the quality of teacher training, policy-makers must invest in its improvement; require schools of education to become accredited; and insist that all teachers pass licensing examinations that demonstrate they can teach well. Shortages must be met by enhancing incentives to teach rather than by lowering standards, especially for those who teach children in central cities and poor rural schools.

The federal government can play a leadership role in providing an adequate supply of well-qualified teachers, just as it has in providing an adequate supply of well-qualified physicians for the nation. When shortages of physicians were a major problem more than 25 years ago, Congress passed the 1963 Health Professions Education Assistance Act to support and improve the caliber of medical training, to create and strengthen teaching hospitals, to provide scholarships and loans to medical students, and to create incentives for physicians to train in shortage specialties, and to locate in underserved areas. Similarly, federal initiatives in education should seek to:

(1) Recruit new teachers, especially in shortage fields and in shortage locations, through scholarships and forgivable loans for high-quality teacher education.

143

(2) Strengthen and improve teachers' preparation through improvement incentive grants to schools of education, and supports for certification reform.

(3) Improve teacher retention and effectiveness by improving their clinical training and support during the beginning teaching stage when 30 percent to 50 percent of them drop out. This would include funding internship programs for new teachers, in which they receive structured coaching and mentoring, preferably in urban schools supported to provide state-of-the-art practices.

If the interaction between teachers and students is the most important aspect of effective schooling, then reducing inequality in learning has to rely on policies that provide equal access to competent, well-supported teachers. The public education system ought to be able to guarantee that every child who is forced to go to school by public law is taught by someone who is prepared, knowledgeable, competent, and caring. That is real accountability. As Carl Grant (1989) puts it:

Teachers who perform high-quality work in urban schools know that, despite reform efforts and endless debates, it is meaningful curricula and dedicated and knowledgeable teachers that make the difference in the education of urban students (p. 770).

When it comes to equalizing opportunities for students to learn, that is the bottom line.

MEDIAN EARNINGS OF WAGE AND SALARY WORKERS

For persons 25 to 34 years old
(in 1994 constant dollars)

Figure 1

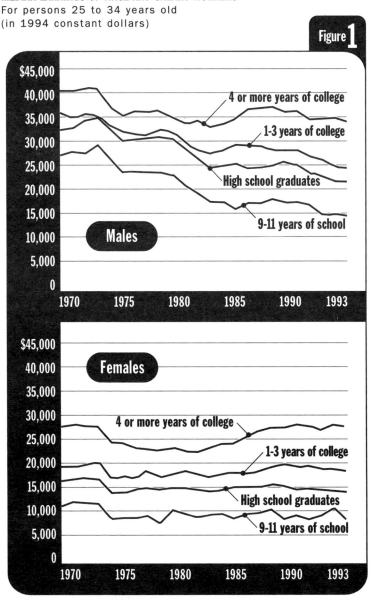

EMPLOYMENT RATES OF HIGH SCHOOL STUDENTS

By graduation status and race/ethnicity:
October 1973-1993

Figure **2**

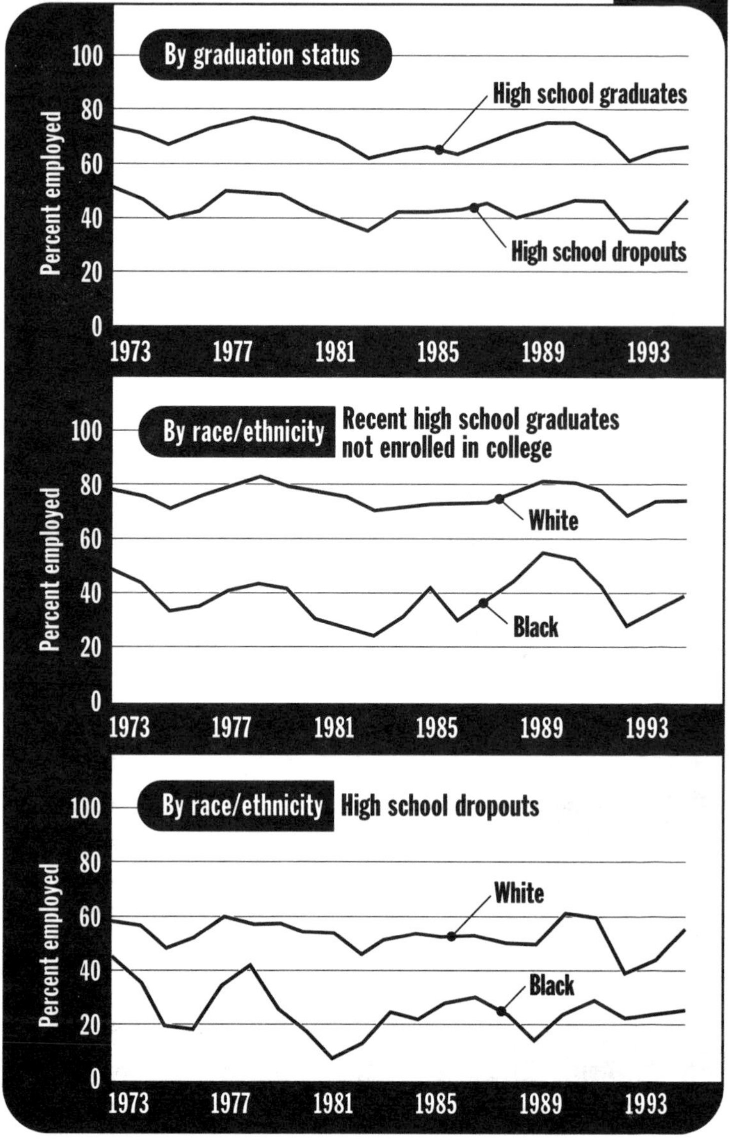

Source: National Center for Educational Statistics, *The Conditions of Education*, U.S. Department of Education, Washington, DC, 1995.

PERCENTAGE OF PERSONS 25-34
WHO RECEIVED INCOME FROM AFDC OR PUBLIC ASSISTANCE
By years of schooling completed: 1972-1992

Figure **3**

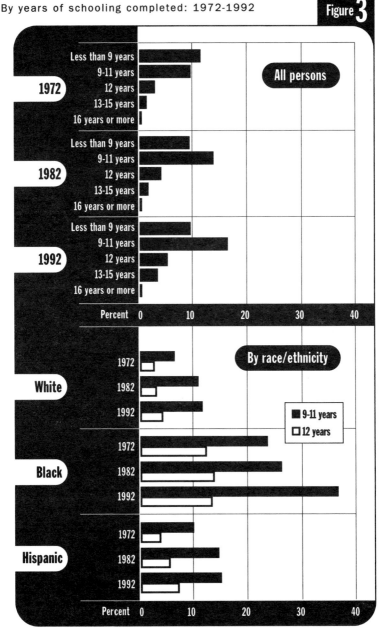

All persons

1972
- Less than 9 years
- 9-11 years
- 12 years
- 13-15 years
- 16 years or more

1982
- Less than 9 years
- 9-11 years
- 12 years
- 13-15 years
- 16 years or more

1992
- Less than 9 years
- 9-11 years
- 12 years
- 13-15 years
- 16 years or more

Percent   0   10   20   30   40

By race/ethnicity

White
- 1972
- 1982
- 1992

■ 9-11 years
□ 12 years

Black
- 1972
- 1982
- 1992

Hispanic
- 1972
- 1982
- 1992

Percent   0   10   20   30   40

Source: National Center for Education Statistics,
The Condition of Education 1995, p. 96

147

EDUCATIONAL ATTAINMENT
BY RACE AND HISPANIC ORIGIN: 1960 TO 1995

For persons 25 years old and over

Figure 4

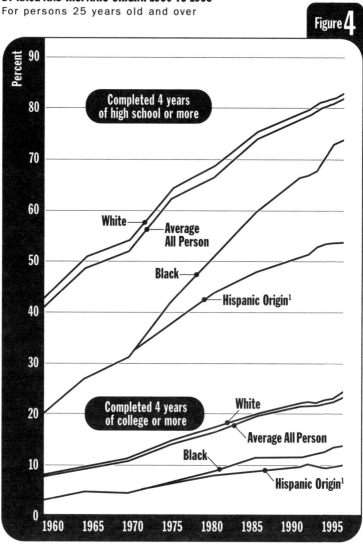

[1]Persons of Hispanic origin may be of any race. Data for 1960 and 1965 not available for persons of Hispanic origin.

Source: Charts prepared by U.S. Bureau of the Census. For data, see table 241.

EDUCATIONAL ATTAINMENT

For persons 25 years old and over (In percent)

Table 1

	Year	Total	White	Black
Completed 4 years of high school or more	1960	41.1	43.2	20.1
	1965	49.0	51.3	27.2
	1970	52.3	54.5	31.4
	1975	62.5	64.5	42.5
	1980	66.5	68.8	51.2
	1985	73.9	75.5	59.8
	1990	77.6	79.1	66.2
	1995	81.7	83.0	73.8

	Year	Total	White	Black
Completed 4 years of college or more	1960	7.7	8.1	3.1
	1965	9.4	9.9	4.7
	1970	10.7	11.3	4.4
	1975	13.9	14.5	6.4
	1980	16.2	17.1	8.4
	1985	19.4	20.0	11.1
	1990	21.3	22.0	11.3
	1995	23.0	24.0	13.2

Source: U.S. Bureau of the Census, *U.S. Census Population, U.S. Summary*, PC80-1-C1 and Current Population Reports P-20-465RV, P20-475; *Statistical Abstract of the United States, 1996.*

SCHOOL ENROLLMENT

Table 2

Students Age	White		Black	
	1990	1994	1990	1994
Total 3- to 34-year-olds	49.5	52.6	51.9	56.4
3- to 4-year-olds	44.9	47.0	41.6	51.9
5- to 6-year-olds	96.5	96.6	96.3	97.2
7- to 13-year-olds	99.6	99.3	99.8	99.6
14- to 15-year-olds	99.1	98.7	99.2	99.2
16- to 17-year-olds	92.5	94.3	91.7	95.4
18- to 19-year-olds	57.1	60.9	55.2	54.0
20- to 21-year-olds	41.0	46.2	28.4	34.9
22- to 24-year-olds	20.2	23.5	20.0	22.6
25- to 29-year-olds	9.9	10.4	6.1	10.5
30- to 34-year-olds	5.9	6.6	4.4	7.2
35-year-olds and older	2.1	2.2	2.1	2.9

Source: U.S. Bureau of the Census, Current Population Reports, P20-487; and earlier reports.

HIGH SCHOOL DROPOUTS — 1975 TO 1994

Table 3

Status Dropouts*	1975	1980	1985	1990	1994
Total	15.6%	15.6%	13.9%	13.6%	13.3%
▶ White	13.9	14.4	13.5	13.5	12.7
Male	13.5	15.7	14.7	14.2	13.6
Female	14.2	13.2	12.3	12.8	11.7
▶ Black	27.3	23.5	17.6	15.1	15.5
Male	27.8	26.0	18.8	13.6	17.5
Female	26.9	21.5	16.6	16.2	13.7
▶ Hispanic	34.9	40.3	31.5	37.3	34.7
Male	32.6	42.6	35.8	39.8	36.1
Female	36.8	38.1	27.0	34.5	33.1

Source: U.S. Bureau of the Census, *Current Population Reports*, P20-487.

* Percent of the population aged 18 to 24 who have not completed high school and are not enrolled.

COLLEGE ENROLLMENT OF RECENT HIGH SCHOOL GRADUATES
Percent enrolled in college

Table 4

Year	Total	White	Black
1976	48.8%	48.9%	41.9%
1981	53.9	54.6	42.9
1986	53.8	56.0	36.5
1991	62.4	64.6	45.6
1994	61.9	63.6	50.9

Source: U.S. Department of Education, *Digest of Education Statistics*, 1995.

STUDENT USE OF COMPUTERS — 1984 and 1993 in percent

Table 5

	1984 Total	1993 Total	1993 by grade level			
			K	1-8	9-12	College
▶ **At Home**	11.5	27.0	15.6	24.7	28.7	32.8
White	13.7	32.8	19.4	31.4	35.9	36.0
Black	4.9	10.9	4.2	9.0	10.4	19.4
Hispanic	3.6	10.4	5.7	7.5	9.8	22.0
▶ **At School**	27.3	59.0	26.2	68.9	58.2	55.2
White	30.3	61.6	29.4	73.7	59.9	54.9
Black	16.8	51.5	16.5	56.5	54.5	56.9
Hispanic	18.6	52.3	19.2	58.4	54.1	51.9

Source: U.S. National Center for Educational Statistics, *Digest of Educational Statistics*, 1994.

PERCENTAGE OF HIGH SCHOOL GRADUATES ENROLLED IN COLLEGE THE OCTOBER FOLLOWING GRADUATION

October 1972-1993

Figure 5

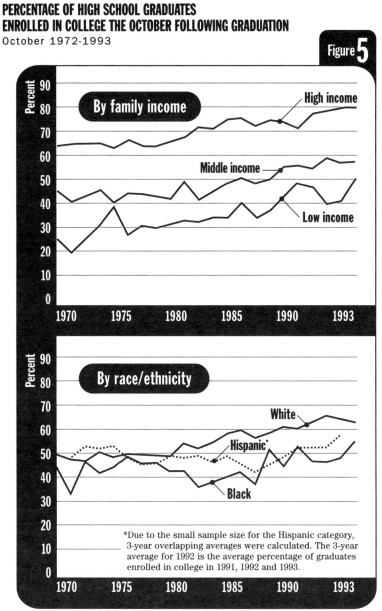

NOTE: Low income is the bottom 20 percent of all family incomes; high income is the top 20 percent of all family incomes; and middle income is the 60 percent in-between.

SOURCE: U.S. Department of Commerce, Bureau of the Census, October Current Population Surveys.

AVERAGE READING PROFICIENCY 1980-92 (scale score)

Average reading proficiency
by race/ethnicity and age

Figure **6**a

	White			Black			Hispanic		
	Age 9	Age 13	Age 17	Age 9	Age 13	Age 17	Age 9	Age 13	Age 17
1971	[1]214	[1]261	[1]291	[1]170	[1]222	[1]239	—	—	—
1975	217	[1]262	[1]293	[2]181	[1]226	[1]241	183	232	[1]252
1980	[12]221	[2]264	[1]293	[2]188	[2]233	[1]243	190	237	261
1984	[2]218	[1]263	[2]295	[2]186	[2]236	[2]264	187	240	[2]268
1988	218	[1]261	295	[2]189	[2]243	[12]274	[2]194	240	[2]271
1990	217	[1]262	[2]297	[2]182	[2]242	[2]267	189	238	[2]275
1992	[2]218	[2]266	[2]297	[2]184	[2]238	[2]261	192	239	[2]271

AVERAGE WRITING PROFICIENCY 1984-92 (scale score)

Average writing proficiency
by race/ethnicity and grade

Figure **6**b

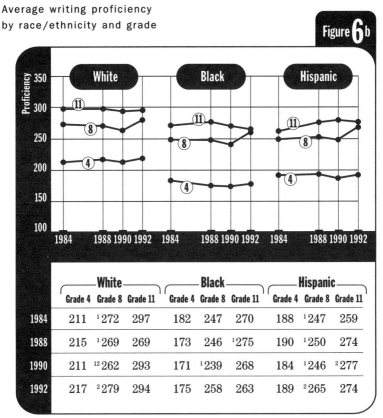

	White			Black			Hispanic		
	Grade 4	Grade 8	Grade 11	Grade 4	Grade 8	Grade 11	Grade 4	Grade 8	Grade 11
1984	211	[1]272	297	182	247	270	188	[1]247	259
1988	215	[1]269	269	173	246	[1]275	190	[1]250	274
1990	211	[12]262	293	171	[1]239	268	184	[1]246	[2]277
1992	217	[2]279	294	175	258	263	189	[2]265	274

155

AVERAGE MATHEMATICS PROFICIENCY 1978-92 (scale score)

Average mathematics proficiency
by race/ethnicity and age

Figure 7a

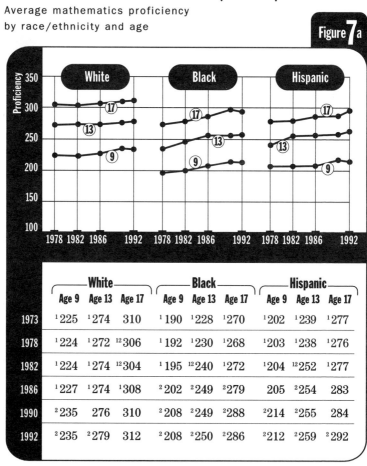

	White			Black			Hispanic		
	Age 9	Age 13	Age 17	Age 9	Age 13	Age 17	Age 9	Age 13	Age 17
1973	[1]225	[1]274	310	[1]190	[1]228	[1]270	[1]202	[1]239	[1]277
1978	[1]224	[1]272	[12]306	[1]192	[1]230	[1]268	[1]203	[1]238	[1]276
1982	[1]224	[1]274	[12]304	[1]195	[12]240	[1]272	[1]204	[12]252	[1]277
1986	[1]227	[1]274	[1]308	[2]202	[2]249	[2]279	205	[2]254	283
1990	[2]235	276	310	[2]208	[2]249	[2]288	[2]214	[2]255	284
1992	[2]235	[2]279	312	[2]208	[2]250	[2]286	[2]212	[2]259	[2]292

AVERAGE SCIENCE PROFICIENCY 1977-92 (scale score)

Average science proficiency
by race/ethnicity and age

Figure 7b

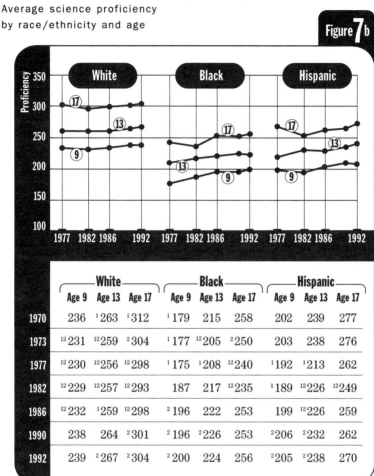

	White			Black			Hispanic		
	Age 9	Age 13	Age 17	Age 9	Age 13	Age 17	Age 9	Age 13	Age 17
1970	236	[1]263	[1]312	[1]179	215	258	202	239	277
1973	[12]231	[12]259	[2]304	[1]177	[12]205	[2]250	203	238	276
1977	[12]230	[12]256	[12]298	[1]175	[1]208	[12]240	[1]192	[1]213	262
1982	[12]229	[12]257	[12]293	187	217	[12]235	[1]189	[12]226	[12]249
1986	[12]232	[1]259	[12]298	[2]196	222	253	199	[12]226	259
1990	238	264	[2]301	[2]196	[2]226	253	[2]206	[2]232	262
1992	239	[2]267	[2]304	[2]200	224	256	[2]205	[2]238	270

157

STRATEGIES FOR FILLING TEACHING VACANCIES

By school type 1994

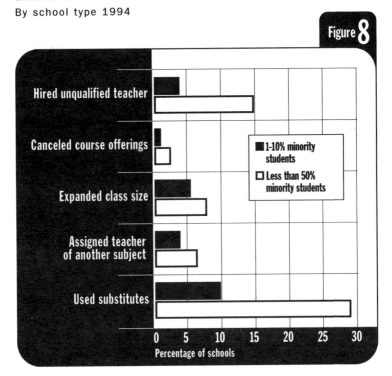

SOURCE: *NCES, America's Teachers: Profile of a Profession, 1993-94, Table A8.12.*

National Commission on Teaching and America"s Future

PROPORTION OF TEACHERS WITH CERTIFICATION AND A DEGREE* IN THE FIELD THEY TEACH

By school characteristics 1994

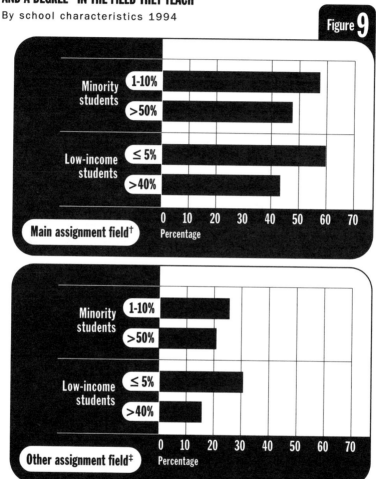

Figure 9

Main assignment field†

	Percentage
Minority students	1-10%
	>50%
Low-income students	≤ 5%
	>40%

Other assignment field‡

	Percentage
Minority students	1-10%
	>50%
Low-income students	≤ 5%
	>40%

SOURCE: †*NCES, America's Teachers: Profile of a Profession, 1993-94, Table A8.12.* ‡*NCES, America's Teachers: Profile of a Profession, 1993-94, Table A3.15a and A3.15b.* *College major or graduate degree.

National Commission on Teaching and America"s Future

TEACHERS QUALIFICATIONS

By school type 1994

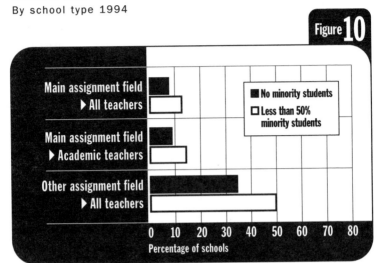

Figure 10

Main assignment field
▶ All teachers

■ No minority students
□ Less than 50% minority students

Main assignment field
▶ Academic teachers

Other assignment field
▶ All teachers

0   10   20   30   40   50   60   70   80

Percentage of schools

Source: NCES, *America's Teachers: Profile of a Profession, 1993-94*, 1997, Tables A3.14a, A3.15a and A3.14b

National Commission on Teaching and America's Future

REFERENCES

Alexander, K.L., & McDill, E.L. (1976). "Selection and allocation within schools: Some causes and consequences of curriculum placement." *American Sociological Review*, 41, pp. 963-980.

Armour-Thomas, E., Clay, C., Domanico, R., Bruno, K., & Allen, B. (1989). An earlier study of elementary and middle schools in New York City: Final report. NY: New York City Board of Education.

Ashton, P., & Crocker, L. (1986). "Does Teacher Certification Make a Difference?" *Florida Journal of Teacher Education*, 38, (3), pp. 73-83.

Ashton, P., & Crocker, L. (1987, May-June). "Systematic Study of Planned Variations: The Essential Focus of Teacher Education Reform." *Journal of Teacher Education*, 38, pp. 2-8.

Barr, R., & Dreeben, R. (1983). *How Schools Work*, Chicago: University of Chicago Press.

Barton, Paul E. & Coley, R. J. (1996). *Captive Students: Education and Training in America's Prisons*, Princeton, N.J.: Educational Testing Service.

Becker, H.J. (1986). *School Uses of Microcomputers: Reports from a National Survey*. Baltimore: Johns Hopkins Center for Social Organization of Schools.

Becker, H.J. (1983). *Computer Survey Newsletter.* Baltimore: Johns Hopkins Center for Social Organization of Schools.

Bents, M., & Bents, R.B. (1990). *Perceptions of Good Teaching among Novice. Advanced Beginner and Expert Teachers.* Paper presented at the Annual Meeting of the American Educational Research Association, Boston, MA.

Berliner, D.C. (1986, August/September). "In pursuit of the Expert Pedagogue." *Educational Researcher*, 15(7), pp. 5-13.

Berliner, D.C. (October 1984). "Making the Right Changes in Preservice Teacher Education." *Phi Delta Kappan*, 66(2), pp. 94-96.

Berne, H. (1995). "Educational Input and Outcome Inequities in New York State." In Robert Berne and Lawrence 0. Picus (eds.), *Outcome Equity in Education*, pp. 191-223, Thousand Oaks, CA.: Corwin Press.

Bledsoe, J.C., Cox, J.V., & Bumbam, (1967). Comparison between selected characteristics and performance of provisionally and professionally certified beginning teachers in Georgia. Washington, D.C.: U.S. Department of Health, Education, and Welfare.

Bliss, T. (1992). "Alternate Certification in Connecticut: Reshaping the Profession." *Peabody Journal of Education*, 69(3), pp. 35-54.

Bowman, B. (1993). "Early Childhood Education." In L. Darling-Hammond (Ed.), *Review of Research in Education* (Vol. 19, pp. 101-134). Washington, D.C.: American Educational Research Association.

Braddock, J. & McPartland, J.M. (1993). "Education of Early Adolescents." In L. Darling-Hammond (Ed.), *Review of Research in Education*, Vol. 19, pp. 135-170. Washington, D.C.: American Educational Research Association.

California Commission on the Teaching Profession (1985). *Who Will Teach Our Children?* Sacramento, CA: California Commission on the Teaching Profession.

California State Department of Education (1984) *California High School Curriculum Study: Path Through High School.* Sacramento, CA: California State Department of Education.

Carter, K., & Doyle, W. (1987). "Teachers' Knowledge Structures and Comprehension Processes." In J. Calderhead (Ed.), ExDlorina Teacher Thinking (pp. 147-160). London: Cassell.

Cicourel, A.V., & Kitsuse, J.I. (1963). *The Educational Decision-Makers.* Indianapolis: Bobbs-Merrill.

Cohen, D., et al. (1990). "Case Studies of Curriculum Implementation," Educational Evaluation and Policy Analysis, 12(3).

College Board (1985). *Equality and Excellence: The Educational Status of Black Americans.* New York: College Entrance Examination Board.

Coleman, J.S., Campbell, E.Q., Hobson, C.J., Mcpartland, J., Mood, A.M., Weinfeld, F.D., York, R.L. (1966). *Equality of Educational Opportunity.* Washington, DC: U.S. Government Printing Office.

Comer, J.P. (1988). "Educating Poor Minority Children." *Scientific American*, 259(5), pp. 42-48.

Commission on Chapter 1 (1992). *High Performance Schools: No Exceptions, No Excuses.* Washington, D.C.: Author.

Cooper, In. & Sherk, J. (1989). "Addressing Urban School Reform: Issues and Alliances," *Journal of Negro Education,* 58(3), pp. 315-331.

Copley, P.O. (1974) "A Study of the Effect of Professional Education Courses on Beginning Teachers." Springfield, MO: Southwest Missouri State University. ERIC Document No. ED 098 147.

Darling-Hammond, L. (1990a) . "Teacher Quality and Equality." In Goodly, J. & P. Keating (Eds.), *Access to Knowledge: An Agenda for Our Nation's Schools* (pp. 237-258). NY: College Entrance Examination Board.

Darling-Hammond, L. (1990b). "Instructional Policy into Practice: The Power of the Bottom Over the Top." *Educational Evaluation and Policy Analysis,* 12(3), pp. 233-242.

Darling-Hammond, L. (1992). "Teaching and Knowledge: Policy Issues Posed by Alternate Certification for Teachers." *Peabody Journal of Education,* 67(3), pp. 123-154.

Darling-Hammond, 1. (1997). *The Right to Learn: A Blueprint: for Creating Schools that Work.* San Francisco: Jossey Bass.

Darling-Hammond, L. & Snyder, J. (1992). "Traditions of Curriculum Inquiry: The Scientific Tradition." In P.W. Jackson (Ed.), *Handbook of Research on Curriculum.* NY: Macmillan.

Davis, D.G. (1986). *A Pilot Study to Assess Equity in Selected Curricular Offerings Across Three Diverse Schools in a Large Urban School District.* Paper presented at the Annual Meeting of the American Educational Research Association, San Francisco.

Doyle, W. (1986). "Content Representation in Teachers' Definitions of Academic Work." *Journal of Curriculum Studies,* 18, pp. 365-379.

Dreeben, A. (1987, Winter). "Closing the Divide: What Teachers and Administrators Can Do To Help Black Students Reach Their Reading Potential," *American Educator,* 11(4), pp. 28-35

Dreeben, P. & Gamoran, A. (1986). "Race, Instruction, and Learning," *American Sociological Review,* 51(5), pp. 660-669.

163

Dreeben, A. & Barr, P. (1987). Class Composition and the Design of Instruction. Paper presented at the Annual Meeting of the American Education Research Association, Washington, D.C.

Drucker, P.F. (1986). *The Frontiers of Management.* NY: Harper and Row.

Drucker, P.F. (1994, November) . "The Age of Social Transformation." *Atlantic Monthly*, pp. 53-80.

Druva, C.A., & Anderson, RD (1983). "Science Teacher Characteristics by Teacher Behavior and by Student Outcome: A Meta-Analysis of Research." *Journal of Research in Science Teaching*, 20(5), pp.467-479.

Ebmeier, H., Twombly, S., & Teeter, (1990). "The Comparability and Adequacy of Financial Support for Schools of Education." *Journal of Teacher Education.* 42 (3), pp. 226-235.

Eckstrom, R., & Villegas, A.M. (1991). "Ability Grouping in Middle Grade Mathematics: Process and Consequences." *Research in Middle Level Education*, 15(1), pp. 1-20.

Educational Testing Service (1991). *The State of Inequality.* Princeton, NJ: ETS.

Evertson, C.1 Hawley, W., & Zlotnick, M. (1985). "Making a Difference in Educational Quality Through Teacher Education." *Journal of Teacher Education*, 36(3), pp. 2-12.

Ferguson, R.F. (1991, Summer) . "Paying for Public Education: New Evidence on How and Why Money Matters." *Harvard Journal on Legislation* 28(2), pp. 465-498.

Ferguson, R.F. & Ladd, H.F. "How and Why Money Matters: An Analysis of Alabama Schools," *Holding Schools Accountable*, Brookings Institution, Washington DC, pp. 265-296.

Finley, M.K. (1984). "Teachers and Tracking in a Comprehensive High School." *Sociology of Education*, 57, pp. 233-243.

Gamoran, A. (1992). "Access to Excellence: Assignment to Honors English Classes in the Transition from Middle to High School." *Educational Evaluation and Policy Analysis*, 14(3), pp. 185-204.

Gamoran, A. (1990). The Consequences of Track-Related Instructional Differences for Student Achievement. Paper presented at the Annual Meeting of the American Educational Research Association, Boston.

Garnoran, A., & Berends, M. (1987). "The Effects of Stratification in Secondary Schools: Synthesis of Survey and Ethnographic Research." *Review of Educational Research*, 57, pp. 415-436.

Gamoran, A., & Mare, R. (1989). "Secondary School Tracking and Educational Inequality: Compensation, Reinforcement or Neutrality?" *American Journal of Sociology*, 94, pp. 1146-1183.

Garcia, E. (1993). "Language, Culture, and Education." In L. Darling-Hammond (Ed.), *Review of Research in Education*, (Vol. 19, pp. 51-98). Washington, D.C.: American Educational Research Association.

Gemignani, Robert J. (1994, October). "Juvenile Correctional Education: A Time for Change. Update on Research." *Juvenile Justice Bulletin.* (U.S. Department of Justice, Office of Juvenile Justice and Delinquency Prevention).

Glaser, P. (1981). "The Future of Testing: A Research Agenda for Cognitive Psychology and Psychometrics." *American Psychologist*, 39(9), pp. 923-936.

Glaser, P. (1990). *Testing and Assessment: O Tempora! O Mores!* Pittsburgh, PA: University of Pittsburgh, Learning Research and Development Center.

Gomez, D.L., & Grobe, H.P. (1990). Three Years of Alternative Certification in Dallas: Where Are We? Paper presented at the Annual Meeting of the American Educational Research Association, Boston, MA.

Good, T.L., & Erophy, J. (1987). *Looking in Classrooms.* NY: Harper and Row.

Grant, C.A. (1989, June). "Urban Teachers: Their New Colleagues and Curriculum." Phi Delta Kappan, 70(10), pp. 764-770.

Greenberg, J.D. (1983). "The Case for Teacher Education: Open and Shut." *Journal of Teacher Education*, 34(4), pp. 2-5.

Grissmer, D.W. & Kirby, S.N. (1987). *Teacher Attrition: The Uphill Climb to Staff the Nation's Schools.* Santa Monica: Rand Corporation.

Grossman, P. L. (1989). "Learning to Teach without Teacher Education," *Teachers College Record*, 91(2), pp. 291-208.

Grossman1 P.L. (1990). *The Making of a Teacher: Teacher Knowledge and Teacher Education*. New York: Teachers College Press.

Hartman, W.T. (1988). "District Spending Disparities: What do the Dollars Buy?" *Journal of Education Finance*, 13(4), pp. 436-359.

Hice, J.E.L. (1970). "The Relationship between Teacher Characteristics and First-Grade Achievement." *Dissertation Abstracts International*, 25(1), p. 190.

Proffer, T.S. (1992). "Middle School Ability Grouping and Student Achievement in Science and Mathematics." *Educational Evaluation and Policy Analysis*, 14(3), pp. 205-227.

Johnston, J.M. & Ryan, K. (1983). "Research on the Beginning Teacher." In KR. Howie & W.E. Gardner (Eds.), *The Education of Teachers: A Look Ahead*. NY: Longman.

Jones, L.V. (1984). "White-Black Achievement Differences: The Narrowing Gap." *American Psychologist*, 39, pp. 1207-1213.

Jones, L.V., Burton, N.W., & Davenport, E.C. (1984). "Monitoring the Achievement of Black Students," *Journal for Research in Mathematics Education*, 15, pp. 154-164.

Kaufman, J.E., & Rosenbaum, JE. (1992). "Education and Employment of Low-Income Black Youth in White Suburbs." *Educational Evaluation and Policy Analysis*, 14(3), pp. 229-240.

Kozol, J. (1991). *Savage Inequalities*. New York: Crown.

Kulik, C.C. , & Kulik, J.A. (1982). "Effects of Ability Grouping on Secondary School Students: A Meta-Analysis of Evaluation Findings." *American Education Research Journal*, 19, pp. 415-428.

Lee, V., & Bryk, A. (1988). "Curriculum Tracking as Mediating the Social Distribution of High School Achievement." *Sociology of Education*, 61, pp. 78-94.

LuPone, L.J. (1961). "A Comparison of Provisionally Certified and Permanently Certified Elementary Schoolteachers in Selected School Districts in New York State." *Journal of Educational Research*, 55, pp. 53-63.

Macphail-Wilcox, B. & King, R.A. (1986). "Resource Allocation Studies: Implications for School Improvement and School Finance Research." *Journal of Education Finance*, 11, pp. 416-432.

Matthews, W. (1984). "Influences on the Learning and Participation of Minorities in Mathematics." *Journal for Research in Mathematics Education*, 15, pp. 84-95.

McKnight, C.C., Crosswhite, J.A., Dossey, JA., Kifer, S., Swafford, S.O., Travers, K.J., and Cooney, T.J. (1987). *The Underachieving Curriculum: Assessing U.S. School Mathematics From an International Perspective*. Champaign IL: Stipes Publishing.

McNeil, J.D. (1974). "Who gets Better Results with Young Children—Experienced Teachers or Novices?" *Elementary School Journal*, 74, pp. 447-451.

McUsic, N. (1991. Summer). "The Use of Education Clauses in School Finance Reform Litigation." *Harvard Journal on Legislation*, 28(2), pp. 307-340.

Miller, J.G. (1997, June). "African American Males in the Criminal Justice System." *Phi Delta Kappan*. K1-K12.

Moore, D., & Davenport, S. (1988). *The New Improved Sorting Machine*. Madison, WI: National Center on Effective Secondary Schools.

Moore, E.G. & Smith, A.W. (1985). "Mathematics Aptitude: Effects of Coursework, Household Language, and Ethnic Differences." *Urban Education*, 20, pp. 273-294.

Moskowitz, G., & Hayman, J.L. (1974). "Interaction Patterns of First Year Typical and Best Teachers in Inner-City Schools," *Journal of Educational Research*, 67, pp. 224-230.

Murnane, P. & Levy, F. (1996). *Teaching the New Basic Skills*. NY: The Free Press.

Murnane, R.J. & Phillips, B.R. (1981, Fall) . "Learning by Doing, Vintage, and Selection: Three Pieces of the Puzzle Relating Teaching Experience and Teaching Performance." *Economics of Education Review*, 1(4), pp.453-465.

Murnane, R.J., Singer, J.D., Willett, J.B., Kemple, J.J., & Olsen, R.J. (1991). *Who Will Teach?—Policies that Matter*. Cambridge, MA: Harvard University Press.

National Assessment of Educational Progress (1994). NAEP *Trial State Assessment* Washington, D.C.: U.S. Department of Education.

National Center for Education Statistics (1985). *The Condition of Education*. 1985. Washington, D.C.: U.S Department of Education.

National Center for Education Statistics (1991). *National Education Longitudinal Survey,* 88, NCES no. 91-460. Washington, D.C.: Office of Educational Research and Improvement.

National Center for Education Statistics (NCES) (1994). *Digest of Education Statistics. 1994.* Washington, D.C.: U.S. Department of Education.

National Center for Education Statistics (1995). *The Condition of Education.* 1995. Washington, DC: U.S. Department of Education.

National Center for Education Statistics (NCES) (1996). *Schools and Staffing in the United States: A Statistical Profile.* 1993-94. Washington, D.C. U.S. Department of Education.

National Center for Education Statistics (NCES) (1997a) *America's Teachers: Profile of a Profession.* 1993-94. Washington, D.C.: U.S. Department of Education.

National Center for Education Statistics (NCES) (1997b) *Characteristics of Stayers. Movers. and Leavers: Results from the Teacher Follow-up Survey,* 1994-95. Washington, D.C.: U.S. Department of Education.

National Commission on Teaching and America's Future (NCTAF) (1996). *What Matters Most: Teaching for America's Future.* New York: Author.

National Commission on Teaching and America's Future (NCTAF) (1997). Unpublished tabulations from the 1993-94 schools and Staffing Surveys.

National Council on Education Standards and Testing (NCEST) (1992). *Raising Standards for American Education.* Washington, D.C.: Government Printing Office.

New York Study Group on Outcome Equity (1993). *The Road to Outcome Equity: Final Report of the Study Group on Outcome Equity.* R. Berne (ed), Albany: New York State Education Department.

Oakes, J. (1992, May) . "Can Tracking Research Inform Practice? Technical, Normative, and Political Considerations." *Educational Researcher,* 21(4) , pp. 12-21.

Oakes, J. (1990). *Multiplying Inequalities: The Effects of Race, Social Class, and Tracking on Opportunities to Learn Mathematics and Science.* Santa Monica: The RAND Corporation.

Oakes, Jeannie (June 1986). "Tracking in Secondary Schools: A Contextual Perspective." *Educational Psychologist,* 22, pp. 129-154.

Oakes, J. (1985). *Keeping Track.* New Haven: Yale University Press.

Cakes, S. (1983, May) . "Limiting Opportunity: Student Race and Curricular Differences in Secondary Vocational Education." *American Journal of Education,* 91(3), pp. 328-355.

Orfield, G.F., Monfort, F., & Aaron, M. (1989). *Status of School Desegregation: 1968-1986.* Alexandria, VA: National School Boards Association.

Pelavin, S.H. & Kane, M (1990). *Changing the Odds: Factors Increasing Access to College.* NY: College Entrance Examination Board.

Peterson, P. (1989). "Remediation is no Remedy." *Educational Leadership,* 46 (60), pp. 24-25.

Resnick, L.B. (1987). *Education and Learning to Think.* Washington, DC: National Academy Press.

Rock, D.A., Hilton, T.L., Pollack, J., Ekstrom, R.B., & Goertz, M.E. (1985). *A Study of Excellence in High School Education: Educational Policies, School Quality, and Student Outcomes.* Washington, D.C.: National Center for Educational Statistics.

Rosenbaum, J. (1976). *Making Inequality: The Hidden Curriculum of High School Tracking.* NY: Wiley.

Rottenbery, C.J. & Berliner, D.C. (1990). Expert and Novice Teachers' Conceptions of Common Classroom Activities. Paper presented at the annual meeting of the American Educational Research Association.

Schofield, J.W. (1991). "School Desegregation and Intergroup Relations." In G. Grant (Ed.), *Review of Research in Education* (17, pp. 335-409). Washington, DC: American Educational Research Association.

Shulman, L.S. (1987). "Knowledge and Teaching: Foundations of the New Reform," in *Harvard Educational Review,* 57(1), pp. 1-22.

Silard, J. & Goldstein, B. (1974, July) . "Toward Abolition of Local Funding in Public Education." *Journal of Law and Education,* 3, p. 324.

Slavin, R.E. (1990). "Achievement Effects of Ability Grouping in Secondary Schools: A Best Evidence Synthesis." *Review of Educational Research,* 60 (3), pp. 471-500.

169

Strickland, D. (1985). "Early Childhood Development and Reading Instruction." In C. Brooks (Ed.) *Tapping Potential: English and Language Arts for the Black Learner.* National Council of Teachers of English.

Sutton, R.E. (1991). "Equity and Computers in the Schools: A Decade of Research." *Review of Educational Research*, 61(4), pp. 475-503.

Talbert, J.E. (1990). *Teacher Tracking: Exacerbating Inequalities in the High School.* Stanford, CA: Center for Research on the Context of Secondary Teaching, Stanford University.

Taylor, W.L. & Piche, D.M. (1991). *A Report on Shortchanging Children: The Impact of Fiscal Inequity on the Education of Students at Risk.* Prepared for the Committee on Education and Labor, US House of Representatives. Washington, DC: US Government Printing Office.

Trimble, K. & Sinclair, R.L. (1986). Ability Grouping and Differing Conditions for Learning: An Analysis of Content and Instruction in Ability-Grouped Classes. Paper presented at the annual meeting of the American Educational Research Association, San Francisco.

U.S. Department of Commerce (1996) *Statistical Abstract of the United States: 1996.* 116th edition. Washington, DC: Bureau of the Census.

Useem, E.L. (1990, Fall). "You're Good, but You're not Good Enough: Tracking Students out of Advanced Mathematics." *American Educator*, 14(3), pp. 24-27, 43-46.

Usiskin, Z. (1987). "Why Elementary Algebra Can, Should, and Must be an Eighth Grade Course for Average Students." *Mathematics Teacher*, 80, pp. 428-438.

Veenman, (1984). "Perceived Problems of Beginning Teachers." *Review of Educational Research*, 54 (2), and pp. 143-178.

Wheelock A. (1992). *Crossing the Tracks.* NY: The New Press.

William T. Grant Foundation, Commission on Work, Family and Citizenship (1988) *The Forgotten Half: Non-College Youth in America.* Washington, D.C.: Author.

Wilson, S. (1990) "A Conflict of Interests: Constraints that Affect Teaching and Change," *Educational Evaluation and Policy Analysis*, 12(3), pp. 309-326.

Winkler, J.D., Shavelson, R.J., Stasz, C.,Abby Robyn, and Werner Feibel (1984). *How Effective Teachers use Microcomputers for Instruction.* Santa Monica, CA: The RAND Corporation.

Wise, A.E. & Darling-Hammond, L. (1987). *Licensing Teachers: Design for a Teaching Profession.* Santa Monica, CA: RAND Corporation.

Wise, A.E., Darling-Hammond, L., & Berry, 13. (1987). Effective Santa Monica, *Teacher Selection: From Recruitment to Retention.* California: The RAND Corporation.

Wong, K.K. (1989, August). "Fiscal Support for Education in American States: The "Parity-to-Dominance View Examined." *American Journal of Education,* 97(4), pp. 329-357.

"Improving Black Student Performance on a Large Scale: The Lessons of EQUITY 2000"

By Vinetta C. Jones, Ph.D.

THE CHALLENGE

American education is failing to live up to its goal: preparing *all* students to meet the standards required to live, learn, work and be productive citizens in the increasingly technological, diverse and global community of the 21st century. More specifically, African-American, Hispanic and poor students are systematically undereducated in American schools in large part, by a tracking system that sets lower standards and expectations for them and herds them into an education track characterized by low-level, watered-down, dead-end courses— limiting their career and higher education options and leading them to a permanent life in the underclass. EQUITY 2000, the districtwide education reform program of the College Board, which aims to close the gap in college-going and success rates between minority/non-minority and advantaged/disadvantaged students, shows impressive interim results at the completion of its six-year pilot program involving over 500,000 students from 14 districts K-12.

Our schools and communities are challenged to equip all youth with the skills to be effective problem-solvers, productive workers and responsible citizens. Students' academic attainment and how well we prepare them affects the future economic security and quality of life of our nation. As the United States becomes more ethnically and racially diverse, education continues to be the major contributor to reducing the gap between haves and have-nots, and to ensuring the success of our youth.

The need for all students to have opportunities to be academically well-prepared and qualified for further study, to find gainful employ-ment, and to lead successful lives after they leave high school—these challenges still face us. Future workers face higher skill requirements; those who are less prepared already find entry-level jobs more difficult to obtain. For well-educated workers, the prospects for earning more are increasing, but real wages for high school graduates are declining. From 1979-94, real earnings of high school graduates fell from 9 percent to 19 percent, depending on age; for dropouts, earnings dropped from 21 percent to 26 percent.

By the year 2000, approximately 60 percent of new jobs will require skills possessed by only 22 percent of high school graduates and dropouts entering the labor market today. Data on the disparity in earnings between underserved groups, particularly blacks and Hispanics, exempli-fy other issues. The future is riskiest for these students because many are inadequately educated.

During the past 20 years, white and Hispanic high school graduation rates have shown little movement, while black rates have increased by about 10 percent. The graduation rate for all whites remains nearly 10 percent above the rate for blacks, and 20 percent above the Hispanic rate. If present trends continue, it will be more than 60 years before Hispanics reach white high school graduation rates. With the perfor-mance of our schools directly affecting the quality of life of all citizens, now and in the future, high expectations and standards for all students must be our first priority.

Glenn T. Seaborg, physics Nobel prize winner of the U. C. Berkeley Lawrence Hall of Science and a member of the National Commission on Excellence in Education, which issued *A Nation At Risk*, points to the consequences of not meeting the challenge of educating *all* of America's children well:

Each year's class of dropouts costs the nation about $240 billion in crime, welfare, health care, and services. Put another way, we spend nine dollars to provide services to dropouts for each dollar spent on education. (Somerton, W. H. *et al, The MESA Way: A Success Story of Nurturing Minorities for Math/Science-Based Careers*, 1994).

SCHOOLS AND SCHOOL DISTRICTS INSTITUTIONALIZE THE GAP

Varying standards and expectations for different students are institu-tionalized in American education by the system of tracking. The system separates students, prescribing curriculums for some that keep all their options open and prepares them for higher education. However, other students are mired in curricula with watered-down, dead-end courses (Oakes, 1985, Braddock & Slavin, 1992, Braddock & Dawkins, 1993, Oakes, 1990, Jones, V. & Clemson, 1996, Jones, V. in press).

A tracking policy makes assumptions and judgments about students' abilities that are often based on socioeconomic, racial, ethnic, or gender status. The result: many students are shunted into dead-end academic paths that deny them a chance to attend college or pursue a variety of careers, particularly in the science- and mathematics-based fields. The pattern is seen consistently, with little variation, in schools and districts across the country. In such a system, poor and minority students are underrepresent-ed in college-preparatory classes—such as algebra, geometry, chemistry and advanced placement—and overrepresented in dead-end classes, such as consumer and business math, and general science. As I travel across the country, I repeatedly see—with few exceptions in urban and suburban school districts—students being prepared to be either masters or slaves in our technological society (with math serving as the "critical filter").

High standards and high expectations for *all* students—these must be a part of any plan to achieve excellence in American education. It is important to note, however, that high standards have no value—and can even be a setup for failure—if they're established without the support to reach them. This is especially true for students from whom little has been expected in the past.

Unfortunately, much of the focus in national discussions on reforming education centers are on standards and ways of assessment *only*. But the issue of supporting *all* students to reach those high standards has been pushed to the margins, and it usually slips through the cracks when the allocation of resources begins. If the goal of American education is to edu-cate all students well, to help them reach the high standards needed for

175

the 21st century, then the discussion of reforming education—which now focuses on standards and assessment—must be expanded to include at the core the issue of equity.

We find general consensus in education research that what works in promoting excellence for *all* students is essentially the same:

Teachers who care about their students; believe that they can learn; hold high expectations for them; are culturally literate about the students' backgrounds; value the cultures and communities that the children come from; are knowledgeable about their subjects; can relate these subjects to the world views and lives of their students; can draw from a rich and diverse repertoire of strategies to meet the learning needs of students; place a high value on and are excited about learning; engage students in active learning; nurture high standards of respect, fairness, acceptance, hard work, cooperation and achievement; encourage creativity; and reward and encourage academic excellence.

Schools that set high standards for all students; build on the strengths of the students; are safe; respect and value their communities; encourage linkages between the school and the community, including substantive parental involvement; expect, demand and provide the resources for all students to excel academically; reward excellence; and provide positive role models with whom the students can identify.

The problem is that if you are an African-American student, your chances of having a teacher and a school as described above are small, particularly compared with a white middle-class student. The result is a huge achievement gap between black and white students.

And yet we do see across the country thousands of isolated examples of programs and schools where minority—so-called "at risk"—students are meeting high standards of academic excellence. This is happening where teachers and schools exhibit the behavior, knowledge and under-standing and characteristics mentioned above. The 1990 Carnegie-sup-ported report, *Education That Works: an Action Plan for Educating Minorities,* listed hundreds of such schools and teachers, found no exam-ples of whole school districts reflecting these characteristics.

With America's changing demographics, where 23 of the 25 largest

176

school districts are majority minority, closing the gap in educational achievement—between minority and non-minority students and between advantaged and disadvantaged students—is one of the greatest challenges facing this nation's education system. If American education fails, the implications for our economy and society will be even more profound in the 21st century. By then, 85 percent of new entrants into the work force will be minorities, females or new immigrants (Somerton, et. al., 1994). The challenge for educators is to confront the systemic deficiencies head-on, establish high academic standards, and ensure that the appropriate support systems are in place to enable all students to meet those high standards (Jones, in press).

EQUITY 2000 - A MODEL TO MEET THE CHALLENGE

EQUITY 2000 addresses all of these issues directly. It uses the power of high standards for all students, coupled with the support to achieve them, to help whole school districts reach the goal of excellence and equity in education. This district-wide education reform model, which builds on what we know helps increase academic achievement, serves as a catalyst. It brings coherence to many isolated disjointed projects and supports what already works in a school district. Results from EQUITY 2000, thus far, are quite encouraging, as it moves beyond its six-year pilot phase in six-cities— involving 14 whole districts, 700 schools K-12, and 500,000 students—and begins to share lessons learned with other districts across the country.

EQUITY 2000 is a comprehensive, research-based, field-developed, districtwide K-16 systemic education reform model of the College Board. Its goal: closing the gap in college-going and success rates between minority and non-minority, advantaged and disadvantaged students, through a series of efforts such as eliminating low-level student tracking policies. To achieve this goal in a district, it uses high standards in mathematics for all students, as a lever to drive reform in K-12 and all disciplines. EQUITY 2000 is based on the fundamental belief that all students can achieve at high levels if given a supportive academic environment traditionally available only to advantaged students. As a *tool* to help districts close the achievement gap, EQUITY 2000 districts sign a formal multiyear agreement to set a goal of having all 9th graders enrolled in algebra or higher, and all 10th graders in geometry or higher. The EQUITY 2000 model supports the districts, teachers, parents, students, counselors, principals, and others to meet the goal.

EQUITY 2000 scales up the reform to the districtwide level while building on what we know about what works in promoting academic excellence in teaching and learning. The model uses the critical filter of mathematics at the middle-grade level as a lever to drive reform in K-12 and all disciplines. Thus, significant changes in course content, instruction, and student enrollment eventually occur at all grade levels and across all fields of study. The model uses the standard of Algebra I by the 9th grade and geometry by the 10th grade for *all* students as a hinge that opens access to rigorous course work and offers them the option of going on to higher education.

EQUITY 2000 builds on the experiences of successful, time-tested precollege interventions, such as MESA (The Mathematics, Engineering, Science Achievement Precollege program, Somerton, *et al*, 1994) and EQUALS, which began at UC Berkeley in 1970; SECME (Southeastern Consortium for Minorities in Engineering precollege program) which began at Georgia Tech; and the MSEN Precollege program (Mathematics and Science Education Network), which began at the University of North Carolina, Chapel Hill, in 1986. These interventions have proven successful with subsets of students in classrooms and schools across the country. EQUITY 2000 borrows not only from these but many other proven initiatives and strategies (e.g., Effective Schools, Comer School Development, Saturday Academies, Family Math, Study Groups) and applies them across entire school districts.

Because bringing about change at the district level is a long-term, complex, multidimensional process—requiring an intensive, simultaneous, sustained and coordinated assault on key subsystems within districts (Dolan, 1994; Knapp, 1997)—the EQUITY 2000 model is built on six key, interdependent components. They produce change by bringing pressure on six critical organizational subsystems in school districts. Dolan describes the subsystems as critical boundaries, indicating that they are both "barriers" and "connections" to the inner workings of the larger district system. He lists subsystems as: 1) the Anchors ... the school board, the superintendent and central administrative cabinet, and the executive committee of the union(s); 2) the teachers (and counselors), support staff, students; 3) the principals; 4) the information system; 5) the central office and specialties; 6) the parents and community, *The External Environment*. (Dolan, 1994, pp. 64-65).

THE SIX COMPONENTS OF THE EQUITY 2000 MODEL ARE:

■ Districtwide policy and major practice changes to alter the requirements and practices of teaching, guidance, and school administration, beginning with the requirement that all students complete the gatekeeper courses of Algebra I by the 9th grade and geometry by the 10th grade. Teachers are expected to embrace the national standards developed by the National Council of Teachers of Mathematics and other discipline-based groups.

■ Ongoing professional development for teachers, counselors, and administrators, to update their skills and reinforce the policy directives. The focus for teachers is on content, pedagogy and equity (the influence of expectations is also explored).

■ Establishment of academic "safety nets"—such as Saturday Academies, Summer Scholar programs and other enrichment experiences—that give students the extra academic support they need to reach high levels of achievement in more rigorous courses.

■ Development of parent/family involvement initiatives that empower them to be effective advocates for their children's education and that help them increase their support for their children's educational growth at home.

■ Formation of school-community partnerships (e.g. business, governmental agencies, higher education and community-based organizations) to gain broad-based support for the goal of academic excellence for all students.

■ Effective use of student enrollment and achievement data—analyzed by race, ethnic group and gender—to drive decisions and monitor the progress of reform.

The strength of EQUITY 2000 resides in the combined development and implementation of each of these six components within the current infrastructure of the school district.

ALGEBRA AND GEOMETRY AS "GATEKEEPERS" TO COLLEGE

The underpinning of EQUITY 2000 is research commissioned by the College Board to find what variables would help achieve the goal set by its board of trustees—to close the gap in college-going-and success rates between minority/non-minority and advantaged/disadvantaged-students. The research, conducted by Pelavin Associates, was published in *Changing the Odds: Factors Increasing Access to College* (Pelavin and Kane, 1989). The 1989 study, using "High School and Beyond" data, found that two or more years of college-preparatory mathematics, and aspirations to attend college are factors strongly associated with college enrollment and completion. In fact, the study found that if you examine those students who take algebra and geometry by the 10th grade and have aspirations or expectations to attend college, the gap practically closes in college-going and success rates between minorities/non-minorities and advantaged/disadvantaged students. However, the study also found that only 19 percent of African Americans and 17 percent of Hispanic students *ever* (not just by the 10th grade) take both algebra and geometry.

It is the tracking system in American education that results in the under-education of a vast proportion of minority students. By the middle-grade level, minority and poor students are placed in a non-college bound mathematics track that they do not get out of. By the time they get to high school, they are so far off track that it is difficult to catch up, even if they realize they are on a dead-end path and try to get the college preparation courses that will keep their options open and prepare them for college. In addition, mathematics, as a critical filter, extends to other disciplines since the math level students are placed in determines (mainly because of scheduling) the science, English and other courses they are assigned. Thus, access to all rigorous coursework is blocked (Jones, 1996; Jones, in press).

These findings led to the development of the districtwide reform model EQUITY 2000 and the partnership between the College Board and six pilot sites in 1990, which aimed at closing the achievement and college-going gap. The six-year pilot phase was completed in June 1996. A more recent study, based on the 1988 NELS data, continued to underscore the strong relationship between algebra and geometry and college-going rates (USDOE, in press). In addition, data from the 1985-93 Bureau of Labor Statistics' National Longitudinal Survey of Youth points to a positive correlation between high grades in mathematics achievement tests and greater earnings and less unemployment (USDOE, in press).

The EQUITY 2000 model has become a catalyst for comprehensive change in school policy, professional development, community and parent involvement, and effective use of data—all of which support higher student achievement. The model helps districts raise expectations and performance, provides more rigorous academic content in key subject areas, and offers assistance in designing support systems for students and additional training for counselors, teachers and administrative staff. During the pilot years, the six pilot sites serving over 500,000 students were Fort Worth, TX, Milwaukee, WI, Nashville, TN, Prince George's County, MD, Providence, RI and San Jose, CA (a consortium of nine districts).

TEACHERS AND COUNSELORS ARE KEY

The obstacles and challenges that the EQUITY 2000 model had to address included the key roles that teachers and counselors play. A teamwork strategy for teachers and counselors, which focuses on the academic development of every child, can be a powerful tool for reaching students. However, teachers and counselors are sometimes seen as obstacles rather than facilitators in improving the academic excellence of all students. This is reflected in how other educators perceive teachers and counselors. In the spring of 1992, the EQUITY 2000 national office surveyed a cross section of educators in several parts of the country who were interested in EQUITY 2000. The purpose of the survey, which included a mix of K-12 and higher education educators, was to identify the perceptions of math teachers and guidance counselors. Among the highlights of that survey were the following:

PERCEPTIONS ABOUT MATHEMATICS TEACHERS

■ Math teachers fail half of their students in algebra and then blame them for the failure.

■ Math teachers build reasons to fail in projects that ask them to change.

■ They act as if it is a "sign of weakness" to teach math to *all* students. They want only their "good" students to succeed and not be bothered with low achievers.

■ Math teachers don't want to teach students from diverse backgrounds, as demographics change.

■ They believe they are only considered good if they have the "aura of being tough."

■ Of all teachers, those who teach math are least flexible.

■ Some math teachers discourage students from taking more math courses than the minimum number required to graduate.

PERCEPTIONS ABOUT COUNSELORS

■ Counselors don't encourage minority students to go to college.

■ Counselors don't encourage students—especially minority students—to take higher level mathematics courses.

■ Counselors are "touchy-feely" people who suffer from math anxiety.

■ In the interest of protecting kids, counselors shelter them from academic challenges.

■ Counselors tend to help students find the "easy way out," rather than putting them into programs that are best for them.

■ Counselors have a negative view of historically black colleges and universities.

■ Counselors do not see themselves as empowered to make changes.

To be effective, teachers must do more than master the course's content (though that is essential, of course). They must also create an atmosphere in which diversity is valued, instruction builds on the strengths of students, and expectations for *all* students are high (Jones, 1996).

PRELIMINARY EVIDENCE OF THE EFFECTIVENESS OF EQUITY 2000

EQUITY 2000 is still very much a work in progress, and its results in closing the college-going and success gaps will not be available for several years. But on interim indicators, the results are impressive and encouraging and indicate that thousands of students—more than ever before—are taking and passing algebra, geometry and other college-prep courses at all of the pilot sites. There is also strong evidence that, though much progress has been made, much more remains to be done to achieve the goal of closing the gap and making a reality of excellence and equity. Districtwide reform truly requires a long-term commitment (Pelavin, March 1996, Jones, in press). Looking at these interim results is illuminating from three perspectives: 1) outside independent evaluators, and the research and development unit from the College Board; 2) site reported data; and 3) my own reflections on the source of the power of EQUITY 2000.

NATIONAL INDEPENDENT EVALUATION

Key findings (June 1997) on the pilot years of EQUITY 2000—in the draft summative report by the independent evaluator, Pelavin Associates—include the following:

■ By the end of the pilot period, the 1995-96 school year, more students were enrolled and successfully *passing* algebra or higher mathematics by the ninth grade and geometry or higher mathematics by the tenth grade than were even *enrolled* before EQUITY 20000. Three of the districts had reached the goal of 100 percent enrollment in algebra or higher by the ninth grade. The average across all of the pilot sites was nearly 90 percent.

■ Grouped by race and ethnicity, students have made substantial progress in both Algebra I and geometry across the sites. Figures I through 4 show the substantial progress in enrollment and passing in these gatekeeper courses.

■ In Algebra I, African-American enrollment by the ninth grade increased from 7,088 out of 15,750 students to 12,600 students out of 17,500. The increase in passing was from 5,355 out of 15,750 to 7,175 out of 17,500. For Hispanic students the increase in enrollment was from 2,600 out of 6,500 to 5,760 out of 8,000. The increase in passing algebra was from 2,015 out of 6,500 to 3,040 out of 8,000 students. For Asian students the enrollment in algebra increased from 2,205 out of 3,500 to 3,120 out of 4,000, and the number of students passing increased from 2,100 out of 3,500 to 2,600 out of 4,000. The increased enrollment in algebra for white students was from 7,080 out of 12,000 to 8,625 out of 11,500. The increase in passing was from 5,880 out of 12,000 to 6,210 out of 11,500 students.

■ In geometry, African-American enrollment by the tenth grade increased from 4,420 out of 13,000 to 7,020 out of 13,500. The increase in passing by the tenth grade was from 3,770 out of 13,000 to 5,400 out of 13,500. The increase for Hispanic students was from 1,208 out of 5,750 to 3,040 out of 8,000 enrolled. The number passing increased from 978 out of 5,750 to 1,885 out of 6,500. For Asian students the number of students enrolled in geometry by the tenth grade increased from 2,065 out of 3,500 to 2,400 out of 3,750. The increase in the number passing was from 1,995 out of 3,500 to 2,175 out of 3,750. The increase in geometry enrollment and passing by the tenth grade for white students was 5,145 out of 10,500 to 5,643 out of 9,250 and 4,620 out of 10,500 to 4,810 out of 9,250.

■ Though it is obvious that thousands of additional students are taking and passing algebra and geometry than before EQUITY 2000, increasing the passing rates remains a challenge.

■ Participation in Advanced Placement courses increased significantly among African-American and Hispanic students at the EQUITY 2000 sites, in contrast to student participation in their respective states.

■ At all the sites, the percentage of students indicating that they plan to attend college after graduation from high school was substantially higher than the national estimate for seniors from school districts with similar economic profiles/backgrounds.

■ There were significantly greater numbers of students at the EQUITY 2000 sites enrolled in higher mathematics such as Algebra II, trigonometry, pre-calculus and calculus than the national enrollments.

■ Teachers, counselors, principals, and site management teams at all sites observed that many more students were talking about going to college, specifically because they were taking algebra and geometry, than had been

talking about college in their school districts at the start of the pilot period.
■ The majority of mathematics teachers and counselors participated in voluntary professional development. They found the activities to influence their attitudes and practice, were helpful in understanding student success and failure, but were unsure what the direct impact was on student achievement.

In addition, a November 1996 report by the Research and Development unit of the College Board, "Signs of Success: EQUITY 2000 Preliminary Evidence of Effectiveness," synthesizes program evaluation data from the six years. The basis of the report is data on enrollment and achievement trends over time, attitudinal surveys of teachers and counselors, classroom observations, and interviews with administrators, school board members, faculty, students, and parents. Among the core findings are:

■ District level reform is a powerful lever for change. The districtwide policy component is central to the EQUITY 2000 reform effort because it allows for organization, consolidation, and collaboration of reform efforts across the district. EQUITY 2000 has acted as a catalyst for reform in the districts.

■ Counselors' and teachers' attitudes and expectations have changed markedly over the years. Professional development has led to changes in counselors' attitudes and expectations regarding students' ability to attend and graduate from college. Teachers' expectations of themselves and students have changed, with the majority believing that their teaching can improve and that students can learn to a higher level of math and succeed in college. Teachers' estimates of the number of students capable of taking and passing algebra and geometry increased substantially.

■ Students were passing algebra in 1994-95 (53-80 percent) at rates comparable to 1991-92 (62-88 percent) even though enrollments had almost doubled. Students were passing geometry in 1994-95 (69-87 percent) at rates comparable to 1991-92 (71-93 percent). Again, this was in the context of much higher rates of enrollments.

■ According to the report, conversations with teachers and surveys of them indicate that professional development provides the bridge from districtwide reform theory to the classroom. The preliminary report concludes that "the empowerment of teachers and counselors is transforming the learning environment and improving quality" (Jones, in press).

SITE REPORTED DATA

The pilot sites used snapshots of their districts to make decisions about allocation of resources, and other matters. They highlighted changes in their districts since beginning to use the EQUITY 2000 districtwide reform model as the "opportunity to learn" vehicle to help all students reach high standards and close the achievement gap. They cite these changes as evidence of the positive impact of systemic reform, using high standards for all as the driver. It should be pointed out that these snapshots come directly from the districts and are not verified through external evaluators. Below are snapshots of three of the sites.

EQUITY 2000 SNAPSHOTS

NASHVILLE SITE

Summer 1991

September 1997

—Had general math courses.

—All general math courses have been eliminated.

—In grades 7-12, approximately 37 percent of math teachers were trained in EQUITY 2000.

—In grades 7-12, approximately 90 percent of math teachers were trained in EQUITY 2000.

—In grades 7-12, approximately 13 percent of counselors were trained in EQUITY 2000.

—In grades K-12, approximately 90 percent of counselors were trained in EQUITY 2000.

—No pre- and post-assessment given to Algebra I students.

—Pre- and post-assessment administered to *all* Algebra I students.

—Career/Resource Centers were in some high schools.

—Centers have been expanded in all high schools (100 percent) and established in all middle schools (100 percent). All high school centers have the ExPAN program available.

—No release time for counselors.

—Counselors now have release time to attend staff development activities.

—No 5th and 6th grade Collaboration Institutes held.

—An EQUITY 2000 5th and 6th grade Collaborative Institute: "Mathematics, Language Arts, and Guidance," modeled after the EQUITY 2000 summer institutes, were offered in summer 1995 and '96 with 90 participants attending each.

—No Saturday Academies offered.

—Student attendance in Saturday Academies is 300.

—Limited college awareness.

—Increased early college awareness (grades 5, 6, 7 and 8).

—No Family Math Workshops.

—More than 3,000 parents have attended Family Math Workshops since 1992.

—No Principal Institute.

—A three-day Principal Institute with 98 percent attendance of principals and assistant principals, 7-12.

—No Pacesetter English.

—10 out of 13 high schools offer English Pacesetters for 11th and 12th grade.

—No vertical team training.

—Trained one team in Glencliff cluster in 1996.

—No "Write" Way Institute.

—Over 400 teachers trained in "Write" Way: Writing Across the Curriculum (40 schools).

—No organized Building Success.

—Building Success workshop conducted in 1996 with 24 teachers trained and four National Trainers.

—1,800 students out of 3,426 taking ACT with composite score of 19.6.

—2,387 out of 2,817 taking ACT with a composite score of 19.1.

—424 students taking SAT with verbal score of 469 and math score of 509.

—In 1997, 526 taking SAT with verbal score of 561 and math score of 552.

—104 Advanced Placement classes offered with: 1,797 enrollment; 757 examinations taken 58.7 percent (444) of AP exam takers scores "3" or above.

—135 Advanced Placement classes offered with: 2,451 enrollment; 1,278

examinations taken 64.7 percent (827) of AP exam takers scores "3" or above.
—Of our 1992 graduates 34.5 percent (1,040) of our white students; 19.4 percent (586) of our black students; 2.7 percent (83) of other students for a total of 56.6 percent (1,708) went on to post-secondary.
—Of our 1996 (2,744) graduates 34.9 percent (1,001) of our white students; 24.4 percent (698) of our black students; 3.9 percent (111) of other students for a total of 63.2 percent (1,810) went on to post-secondary.
—Of our 1992 graduates 24.5 percent (738) of our male students; 32.1 percent of our female students for a total of 56.6 percent (1,708) went on to post-secondary.
—Of our 1996 (2,744) graduates 26.7 percent (764) of our male students; 36.5 percent (1,046) of our female students for a total of 63.2 percent (1,810) went on to post-secondary.
—PSAT: In 1990 total tested was 1,045 with mean of 40.0 on verbal; 43.4 on math.
—PSAT: In 1996 total tested was 1,085 with mean of 47.6 on verbal; 47.6 on math.
—PLAN: In 1992 total tested was 2,111 with average PLAN composite score of 16.7.
—PLAN: In 1995 total tested was 2,903 with average PLAN composite score of 16.3.

EQUITY 2000 SNAPSHOTS

SAN JOSE SITE

Summer 1991

September 1997

—Not all middle schools offered algebra classes; only pre-algebra.
—As a result of EQUITY 2000 most of the middle schools in the San Jose Site are offering Intro to algebra, Algebra I and geometry.
—No student "safety nets."
—Saturday Academy available for middle and high school students. Homework centers open after school collaboratively sponsored by the city and the districts.

—Only 52 percent of the students enrolled in algebra by the 9th grade in both ESUHSD and SJUSD.

—Over 90 percent of the 9th grade class is enrolled in Algebra 1 or a higher math course.

—At ESUHSD and SJUSD 63 percent and 45 percent respectively were passing algebra.

—The pass rate in the EQUITY 2000 math program with a grade of C or higher, is 68 percent for the Spring semester of 1997. We now have a significantly higher number of students passing Algebra 1 than what we use to have enrolled in that course prior to the EQUITY 2000 program.

—No articulation between the feeder schools.

—Ongoing articulation between middle and high schools, as well as influencing elementary schools to "enter the picture."

—At SJUSD only 50 Hispanic students were passing the Advanced Placement exams in calculus.

—The number of students participating in the Advanced Placement Program has more than tripled.

—Little to no family math involvement with parents.

—As a result of EQUITY 2000, family math nights and math workshops for parents have been adopted at the majority of middle schools and elementary schools, as well as in some high schools.

—The enrollment in the higher math courses Algebra 2, Trigonometry, and calculus) has more than doubled.

—The EQUITY 2000 program has been a catalyst to the untracking of the curriculum in other core curricular areas. In particular, the science department in the East Side has eliminated significantly the remedial non-college prep courses. The current 9th grade students will have to complete two college prep laboratory-based courses for graduation in the year 2001.

—We have established collaborative partnerships to address student success with San Jose State University, the Hispanic University and the University of California at Santa Cruz.

—The summer school program is now being used more intensively as a support system for student success in the area of mathematics.

—The tutoring program is being improved with the help of the institutions of higher learning.

—We are in the process of setting up a Saturday Academy to work with students in the areas of Algebra I, geometry and the SAT.

—In collaboration with the CPMSA, we have released four "star" teachers in the areas of math and science to work with teachers as mentors to improve student success.

EQUITY 2000 SNAPSHOTS

P R I N C E   G E O R G E ' S   C O U N T Y   S I T E

Summer 1991

September 1997

—A five-area administrative area organization.

—School system organized into 20 pre-K-12 "Communities Committed to Children."

—Oasis center program committed to family and community involvement.

—No strategic plan.

—EQUITY 2000 institutionalized through inclusion in 3-year Strategic Plan document.

—Lower level mathematics courses.

—All lower-level mathematics courses have been eliminated (except math labs).

—58 percent of 9th graders enrolled in Algebra I or above.

—91 percent of 9th graders enrolled in Algebra I or above.

—48 percent of 10th graders enrolled in geometry or above.

—84 percent of 10th graders enrolled in geometry or above.

—$45K district funds committed to support EQUITY 2000.

—Over $2.1 million district funds committed to support EQUITY 2000 in FY 1997.

—No student relational database system.

—READ, a student relational database, in place to guide managerial and personnel decisions.

—Two math credits required for graduation.

—Algebra and geometry required as 2 of 3 credits to graduate.

—Little coordinated professional development for mathematics teachers and guidance counselors.

—Over 70 percent of K-12 counselors and secondary mathematics teachers received professional development, as well as more than 750 elementary mathematics teachers.

—Few principals involved in EQUITY 2000 training or activities.

—Each district principal has participated in an EQUITY 2000 activity.

—No "safety nets" required.

—"Safety nets" to support high achievement in mathematics required for each school.

—Pre-K-12 Mathematics Program revised to align with NCTM standards.

—Pre-K-12 guidance program revised to keep options for college and career open for all students.

—All programs and practices under "excellence/equity" review.

REFLECTIONS ON THE SOURCE OF THE POWER OF EQUITY 2000

Finally, I will share my view of the source of EQUITY 2000 's power as a districtwide force to drive standards higher and to support all students to reach them, thereby closing the achievement and college-going gaps.

■ It involves a long-term commitment—no quick fixes. It establishes high standards for all students as a goal, and it changes the culture of teaching and learning in the districts to be supportive of meeting that goal. It targets resources for *all* students, so they can reach the high standards.

■ It is focused. It uses the power of mathematics, initially at the middle-grade level, to change algebra and geometry from gatekeepers that block access to high standards access that open—and to drive reform in K-12 and in all disciplines.

■ It serves as a catalyst. Within a district, it brings cohesion to many isolated, disjointed projects and programs—thus helping students reach high standards. It fosters the alignment of goals, resources, programs and evaluation.

■ It builds on what is already working in the district. It does not try to reinvent the wheel.

■ It uses guidance counselors as an essential part of the leadership team to achieve the goal of all students reaching high standards. EQUITY 2000 transforms the role of the guidance counselor into that of an advocate for all students' full academic development. It is one of the only national education reform initiatives to foster this role for counselors. In doing so, it changes the role, vision and assessment of guidance counseling for the 21st century.

■ It is districtwide, serving as a catalyst to "scale up" the effective, isolated efforts in a district. In looking at the continuum of reform—from the state level to the individual classroom—the district-level reform appears to be a powerful lever for change.

■ It works top-down, bottom-up and in the middle. It draws on the leadership's involvement and support of the entire district, from the planning through the implementation and evaluation phases.

■ It is data driven. It uses student enrollment and achievement data, analyzed by race and gender, to inform decisions and guide reform. With money limited, it increases the likelihood of shifting resources to what is working and away from what is not.

■ It establishes as a norm the need to invest in the ongoing professional development of school and district personnel—the human capital who must deliver the reform, and who must change themselves and the environment in ways that result in excellence and equity.

■ It connects educators to a network of colleagues across the country who are facing the same challenges, and it provides ongoing opportunities for joint problem-solving. It is part of a national effort.

■ Its association with a national organization—such as the College Board, with its high standards—works against the stereotype that says, if it is for *all* students, it must not reflect high standards. This association can give districts the lead time they need to show some positive results.

■ It is comprehensive. Each of the six components of the model taken alone is nothing new. Together, they are more than the sum of their parts, and address the critical pressure points in order to have all students reach high standards.

■ Finally, it makes high expectations for all students a primary focus for the whole effort. It does this not just in words, but in plans that address the implications of making high expectation for all a reality throughout the district. If I were to pick the single most powerful variable in how much students achieve, I would say expectations—particularly teachers' expectations. They reflect the standards to which we hold students—and they are self-fulfilling expectations.

BIBLIOGRAPHY

Braddock, J.W., and Dawkins, M.P. (1993). "Ability Grouping, Aspirations, and Attainments: Evidence from the National Longitudinal Study of 1988." *Journal of Negro Education.* 62 (3), pp. 1-13.

Braddock, Jomills Henry, II, and Slavin, Robert E. (1992). *Why Ability Grouping Must End: Achieving Excellence and Equity in American Education.* Paper presented at the Common Destiny Conference at Johns Hopkins University (Baltimore, MD, September 9-11, 1992). ERIC Document Reproduction Service, Number ED355296.

Dolan, W. Patrick (1994). *Restructuring Our Schools: A Primer on Systemic Change.* Kansas City, KS: Systems & Organizations.

Education That Works: An Action Plan for Educating Minorities (1990). New York, NY: Carnegie Corporation.

EQUITY 2000 Planning Document (1997). Unpublished document produced by the EQUITY 2000 National Office.

Herrnstein, Richard J., and Murray, Charles (1994). *The Bell Curve: Intelligence and Class Structure in America.* New York, NY: Free Press.

Jones, Vinetta C. (in press). "What a Difference a Standard Makes." In D. Bartels & J. Opert Sandler (Eds.), *Implementing Science Education Reform: Are We Making an Impact?* Washington, D.C.: American Association for the Advancement of Science.

Jones, V.C., and Clemson, R. (1996). Promoting Effective Teaching for Diversity (pp. 149-167). In Rendon and Hope (Eds.) *Educating a New Majority.* San Francisco, CA: Jossey-Bass Publishers.

Judy, Richard W., and D'Amico, Carol (1997). *Workforce 2020: Work and Workers in the 21st Century.* Indianapolis, IN: Hudson Institute.

Knapp, Michael S. (1997). "Between Systemic Reforms and the Mathematics and Science Classroom: The Dynamics of Innovation, Implementation, and Professional Learning." *Review of Educational Research.* Volume 67, Number 2, pp. 227-266.

Oakes, J. (1985). *Keeping Track: How Schools Structure Inequality.* New Haven, CT: Yale University Press.

Oakes, J. (1990). *Multiplying Inequalities: The Effects of Race, Class, and Tracking on Opportunities to Learn Math and Science.* Santa Monica, CA: RAND.

Pelavin Research Institute (1997). *The EQUITY 2000 Evaluation, A Summative Report: Impact and Implementation.* New York, NY: The College Board.

Pelavin Research Institute (1996). *EQUITY 2000 1994-95 National Implementation Report.* Draft Report. New York, NY: The College Board.

Pelavin, S., and Kane, M. (1989). *Changing the Odds: Factors Increasing Access to College.* New York, NY: The College Board.

Signs of Success: EQUITY 2000 Preliminary Evidence of Effectiveness (1996). New York, NY: The College Board.

Somerton, W. H. *et al.* (1994). *The MESA Way: A Success Story of Nurturing Minorities for Math/Science-Based Careers.* San Francisco, CA: Caddo Gap Press.

Standing at the Edge of the Digital Divide[1]

By Allen S. Hammond IV[2]

INTRODUCTION:

Change has always been a fact of life. Philosophers and poets have proclaimed (and bemoaned) its inevitability for thousands of years. But today's changes are different and astonishing—in the rapidity with which they are taking place and in their global scale. Knowing about them and reacting appropriately will be important for all Americans. Their significance for minorities and the poor in this country can hardly be overestimated.[3]

Any Change may bear seeds of benefit.

Seek them out.

Any Change may bear seeds of harm.

Beware...[4]

Each time a new medium comes along, great hopes are raised. But the lesson of history is that every new medium provides new opportunities for selling as well as for education, for monopolists as well as for democracy, and for abuse as well as for benefit.[5]

NEWS OF THE INFORMATION SUPERHIGHWAY: PROMISES MADE, PROMISES TO KEEP

By now most of us have heard about the information superhighway. In television commercials, a telephone company promises us we'll be able to send handwritten faxes from the beach, while another promises we'll be able to participate in office presentations without getting out of our pajamas. In still other commercials, banks and computer manufacturers promise we'll never have to stand in another dreary, slow-moving teller line, waiting to deposit our paychecks once we bank by computer. Meanwhile, a software manufacturer's commercial asks, "Where [on the Internet do we] want to go today?" And in numerous speeches, the president, the vice president and members of Congress extol the value and importance of the Internet to the nation as the Supreme Court rules on the constitutionality of internet regulation.

It is expected (and promised) that the networks of the information superhighway and the telephones and computers connected to them will revolutionize the finance, manufacturing and advertising businesses[6]; stimulate economic development[7] and facilitate electronic commerce[8]; enhance educational pedagogy and service delivery[9]; extend health care to remote locations[10]; and create new opportunities for electronic democracy.[11]

THE TELECOMMUNICATIONS ACT OF 1996

We may have heard about the deregulation of the telephone, cable and broadcast companies, accomplished by the Telecommunications Act of 1996. Perhaps we are even aware of the Congressional, administration and industry voices promising that, through this deregulation, Americans will be the beneficiaries of lower consumer prices and new services created by the increased competition between the newly freed companies. And maybe we have become aware that the act seeks to assure every American will have access to basic telephone services (touch tone, single party, operator assistance, directory assistance and emergency/911 services—with discounts for the poor)[12]; and eventual access to advanced telecommunications services (e-mail, the Internet, distance learning and other multimedia services).

THE DIGITAL DIVIDE: MAKING IT REAL COMPARED TO WHAT?

Amid the media voices (as we frantically try to learn techno-speak) are, however, other voices. Some within the civil rights community warn that the new law does very little to slow technology's tendency to separate American society into the information rich and poor. Some say that much of the new act may actually make things worse. This concern about information haves and have-nots may seem troubling to some, but efforts to explain why African

Americans should be concerned are often unsuccessful. To many of us, the passage of a law to increase competition and lower consumer prices, while making sure everyone has a phone, may seem to raise consumer fairness issues at best. A law that makes it possible for companies to help us send faxes from the beach, attend business presentations in bathrobes, and bank without leaving our home is not necessarily a law that seems relevant to us.

Many black communities are embattled. We are reeling from the impact of "welfare reform;" chronic unemployment; unsafe streets; underfunded, understaffed and underperforming schools; poor health care; financial redlining; the burning of our churches; deteriorating cities; police brutality; racial violence; and the slow demise of affirmative action. Given blacks' status, it would not be surprising if we were to dismiss the information superhighway and the Telecommuncations Act of 1996 as irrelevant.

But the telecommunications networks—and the telephones, computers, televisions and other equipment connected to them—have a significant impact on the lives of all Americans as individuals, learners, citizens and consumers. Access to these networks increasingly determines the ease with which we can conduct and control our financial affairs; pursue an education[13]; acquire the skills to become employable; call for emergency police, fire or medical assistance[14]; apply for a job, work at a distance,[15] or participate in the political process. Through them we are connected to family, friends, schools, employers, spiritual leaders, political representatives, markets and society. For many Americans, this statement reflects the fact that access to the basic and advanced networks provides a broad range of services from which to choose.[16] But, for many Americans, and especially many African-Americans, the choice is diminishing.

As we identify and anticipate the potential of network technology to benefit society, we in the African-American community must be wary that the technology not become a new tool of disenfranchisement rather than a tool of empowerment. Many are concerned that a significant portion of America's inner-cities and rural communities will become the domain of "information and technology have-nots" because of unequal access to telecommunications network technologies and the telephones, computers and other customer equipment that may be attached to the networks.[17] The telecommunications and electronic network infrastructure serving the communities in which many African Americans reside is older and less able to provide the newer services that many middle- and upper-class neighborhoods take for granted.[18] Already, consumer and civil rights groups allege that network providers are bypassing low-income and minority communities when planning to enhance older networks or build new networks.[19] There is legitimate concern that networks will be deployed or built in communities perceived to be "more profitable."[20] Such strategies will preclude near-term access to advanced network infrastructures for many inner-city, rural and near-suburban communities that aren't viewed as desirable markets, regardless of their actual consumption of telecommunications and video services.[21]

African Americans in these same communities often are less likely to own or have access to the telephones and computers that are necessary to take advantage of the basic or advanced network services and efficiencies.[22] In part, as a consequence of limited access to networks and equipment, their access to the information necessary to function as citizens, students, workers and consumers in Amercan society is also diminishing. Chief among the reasons for these Americans' critical access deficiencies is their relative lack of wealth.[23]

Their access to information is also diminishing, as more and more previously public information is becoming private, and access to it must be purchased. For instance, competition and innovation in the video-distribution market are creating a shift from advertiser-supported to subscriber-supported delivery of video information.[24] This means that programs previously available for "free" on broadcast television are increasingly shown on cable and satellite television for a subscription fee. And information previously found in public libraries is now repackaged and sold by online subscription services.

THE WRONG METAPHOR: NOT HIGHWAY BUT NERVOUS SYSTEM

Viewing this lack of access to networks, equipment and information as a lack of access to the "information superhighway" mischaracterizes the seriousness of the situation. It is not just that some people will be unable to travel "virtually" to various informations sources, just as many of us today cannot afford vacations. Nor is it the fact that some Americans will be unable to instantaneously correspond with others. The impact of these deferred connections and disconnections is far more profound, touching the fundamental nature of who we are as Americans. As the networks and the equipment attached to them become the preferred vehicles for political participation, lifelong learning, employment and commerce, as well as personal expression, non-access and non-connection could become tantamount to "non existence."

In this sense, the "information superhighway" metaphor is inapt. A more appropriate metaphor is "the national nervous system." Taken as an integrated, transparent whole, the national system of networks is a collection of transmission pathways connecting individuals, homes, schools, businesses and organizations that communicate by electrical and photonic signals. In much the same manner, our nervous systems are collections of nerve transmission pathways connecting all the parts of our body which communicate with each other via electrical impulses switched through our brain.[25] When major nerve pathways are severed or undergo severe atrophy, the result is the disconnection of essential body parts and/or the impairment of body functions. In more extreme cases, total atrophy of significant portions of the human nervous system results in paralysis, wasting away of critical body functions or parts, and eventual death. Appropriate medical analogies include Alzheimer's[26] and Lou Gehrig's diseases.[27]

Viewed through the lens of the nervous system metaphor, many American inner cities, nearby old suburbs and rural areas—and their African-American residents—are experiencing diminishing and/or limited access to basic and advanced networks and services, and to telephones and computers—which resulting in losses in network connections and access to information. This lack of connection subjects these communities to the equivalent of Lou Gehrig's[28] disease, and the nation, which they are part, to Alzheimer's.[29] If there is any doubt about the truth of these statements, consider the following story.

LIVING JUST ENOUGH FOR THE CITY [30]

Tamika, a teen-ager in Inner City, USA, rushes out of her apartment to call for family or emergency help. During the night, her grandmother had become seriously ill. Tamika's family does not own a phone. The family was forced to give up phone service when it was unable to pay its grow-ing long-distance phone bill. The phone bills had escalated because of collect calls from her incarcerated uncle and from the extensive phone usage by her and her teen-age sister. Many of her family's neighbors do not own working phones either. Concerned for Tamika's safety, her fam-ily would not let her call for assistance during the night. Now, in the morning, she's allowed to venture out, quarters in hand. But there are precious few pay phones, and those that are available don't work.

She decides to find a cab, so she can take her grandmother to the hos-pital, but she doesn't have enough money with her. Because she works at a local fast-food restaurant, she has a small bank account from which she can make a withdrawal. Unfortunately, as a cost-saving measure precipitated by a merger, her bank recently closed the branch in her neighborhood. She has to find an ATM, but this search fails, just as her search for a working phone. She heads for the check-cashing store to write a check and pay a large fee, so she can finally get back to her grandmother and take her to the hospital. ...

When Tamika returns home, her mother decides to take "grandma" to the hospital, so Tamika can attend school. Tamika gives her mother the money. As her mother and grandmother leave for the hospital, Tamika leaves for school.

Tamika's high school is like many others in Inner City, USA. Overcrowded, its walls and ceilings are in serious need of repair; there are too many students per class; and very few telephones or computers are available. The school is not even wired for much of today's technology. And with the meager tax base on which the school must rely for funds, there is little possibility that its insufficient budget can cover building upkeep and renovation, current textbooks, competitive teacher salaries and can be stretched to pay for sophisticated computers, software, and network access, not to mention technology training for the teachers.

Tamika sits in a computer laboratory watching, as a classmate uses a remedial math software program on an old 286 computer. She is one of several students standing in groups of five or more behind one of the five terminals in use. The computers, which were donated by a local business, are the only ones in her school. None of the computers allows students access to the Internet, and none are networked. Often there are days when at least one of the computers breaks down, and PC access is even more limited. Tamika, a few of her classmates, and the computer lab teacher have learned how to repair minor glitches in the computers. But parts are scarce, and all fear that it's just a matter of time before they have no working computers at all.

After school, Tamika goes to work. She is a smart, diligent worker, relied on to organize and supervise her co-workers. As a result, her fast-food employer allows her to work as many hours as her school schedule permits. Her manager has told her that she has management potential and should go to college. Her mother and grandmother have told her that college is the key to a good job and a good future. Her teachers have also encouraged her. Tamika would very much like to attend college, but she's concerned that she doesn't have all the training and access to good equipment that other high school students may have. And, if she's unsuccessful in attending college, she's concerned that she may never find a better job than her current one, because there are so few businesses in her community. And the ones outside her community increasingly require a college degree and technology training. Some may consider Tamika's story to be fanciful, but the current technology-based reality is far closer to causing Tamika's plight than we might think.

CITIES AND ACCESS TO FINANCE AND COMMERCE

There are two popular images of the "city of the future, based on the impact of technology: dead or dying; its trash-filled streets looked upon by empty, graffiti-marked buildings; its only signs of life a few remaining smoke stacks pumping effluents into the air; its unemployment offices marked by block-long lines of the hopeless, the unskilled, the illiterate—the human effluent of an economic storm. Or thriving, ribboned by green parks, its clean air humming with electronic commerce and the happy jingling of the cyber-cash-register in the sky. ...[31]

Advanced network-infrastructure efficiencies are allowing businesses to abandon cities, nearby suburbs and rural areas for lower property taxes, better services, and more highly skilled and/or cheaper labor pools. By providing faster, more efficient communications, networks facilitate businesses' ability to out-source manufacturing and back-office jobs previously held by urban residents.[32] For the minorities and women workers who constitute the majority of urban-core residents, the net result is that there are fewer available jobs for which they are trained. In addition, urban core residents increasingly find there are far fewer businesses providing the basic goods and financial, medical and social services where they live. Where such goods and services are provided, too often they are provided at an increase in price, and the businesses that provide them are often less efficient than their network enhanced counterparts. While many other developments have contributed to "urban blight," the reliance on network efficiencies is exacerbating the problems.[33]

The business outmigration experienced by inner-city and rural communities, as a result of relocation, is only the first wave of abandonment. The second wave is the movement to electronic finance and commerce.[34] An increasing number of public-and-private sector financial transactions are migrating to telecommunications networks. Retail commerce, now housed in brick-and-mortar stores, is beginning to migrate to electronic networks and online services.[35] It is estimated that as much as $6 billion dollars in consumer transactions will have migrated to the Worldwide Web by 1998.[36] Not surprisingly, the demographics of online consumers show an absence of those without access to the advanced network and equipment technologies necessary to take advantage of the shift to the Worldwide Web and online services.[37]

The migration does not end here. As much as $13 billion dollars in business-to-business transactions will have migrated to electronic networks by the year 2000.[38] Even the federal government has decided to place a substantial portion of its procurement business online.[39] Thus, for minority-owned and small-business providers, contracting with the government necessitates investing in electronic networks to continue in business. This federal procurement development mirrors procurement efforts already under way in large commercial firms relying on value-added and private networks.[40] Increasingly, the network serves as a means of reducing costs, enhancing efficiencies and expanding the markets of firms. Given the value of networks, businesses seek out communities that have made the necessary investments in network infrastructures, as part of their competitive strategies.[41] Consequently, officials of many states, municipalities and rural communities realize that, without the investment in infrastructures to support electronic commerce and other services, they will be bypassed by businesses of all types to the detriment of those who reside therein.[42]

COMMERCE AND COMMUNITY ECONOMIC DEVELOPMENT

The efficiencies of network technology allow more of the economy to operate at a distance. Many U.S. firms outsource substantial amounts of clerical back-office work to English-speaking nations in Europe and Asia, thereby reducing the pool of jobs recently held by minority and female workers.[43] Businesses previously located in the urban core migrate to communities with lower taxes, higher concentrations of highly skilled workers and a better quality of life. To the extent that there is a continuing need to interface with a corporate headquarters' resident in the central business district, it can be done electronically via telecommuting.

The inner cities in which our teen-agers live are likely to be the weakest parts of a metropolitan economy. Without economic-development initiatives, inner-city communities and residents will find it harder to compete. The cities of which these communities are a part face a substantial challenge: They must bridge the growing gap between the skills required for employment in advanced services concentrated in urban cores, and the limited skills that many inner-city residents like our teen-agers bring to the job market.[44] The road to employable skills and individual economic self-sufficiency passes through education and access to technology. But the telecommunications infrastructures in many urban and rural areas are incapable of providing access to the advanced services necessary to make passage on this road successful.[45]

CONTROL OF PERSONAL AND COMMUNITY WEALTH

Despite state and federal laws requiring that banks and financial institutions serve all segments of society,[46] numerous banks have closed branches in inner-city areas because of mergers and consolidations, cost reductions or discrimination.[47]

For instance, urban African-American residents in New Jersey are four times more likely to have a bank branch in their communities close.[48] As a result, many people in inner-city communities cannot make a deposit or withdrawal at a bank branch or at an automatic teller machine [ATM] within walking distance of their homes.[49] Given the limited access to phones and the virtual absence of computers, few inner-city residents bank by phone or PC.[50] Yet one of the chief impacts of an increase in the use of telecommunications networks is the closing of local branches and mounting reliance on less-expensive electronic-banking methods based on the phone and computer, as bank consolidations and competition increase.[51]

Welfare recipients and their communities will be particularly hard hit. By the end of 1998, persons receiving public-assistance[52] will be required to have accounts that can receive their benefits, which will be transmitted over private telecommunications networks. For public-assistance recipients living in neighborhoods where bank branches have closed, this change in policy and practice creates significant inconveniences. The recipients will then have to frequent banks[53] or supermarkets in distant communities that have ATMs, allowing them to use their debit cards. For small merchants that accept food stamps and welfare checks as legal tender, it will mean an immediate loss in money-changing fees and cash flow, as their clients bank and shop elsewhere. This new practice is likely to remove a significant amount of legal tender from the cash economies of inner cities.

In addition, studies have shown a significant correlation between the existence of an operating bank branch in a community and success in securing a house mortgage or business loan.[54] As bank branches close, communities lose more than convenience and access to services; they lose control of their economic resources and a measure of economic viability.[55] Without access to phones, computers and the networks to which they are attached, the gap in access to financial services and economic development will surely widen.

Increasing bank and government reliance on network-delivered financial and benefit services means that people in underserved communities will have to acquire greater access to phone and computer services to gain access to financial resources. If they are unsuccessful, they will lose more control over their already limited economic resources. And their ability to stimulate economic activity in their communities will be further compromised.

EDUCATION AND EMPLOYMENT

More than 60 percent of the new jobs being created today require computer skills.[56] Children in poor inner cities, near suburban and rural schools are least likely to have access to learner-centered, skill-enhancing computer hardware and software. According to a 1994 report by the U.S. Census Bureau, only 39 percent of African-American students and 56 percent of European-American students use computers in school. Statistics on home-computer use are even more dismal. Fifteen percent of African-American students and 36 percent of European-American students reported using a computer at home. Because so many jobs in our economy are going to require some computer skills, children without such skills will be increasingly left behind. Access is essential to develop the skills necessary for employment today and in the next millennium. While the amount of usage is growing,[57] far too few Americans use a PC to access the Internet, remote databases and Websites for work, school, shopping or recreation.

If our children do not attend schools that provide meaningful access to a learner-oriented, computer-use curriculum, they are less likely to qualify for the better-paying technology jobs. They already have a less than 50 percent chance of attending such a school. Approximately half of the states have been sued for the inequitable distribution of revenues to schools in neighborhoods like many of those in which we and our children reside.[58]

Although academia, industry and government demand increased performance from American students,[59] disparities in economic wealth cause unequal access to computer and Internet technologies and services. As a result, children like Tamika cannot get access to the tools necessary to gain proficiency in the skills that future employers will demand.[60] Her chances of educational and economic success suffer as a result.[61]

POLITICAL EXPRESSION AND POLITICAL POWER: MIS-REPRESENTED, UNDER-REPRESENTED AND MIS-UNDERSTOOD

> The outcome of the election [of 1994] was due in great measure to the Republican Party's ability to mobilize voters through technology—television, talk radio, voice mail, online services, and fax communication. Whether you agree or disagree with the outcome of the election, the fact is that those who best controlled technology came out on top.[62]

Members of the African-American community have criticized the media for years. Many times, broadcast licensees and their advertisers have been criticized for not presenting programs to address the needs, interests or perspectives of our communities.[63] When we were portrayed, the portrayals were overwhelmingly stereotypical.[64] To address these problems, efforts focused on increasing diverse viewpoints by expanding the number of African Americans on a broadcaster's staff (EEO),[65] requiring the broadcaster to fairly present controversial issues of public importance (fairness doctrine),[66] requiring broadcast to talk with members of our community (ascertainment), challenging broadcasters license renewals,[67] and increasing the number of broadcast stations owned by minorities, to provide minority-oriented perspectives. Most of these efforts have been undermined or abolished in the last 15 years.[68] More recently, the current Supreme Court ruling declared government efforts to increase minority ownership of broadcast media unconstitutional.[69] And while the addition of public and educational cable channels has increased opportunities for African Americans to speak to other members of their community, even today, some of our communities still do not have access to cable.[70]

By comparison, computer and Internet technologies and services such as e-mail have created increased opportunities for personal and political electronic expression.[71] They are expected to be used widely in the next presidential election.[72] And some believe they're a necessary antidote to the large media conglomerates that own newspapers, broadcasts stations and cable companies.[73] As one commentator has stated:

> In the age of mass media, citizens and grassroots groups need an equalizer. The combination of personal computers and the telephone network might prove as important to citizens in the information age as the printing press has been for several centuries. The use of electronic mail services, computer bulletin-board systems, and computer conferencing systems as channels to make decisions and disseminate information can help grassroots political organizations, nonprofit groups, and other public interest groups to gather critical information, organize political action, sway public opinion and guide policy-making.[74]

Our limited access to and control of media is a matter of critical concern for at least two reasons. The first is the media's historical tendency to portray African Americans in a largely unflattering, stereotypical manner. The second is our current and historical political under-representation. For instance, recent Supreme Court decisions ban many efforts to redraw Congressional districts by taking race into account. These redrawing efforts by civil rights groups and the Justice Department created districts with sufficient percentages of minority voters to increase the likelihood of electing minority representatives. Such districts are credited with doubling the number of African-

American representatives in Congress in recent years.[75] It is predicted that the Supreme Court's decision will result in a loss of political power in Congress and may have repercussions in the states.[76]

In spite of the Supreme Court's rulings, however, African Americans can still associate across geographic and political boundaries by using computers and the Internet. With these tools we can pursue our common community agendas with great efficiency. Given the current political realities, we must make use of e-mail, participate in online and/or Internet user groups, and create Web sites to help accomplish our goal.

The failure to meet and conquer this challenge will leave us at a decided disadvantage in the 1998 and 2000 year elections. If anyone needs convincing, consider that one of the chief results of our failure to master technology in 1994 was the substantial influx of conservatives into Congress. They in turn were instrumental in shaping and controlling the affirmative action, minority set-aside and welfare debates. This change in Congressional composition has been substantially responsible for the demise of the tax-certificate policy which assisted minorities trying to buy broadcast stations, and for changes to the nation's affirmative action and welfare policies.

For example, because of their increase in numbers, conservative Congressmen, along with many in the media, were able to misrepresent the welfare issue as a "black" issue. Erroneous perceptions about welfare recipients flourish in this nation, despite the fact that we do not constitute the majority of welfare recipients. Nationally, non-Hispanic European-Americans comprise 48 percent of welfare recipients, African Americans 27 percent, and Hispanics 22 percent.[77] Yet, too many Americans believe what the conservative Congress' and media has portrayed Americans on welfare as being—African American and Latino.[78] Our absence as an unmediated, representative, electronic presence in the welfare debate was critical to the misuse of race as an issue in the debate's outcome.[79] Unless we gain access to the new tools of electronic political expression, we will be misrepresented and under-represented again and again.

FREEDOM OF SPEECH AND FREEDOM OF ASSOCIATION

Computer and Internet technologies have created opportunities for greater electronic expression. Newer media such as the Internet, and services such as e-mail have occasioned greater opportunities for electronic expression by individuals and groups who use but do not own media. The opportunities have resulted in increased personal and political electronic expression. For instance, the use of computers and telecommunications networks can provide a much needed counterbalance to the concentrated, private control of the traditional mass media.[80] Through the use of PC and telephone networks, communities can gain access to electronic-mail services, computer bulletin-board systems; communities using computer-conferencing systems can make decisions, gather and disseminate critical information, organize political actions, sway public opinion and guide policy-making.[81]

Decentralized, user-based, interactive communications afforded by computers and the Internet can provide a critical, necessary, democratic alternative—assuring speech and association opportunities for individuals and communities. Such communications serve as a potential counter to the increasing centralization of control in the converging, traditional media of broadcasting, cable, print and telephony. However, these technologies and services can do so only if all individuals and communities have access to them, the training necessary for their proper use, and inexpensive means to reach the information. The current picture is not good.

ACCESS TO BASIC NETWORK TECHNOLOGY AND TELEPHONES

According to the Communication Act of 1934, Title I, Section 1, the primary goal of American communications policy is "to make available, so far as possible, to all people of the United States a rapid, efficient, nationwide, and worldwide wire and radio communications service with adequate facilities at reasonable charges."[82] The law is interpreted to mean that the major local and long-distance telephone companies are required to provide services to as many Americans as possible.[83] The government allowed telephone companies to subsidize their costs of serving poor, rural, or other less-profitable customers by charging their higher-margin clients, such as downtown businesses, more.[84] The access policy, coupled with a policy of non-discriminatory common carriage, allowed individual telephone subscribers to acquire relatively cheap access to telephones with very little constraint on what could be said.[85]

However, despite the inclusive goal of universal service, there are still substantial gaps in service.[86] Roughly 20 percent to 25 percent of low-income families in many communities lack phone service.[87] Even pay-phones, the traditional substitute for a phone in the home, are becoming less and less available for a variety of reasons.[88] Without access to a phone, poor people lose opportunities to acquire government benefits and to secure employment, emergency care and other essentials such as connection to the larger society.[89]

ACCESS TO ADVANCED NETWORKS AND COMPUTERS

The four places where Americans are likely to have access to computer technology are at home, at school, at the local library or at work. Although the gap in access is closing, far fewer African Americans enjoy access comparable to that of European-Americans. And the poorer one is, the less likely one is to have access at all.

In 1993, less than half of Americans had access to computers. For instance, across the board—taking into account access at home, of school or work—census data indicate that roughly 25.6 percent of Americans have access to computers. According to the U.S. Census Bureau, approximately 25 percent of African Americans used computers at home, work or public locations such as a library. By comparison, 37 percent of European-Americans used computers at home, work or public locations. Roughly 32 percent of all American children between the ages of 3 and 17 had access to a computer. However, only 13 percent of African-American children had access to a computer at home, school or elsewhere.[90]

Based on the sample of Americans surveyed, European-Americans were more than twice as likely to have a PC at home than African-Americans.[91] Recent data published by NTIA confirm these conclusions. However, depending on whether the comparison is between rural, urban or inner-city African- and European-American residents, European-American households are closer to three times more likely to own a computer than their African-American counterparts.[92]

Access to computer technology is even more skewed when income is considered irrespective of race. American families earning $15,000 or less annually are more than seven times less likely to own a computer than families earning $75,000 or more annually.[93] By comparison, some researchers have found there is little disparity in ownership between African-American and European-American households making $75,000 or more annually.[94] Disparities in computer access are reflected in Internet usage.[95] Even if, as some forecasts suggest, as much as 60 percent to 65 percent of U.S. homes will have a PC by the year 2000,[96] the cost of computers relative to the income of poor Americans is likely to preclude such penetration rates among the poor.[97]

According to a 1995 report by the U.S. Education Department, while half the nation's public schools have hooked up to the global computer network, minority and low-income students are less likely to have classroom access to the Internet than wealthier students.[98] A 1994 U.S. Census Bureau report estimates that 39 percent of African-American students use computers in school versus 56 percent of European-American students.[99] Even where corporate and government efforts provide Internet access to schools and give some children greater access to the use of computers during the day, the absence of computers at home places many low-income children at a distinct and growing disadvantage.[100] Only 15 percent of African-American students reported using a computer at home. By comparison, 36 percent of European-American students reported using computers at home.[101]

A CRITICAL POINT IN TIME

The confluence of communications convergence and concentration, and the rapid expansion of government and business reliance on network efficiencies, are occurring at a time of uneven and often inequitable deployment of technology and information, rising costs of access to technology and informations and growing disparities in personal and geographic incomes. In this context, the passage of the Telecommunications Act of 1996 comes at a critical point in time. It is a time pregnant with opportunity for substantial gain and fraught with the potential for irreversible loss. Communications technology can be used to either expand and equalize access to education and electronic political empowerment or disenfranchise the growing number of Americans who are at risk. It can be used to either provide much needed efficiencies in service delivery and economic development to urban and rural communities or bypass and abandon them.

Changes during this time of confluence will determine which Americans will have access to electronic communications to speak what we will be allowed to say and listen to what we will be allowed to hear.[102] The interactive communication afforded by computers and the Internet can provide a critical, necessary democratic alternative—assuring speech and association opportunities for individuals and communities. Such communications serve as the potential counter to the increasing centralization of control in the converging, traditional media of broadcasting, cable, print and telephony. However, these technologies and services can do so only if all individuals and communities have access to them, the training necessary for their proper use, and inexpensive means to reach the information.

To the extent that all members and groups within American society do not have equitable opportunities to create, speak and be heard electronically, our collective notions of individual self-worth, equality and equity cannot be fully inclusive. This is the substantial risk of basing opportunities—to create, speak and hear electronically—on economic wealth expressed in the marketplace. For, in a society with the greatest gap in economic wealth between the wealthy and the poor of any industrialized western nation, basing such opportunities on economic wealth is to consign many to silence, invisibility and potential extinction.

In addition, enhanced networks present us with the opportunity for improved, cost-efficient delivery of needed goods and services. But, if inequitably deployed, they will eventually result in further urban atomization and rural stagnation, as the business and service institutions exit or atrophy because of the escalating costs of providing and securing goods and services in relation to their diminishing levels of availability. Meanwhile, new technology and network-based reliant businesses will decline to enter or be delayed in their move into remote rural areas and urban cores. In summary, without equitable access to speak and to acquire information, without equitable access to network technologies and efficiencies, there will be far less equality in the 21st century.

ASSESSING THE STRATEGIES OF DEPLOYMENT

A number of strategies have been implemented by federal and state governments, public and private foundations, and community organizations and churches, to address the current disparity in access. These strategies seek to increase the percentage of the population with access to basic telephone services, while expanding opportunities for access to computers and advanced telecommunications services. The chief set of policy initiatives is being implemented at the federal level via the Telecommunications Act of 1996 and responsive rule-makings by the Federal Communications Commission. In addition, the National Telecommunications Administration, Department of Housing and Urban Development and the Department of Education have efforts underway. State efforts are underway as well, most notably in California, Pennsylvania and Wisconsin. Finally, various foundation and/or community organizations have also begun initiatives.

For many Americans, the ultimate measure of the success of these initiatives will be the number of at-risk Americans enabled to become full, contributing participants in the intellectual, political, economic and social fabric of American life in the 21st century.

For many Americans, the ultimate measure of the success of these initiatives will be the number of at-risk Americans enabled to become full, contributing participants in the intellectual, political, economic and social fabric of American life in the 21st century. The key test for any telecommunications reform measure is whether it helps the American people. Legislation should provide benefits to consumers, spur economic growth and innovation, promote private sector investment in an advanced telecommunications infrastructure, and create jobs.[103]

The chief policy and legal instrument for assuring access to network services is the Telecommunications Act of 1996. Congress' primary goal in passing the legislation was to ensure that all Americans have affordable, non-discriminatory access to communications services. To accomplish its goal, Congress instituted a number of regulatory changes via this Act. For the most part, these changes reflect a preference for "marketplace and market demand" driven methods for accomplishing the legislative goal of non-discriminatory, affordable access. However, while the legislation evidences a distinct and deep-seated Congressional preference for reliance on the market, there are some provisions that seek to address the market's inability to assure access to all. These provisions include a revision to the non-discrimination provision of the Communications Act of 1934, a revision to the nation's universal service policy, and the retention of Lifeline and Link-Up subsidies for the poor.[104]

Among the market-reliant regulatory changes enacted in the legislation are the introduction of greater competition in the provision of local and long-distance telephone services; the deregulation of cable television rates; the creation of opportunities for competition between telephone and cable firms in providing video programming services; and the relaxation of the broadcast media concentration rules.[105] Many in government and industry anticipate that increased competition in the local and long-distance telephone markets, as well as in the video market, will result in reducing prices consumers pay for access to existing telecommunications and video services. In addition, it is argued that increased competition will result in more rapidly deployed new, innovative and responsive services.

Eighteen months after its enactment, and six months after the commission's implementation of Congress' directive, difficulties encountered in the Act's implementation call into question the likelihood of reaching a significant portion of Congress' goal. Many consumers are finding that their telephone and cable subscription rates are higher rather than lower.[106] And while some find their access to service options have increased, the number of firms from which such access may be purchased has shrunk.[107] Consumer access to advanced telecommunications services such as the Internet has not increased significantly since the Act's passage. Some consumer groups complain that the implementation of provisions such as the Act's local-market competition and universal service requirements, is resulting in an increased cost to consumers.[108]

Despite the establishment of a universal service discount for schools and libraries,[109] only 9 percent of all instructional rooms (classrooms, labs and library media centers) are currently connected to the Internet because of, in large measure, inadequate funding.[110] But the current lack of access is not the most pressing problem related to the implementation of the discount. Rather, the problems are the filing of numerous legal challenges to the Federal Communications Commission's methods for funding the Universal Service discount,[111] and a Congressional threat to the funding of the discount.[112] The initiation of litigation assures that the implementation of the Universal Service discount will most certainly be delayed in the short term. Meanwhile, a decision to use Universal Service funds to augment the deficit in the general treasury would establish a dangerous policy that could eviscerate any meaningful national attempt at equitably deploying technology.[113]

ACCESS TO BASIC TECHNOLOGY

The strategy, envisioned by Congress and the Federal Communications Commission, to increase the percentage of Americans having access to a phone is to maintain and expand the lifeline and link-up programs. The Link-Up program provides telephones installed at reduced prices, to people eligible for welfare. Life Line makes basic phone service available at a discounted rate.[114] In this way, it is hoped that the percentage of

215

Americans having access to phones will be further increased. This strategy enjoys the support of a majority of the telecommunications industry.[115] However, because these programs have essentially been in place at the federal level and in many states, something additional seems called for.

It is pointed out that, even with these programs, approximately 19 percent of rural and urban residents with incomes under $10,000 do not own a phone.[116] At least two reasons are offered for the current shortfall. First, as one study suggests, the current telephone access deficit is created by a lack of knowledge of the discount on the part of those Americans who are eligible to receive the lifeline discount. In addition, another study suggests that those who at one time may have acquired access to phone service but are currently disconnected for failure to pay may not be able to afford the reconnection fees.[117]

Others have suggested that the Lifeline and Link-Up programs may not be capable of significantly increasing phone penetration among those not already connected. They also suggest that the programs mostly accomplish a redistribution of income among those members of the poor who would have been connected even without the programs.[118] Based on their economic estimates, the programs have a minimal impact at best on the telephone penetration rate among the poor in the United States.[119] So they suggest, a more efficient Lifeline program would target low-income, poor households that would not otherwise subscribe.[120]

Even if one accepts the estimates and calculations upon which the criticism of the programs is based, an increase in the number of people enjoying access to telephone service that they heretofore could not afford is critically important. For, as is increasingly clear, "[t]elephone service is no longer considered a luxury in today's society where communications are vital to finding and holding a job, calling for emergency help and staying in touch with friends and family."[121] Even a minimally significant increase in access rates among the 6.3 million households currently without phones[122] results in a substantial increase in the quality of life, heightened chances for economic survival and greater opportunities to become a contributing member of society.[123]

216

ACCESS TO ADVANCED TELECOMMUNICATIONS SERVICES AND THE LEGISLATIVE DISCONNECT

In addition to assessing the success of the Act's current implementation, it is reasonable to raise fundamental questions about the practical advisability of Congress' reliance on marketplace solutions in an era in which so much of American society is economically stratified. An analysis of the legislation, in light of the needs established earlier in this article, underscores this point.

REDLINING: EQUATING ANTIDISCRIMINATION WITH ANTIREDLINING

Despite early efforts to include specific language prohibiting the electronic redlining of poor and minority communities in earlier drafts of legislation, the Act does not address electronic redlining. Instead, the redlining issue is addressed as part of the amendment to Section 151 of the Communications Act of 1934, which now states in pertinent part: "... to make available, so far as possible, to all people of the United States without discrimination on the basis of race, color, religion, national origin, or sex, a rapid, efficient, nation-wide and world-wide wire and communications service with adequate facilities at reasonable charges ..."[124]

The Act thus amends the Section 151 language, which many have been interpreted as the first and heretofore sole statutory basis for Universal Service, by prohibiting discrimination in the provision of service on the basis of race, color, religion, national origin, or sex. This is clearly an important revision, but it fails to address the concerns of minority and poor communities—that they are being electronically redlined because they are perceived as being less economically desirable, not necessarily because of religion, ethnicity race, or sex.

Section 254 establishes the procedure whereby the FCC will develop the new and evolving definition of Universal Service, including which services will be deemed basic or advanced, what subsidies will be created and who will be eligible for them. The FCC has since established the definitions for basic and advanced telecommunications services.[125] However, given the bifurcated definition of services, the section essentially contemplates that

217

all Americans will not be able to afford all services immediately and thus will not be economically entitled to have access to them.

As a result, even with the non-discrimination principle in Section 151, and even if access to basic services is actually achieved via Section 254, the Telecommunications Act does not prohibit or discourage business- es from deciding to delay or decline to upgrade architectures or provide new services in many communities.[126] Nor does it create a positive incentive structure for encouraging earlier deployment.[127] So long as competitive business decisions are based on perceptions that commu- nities possess limited wealth or constitute less desirable markets, those communities will continue to be left out for the near term when it comes to the provision on all services not deemed basic.

UNIVERSAL SERVICE: ALL REGIONS OF THE NATION

The guiding principles of Section 254 do little to blunt this economic reality. Subsection (b)(3) of Section 254 requires that the FCC must develop the nation's Universal Service policy such that:

> Consumers in all regions of the Nation, including low-income consumers ... should have access to telecommunications and information services, including interexchange services and advanced telecommunications and information services, that are reasonably comparable to those services provided in urban areas and that are available at rates that are reasonably comparable to rates charged for similar services in urban areas.

At minimum, the subsection's guiding principle that access be pro- vided in "all regions of the nation" is a directive assuring that rural, low- income urban and suburban consumers are afforded at comparable rates, access to reasonably comparable basic and advanced telecom- munications and information services. But, the subsection still contem- plates payment for bifurcated panoply of services available at rates comparable to those available in the more desirable urban regions. These are likely to be rates that many will be unable to afford.

218

Even if the FCC should ultimately determine that the service roll-out is too slow or inequitable because of electronic redlining, the FCC may only stimulate faster deployment of services by facilitating more competition that presumes market rather than equitable social considerations. If the delay or failure to provide service is due to misperceptions or accurate perceptions of a market segment's desirability, more competition is not likely to solve it.

UNIVERSAL SERVICE: TARGETED SUBSIDIES

Aside from the legislative intent embodied in Section 151 as amended and Section 254(3)(b) of the 1996 Act, Congress sought to assure that those Americans deemed poor by established criteria are also protected from a loss of service via the continued provision of lifeline services.[128] In addition, the FCC, on the advise of the Joint Board, has promulgated and seeks to implement regulatory policies that assure that low-income communities are provided access to advanced telecommunications and information services via their schools and libraries.[129]

The services are to be provided to schools and libraries at a discount, ranging from 20 percent to 90 percent based on established need criteria.[130] The proposed discount structure is currently subject to litigation.[131] Aside from the heated debate raging over the size and scope of the discount and who will pay to subsidize it, the framework in which the debate—over subsidies, payment responsibility, and services—is conducted presumes the existence of a bifurcated service model based on price. Such a model establishes two tiers of access and concedes the continued existence of the digital divide.

The provisioning of libraries and schools is laudable and pragmatic, but it is also problematic. Based on the number of school finance suits filed and the budgetary wars over education funding in Congress and many state legislatures, it is reasonable to conclude that the pool of existing state education dollars is often inequitably distributed, and the pool of federal and state education dollars is likely to shrink relative to need, rather than grow.[132] Thus, any technology dollars made available to schools without regard to the current disparity in, and pressures, on educational allocations may exacerbate rather than ameliorate the disparity. Second, many communities are closing local library branches for budgetary reasons. Thus, an access policy for low-income communities based solely on access via schools and libraries will inadequately serve some communities while leaving out many other communities. In other words, even where the bifurcated access model is implemented, Americans in many communities will still be underserved or remain unserved.

And where the opportunity to prove access is taken, using the school/library discount strategy—to benefit working parents, guardians and local businesses—will often times be problematic. Even where sufficient finances are found to purchase discounted access over time, to acquire the necessary end-user equipment and software, and to train teachers and librarians in the technology's use as a pedagogical and research tool, added financial resources will be necessary to keep schools and libraries open during the day and evenings, and on weekends. Absent technology's availability to parents, guardians, businesses and community organizations, the digital divide will be aggravated by parent-child, school-business, and school-community divides. First, successful school-based meldings of technology and education have included a substantial participation by parents and communities as users/adopters of the technology. Second, since as the vast majority of new jobs in this nation are created by small businesses, reliance on a technology deployment strategy that does not facilitate the early adoption of technology by viable small businesses severely reduces the prospect that they will maintain a sufficient level of competitiveness. This in turn leads to a situation in which children conversant with technology will have fewer opportunities for gainful employment when they later become eligible to work. Downsized, technology corporations are not likely to be the primary source of employment. Third, sole reliance on the school/library deployment strategy excludes community-based organizations that have successfully helped bridge the parent-child, school-business and school-community technology divides. In the final analysis, it is not that the school-library deployment strategy is ill-advised; it is essential, pragmatic and must be enthusiatically supported.

However, sole reliance on this strategy to the exclusion of other complementary strategies is ill-advised for all the aforementioned reasons.

Despite these reasons, the Act and the FCC's implementation order allow significant discounts only to schools and libraries acquiring access to the Internet, distance learning and other telecommunications services.[133] And despite expressions of public concern,[134] the FCC's Order, like Congress' Act, did not make discounts for advanced telecommunications services available to community–based–organizations (CBOs) that bridge the education, economic and service delivery gaps left by the current social-service and education-delivery systems.

Many CBOs are playing a key role in efforts to provide access to computer technology to enhance educational achievement, employment opportunities and civic engagement.[135] There are numerous stories of Americans whose lives have been profoundly changed in positive ways because of CBOs' provision of access to computers. Possessing enhanced skills learned at community centers, the working poor find better paying jobs, parents become users of technology as they participate in the education of their children, and residents engage in civic organizing for the betterment of the community.[136]

Unlike Congress, which has failed to extend the discount to CBOs and is ambivalent toward administration programs to assist community organizations in acquiring technology,[137] in response to community concerns,[138] the California legislature and the Public Utility Commission have recognized the critical role that CBOs can play in making the benefits of advanced telecommunications networks and services available to their communities.[139] As the California PUC stated:

Because of their economic and social impact ... community ... institutions must be positioned to be early recipients of the benefits of the information age.

"In accordance with state ... directives, qualifying ... community based organizations (CBOs) shall be entitled to discounted rates for certain services.[140]

The PUC went on to adopt rate discounts for CBOs. It determined that, in California, "Qualifying community-based-organizations (CBOs) shall be entitled to a discounted rate for switched 56, ISDN service, and T-1, or their functional equivalents. ... Only a tax exempt organization [as described in Section 501(c)(3) or 501(d) of the Internal Revenue Code, Title 26 of the United States Code], offering health care, job training, job placement, or educational instruction, ... qualify for the discounted rates for CBOs." Similar efforts are underway in Wisconsin and Pennsylvania.[141]

It may be argued that making the discount available to CBOs would increase the proposed yearly discount amount by $2.25 billion, (roughly the cost of one B-1 bomber), thereby placing an even greater burden on those consumers and firms paying into the fund. While there is certain to be some increase if CBOs become eligible for a discount, the size and impact of such an "increase" can be minimized in several ways. The scope of services for which a discount is provided could be more limited than that for schools and libraries; the relative size of the discounts might be smaller; and eligibility criteria could fairly limit the number of organizations receiving the discount. In addition, CBOs could be required to aggregate the community demand for services by joining with schools and libraries and by partnering with telecommunications, video or service firms to provide telephone, Internet, financial, and telecommuting services. The not-for-profit CBO through for-profit subsidiaries, would share the cost and profits of the service provision with the commercial providers. In this way, the discount serves as an investment in the CBOs as joint partners which is repaid in a reduced [shared] cost of doing business, relative to the provider's return on investment.

For example, as this article documents, many urban and rural communities are suffering from limited access to basic telephone communications and a loss of access to financial services. In neither case is this mainly a function of a lack of profitability in these communities. Rather, it is arguably a function of an increase in the cost of providing services relative to the revenues to be gained, because of a change in the competitive environment in which local telephone companies and banks operate. A technology deployment strategy that engages the CBOs as joint partners in aggregating telephone and banking service demand in, marketing current and future services, and in providing a brick-and-mortar presence for providing services creates opportunities for shared costs, shared risks, and volume discount-based resale revenues in phone parlor, phone card, ATM, kiosk/point-of-sale and bill-payment services.

In addition, inner-city and rural communities are not likely to be early recipients of advanced technology and services. It is argued that, in many cases, these access problems are a function of the perceived costs of the network upgrade and of marketing new services, relative to the revenues to be generated, given the low penetration of necessary consumer-electronic equipment and the relative lack of wealth. Here again, the use of the CBOs as the focal point or presence for deploying donated (new or used) computers, an advanced network gateway for multimedia and Internet access, and telecommuter and rented small business services—such as e-mail, Internet access, postal and parcel delivery services, copy, just-in-time inventory, and software—defined tax preparation and accounting services—provide opportunities for consumer education in the marketing of new services to residents and local businesses at a fraction of the cost associated with a communitywide upgrade. Moreover, as already mentioned, the community participates in sharing the costs, risks, and attendant benefits of the technology and service deployment and marketing efforts.

THE RURAL HEALTH CARE PROVIDER DISCOUNT: DISCRIMINATION AGAINST POOR URBAN RESIDENTS

In addition, the Telecommunications Act of 1996 did not extend the rural health-care provider discount to urban health-care organizations providing medical services to the poor and elderly. The omission is discriminatory toward those with comparable needs. Ironically, the FCC's decision to provide school, library and rural health-care discounts is now being appealed in the courts, not on leaving CBOs and urban health care providers out, but on the issue of the size of the discount and what it should include.

223

ACCESS TO COMPUTERS: DUMB OR SMART, USED OR NEW

As governments and communities explore and implement strategies to deploy advanced telecommunications services, they have also had to assure that communities have access to a sufficient number of working computers. Three basic strategies that have been proposed. Two strategies on acquiring new or used computers are currently being implemented. The third strategy is based on developing an inexpensive network computer. An assessment of the three strategies is given in the following chart.

STUDENT USE OF COMPUTERS – 1984 and 1993 in percent

Table 5

	1984 Total	1993 Total	K	1993 by grade level 1-8	9-12	College
▶ At Home	11.5	27.0	15.6	24.7	28.7	32.8
White	13.7	32.8	19.4	31.4	35.9	36.0
Black	4.9	10.9	4.2	9.0	10.4	19.4
Hispanic	3.6	10.4	5.7	7.5	9.8	22.0
▶ At School	27.3	59.0	26.2	68.9	58.2	55.2
White	30.3	61.6	29.4	73.7	59.9	54.9
Black	16.8	51.5	16.5	56.5	54.5	56.9
Hispanic	18.6	52.3	19.2	58.4	54.1	51.9

Source: U.S. National Center for Educational Statistics, *Digest of Educational Statistics*, 1994.

The first two strategies rely on the use of PCs containing the software necessary to allow a user to run various programs. Fully functional PCs allow users to store, edit, manipulate, send or receive information and to access the Internet and online services. The third strategy contemplates the use of network computers, which relies on the network to which a PC is connected for all the software necessary to conduct the above-mentioned functions. Great care must be given in assessing which strategy to employ. The value of the new PC strategy is that it assures maximum user empowerment. However, new PCs are too expensive for many African Americans, especially those of us who are poor. Reliance on a used PC strategy assures user empowerment at a lower immediate cost. However, the quality of the hardware and software will vary considerably; issues of replacement parts make repair problematic; and software applications may be limited. Reliance on network or "dumb" computers assures access to relatively inexpensive new computers and, hence, faster penetration. User flexibility however will be only as great as the software applications resident on the network. And there is a downside risk that the network provider may place restrictions on allowable software applications, user access and user speech. Finally, there are potential issues of user privacy, regarding who one can speak to and associates with. Because these issues arise on a "private" network, users are not likely to have federal or state protection, either constitutional or statutory.

Under the circumstances, reliance on a combination of the first two strategies may be more advisable, as the third brings us closer to the speech problems African Americans have encountered with the broadcast and cable industries, where speech rights resides with the network owner. Moreover, there are efforts afoot to produce a fully functional PC at $500 dollars, and there are successful community-based computer refurbishing and recycling programs that other communities could emulate.

CONCLUSIONS

The Congress has established a nascent market-based regulatory paradigm that has, as its stated goal, the provision of affordable communications services to all Americans. Its effort can be fairly said to fall far short of its intended result. Because the Act's implementation is to be evolutionary in development, it is possible for one to offer a potentially hopeful assessment of its final impact. However, at this point in time, the Act, whatever Congress' intent, codifies the digital divide that currently exists, constrains the FCC and NTIA in their efforts to achieve an equitable deployment of increasingly necessary advanced technology, and provides no mechanism for timely resolution of the growing number of lawsuits that challenge FCC decisions. In all likelihood, the dawn of the millenium will have arrived and moved on before equitable access to technology is achieved. If it does, it will have moved on with as much as half of America left behind.

There are some critical short-term actions that would assure more Americans are technologically empowered. They include extending the telecommunications discount to eligible CBOs and urban health-care providers; funding NTIA's TIIAP program at a level more commensurate with its pivotal role in facilitating the equitable, timely deployment of advanced technology; and adopting a national Congressional perspective on Americans that recognizes us as not just consumers, but citizens and students and workers deserving of the legitimate opportunity to contribute fully and responsibly to the nation, regardless of geography, race, sex, national origin, religious belief, physical impairment, or wealth.

Imagine a time in the near future when Tamika's grandmother can communicate with her health-care provider by computer and video technology, without leaving her apartment. The doctor or nurse practitioner can see Grandma and can take readings on her vital signs while speaking with her. Any medications can be electronically prescribed during the consultation, with future refills ordered simply by running the prescription's bar code under the household infrared scanner. The prescription is later delivered by the local pharmacy whose just-in-time inventory system has already noted the reduction in the prescription drug and has ordered more.

Tamika uses the household computer for school reports, inexpensively surfing the Internet, communicating with her peers and teachers or her uncle, who is becoming computer proficient. The household acquires Internet access through the local CBO which is a subsidiary of their church.

The CBO also provides discount telephone service to the community. It has recently begun a credit union, and has installed an ATM, a bill payment kiosk for the utility company, and a license- and tax-payment kiosk for the local government. In fact, the CBO has become the technology gateway for a host of advanced telecommunications services provided to the community's schools, libraries, businesses and local churches. It acquires new and used computer equipment and distributes it, at cost, to community members. It has established training classes in computer repair, inside the home wiring, and computer-based office work. Through the CBO the community has direct communication with its political representatives. Recently, the community was instrumental in the defeat of a politician hostile to equitable funding for the community's schools and libraries. Future plans include a consumer-electronics cooperative and participation in an electronic mall for local entrepreneurs. Some may think the above scenario is far-fetched. In reality, many of the above referenced actions are under way in CBOs around the country. Technological change is upon us. Before it changes us in ways we do not like, it is time for us to make some changes of our own. "The changes are inevitable. The choices are ours."[141]

FOOTNOTES

[1] (c) 1997 by Allen S. Hammond IV, Professor, New York Law School. Thanks are due to the trustees and administration of New York Law School, whose research grant made major portions of this article possible. Thanks are also due to the Honorable New York State Assemblyman Albert Vann, Ceasar McDowell of the Civil Rights Project, and Jeff Chester of the Center for Media Education for their encouragement and support. Very special thanks are due to Dr. Bernard Watson, who has offered counsel and encouragement for so many years, and to President Hugh Price for allowing me this opportunity to share my thoughts with the National Urban League readership. Finally thanks are due to my research assistants, Anjali Singhal, Gamal Hennessey, Ann Schoffield, Nancy Bloom, Sharon Hong, Nejla Cadet and Catherina Chang for their substantial assistance in researching portions of this article.

[2] This article may not be cited, referenced or used in any manner without the express, written consent of the author.

[3] Dr. Bernard C. Watson, *Changes and Choices*, (c) 1991, National Urban League, Inc., p. 1.

[4] Octavia Butler, *Parable of the Sower*, (c) 1993, by Octavia E. Butler, Warner Books, Inc., New York, 1995, p. 103.

[5] Steve Lohr, Wired Life; "The Great Unplugged Masses Confront the Future," *The New York Times*, April 21, 1996, Sec. 4; p. 1 (quoting Erik Barnouw, professor emeritus at Columbia University.

[6] "Telecommute America," New national survey reports sharp rise in telecommuting, M2 PRESSWIRE, July 3, 1997.

[7] Studies have identified a significant economic multiplier effect that occurs as a result of a nation possessing an efficient telecommunications infrastructure. "Rural Comms: Wishful Thinking Versus Reality; Rural Communications," Martyn Warwick, *Communications International*, July 1993, p. 44.

[8] Many retail firms are moving a portion of their consumer marketing and sales transactions on-line as the number of potential consumers on the Internet and online services has grown rapidly. See "More National Retailers Weave Web Sites Into Sales Strategy, Wired For Shopping," John M. Moran, *The Hartford Courant*, November 28, 1996, p. E1; "Prodigy to launch first personalized virtual mall with secure transactions on the Internet," *Business Wire*, November 27, 1995; and "Net results; sporting goods industry links up with the Internet," Hollee Actman, *Sporting Goods Business*, June 1995, Vol. 28; No. 6, p. 36. Business to business transactions are rising as well. See "It's No Longer Too Early to Get In," T.C. Doyle, *VARBusiness*, May 1, 1995, p. 54. The federal government is also planning to conduct three quarters of all practicable transactions electronically by the year 2000. See "Managing electronic commerce on the Federal acquisition computer network (FACNET)," Christopher Yukins, *National Contract Management Journal*, 1996, Vol. 27, No. 1, p. 35-49.

[9] Researchers have documented impressive learning gains achieved through the use of interactive video and computer based instruction. In some cases, such instruction has been found to be 30% more effective than more traditional instructional formats. Testimony of Madeline Kunin, Deputy Secretary of Education, before the Senate Committee on Appropriations, Subcommittee on Labor, Health and Human Services, Education and Related Agencies, Federal News Service, April 4, 1995. Other education officials have acknowledged the importance of technology to education. See, Prepared Testimony of Dr. Linda G. Roberts Director, Office of Educational Technology, U.S. Department of Education, before the Senate Committee on Commerce, Science, and Transportation Science, Technology and Space Subcommittee, Federal News Service, April 24, 1996; and "Council of Chief State School Officers Releases Recommendations for the National Education Summit," PR Newswire, March 20, 1996.

[10] Mary Gardiner Jones, President, Consumer Interest Research Institute, "Telemedicine and the National Information Infrastructure: Are the Realities of Health Care Being Ignored? A Call to Action," Keynote Address before the American Medical Infomatics Association Spring Congress Information Technology in Community Health, San Jose, California May 29, 1997. See also, "Distance health care' is latest medicine," Margaret Ryan, *Electronic Engineering Times*, April 29, 1996, p. 55; "Digital DOCTORS:

Physicians on L.I. are practicing telemedicine, a new high-tech way in treating patients,"
Michael Unger, *Newsday*, January 29, 1996, p. C1; "Networked M.D.s Share X-Rays,
MRIs," MARK ROCKWELL, *Communications Week*, November 27, 1995, p. 26; "ISDN
and ProShare zap X-ray images to doctors," David Rhode, *Network World*, November 27,
1995, p. 18; "Bell Atlantic Helps Major Medical Group Establish First Teleradiology
Network To Use PCs and Desktop Video," *PR Newswire*, November 16, 1995; "The
economic impact of information technology," Robert B. Cohen, *Business Economics*,
October, 1995, p. 21; "NYNEX Telemedicine Solutions-Just What The Doctor Ordered;
NYNEX Teams Up with Healthcare Industry to Improve Patient Care," *Business Wire*,
July 20, 1995.

[11] Proponents say that linked computers have the ability to profoundly affect everything
from commerce to democracy, dramatically changing society. "No universal agreement
on 'Net; Debate on need for access spirited," Dwight Silverman, *The Houston Chronicle*,
July 5, 1996, p. 1.

[12] Section 254 (j) provides that "Nothing in this section shall affect the collection,
distribution, or administration of the Lifeline Assistance Program provided for by the
Commission under regulations set forth in section 69.117 of title 47, Code of Federal
Regulations, and other related sections of such title. The Commission has implemented
Congress' directive. See Common Carrier Action Commission Implements Telecom Act's
Universal Service Provisions: Adopts Plan to Ensure Access to Affordable
Telecommunications Services for All Americans (CC Docket No. 96-45), Report No. CC
97-24; CC Docket No. 96-45, May 7, 1997.

[13] "Computer Access Found to Vary Widely In Fairfax Schools," Robert O'Harrow Jr., *The
Washington Post*, May 18, 1997, p. B1; "Computer Dreams: Educators Want to Give All
Students Access to Technology, But Schools Often Lack Funds and Necessary
Equipment," Beth Frerking, *The Plain Dealer*, February 26, 1996, p. 5D;, "Technology and
equity issues; assuring fair access to all," Michael N. Milone, Jr. and Judy Salpeter,
Technology & Learning, January 1996, p. 38.

[14] A recent study of obstacles which predict a lack of a regular medical provider and delays
in seeking medical care for patients at an urban public hospital, disclosed that 20% of
respondents cited a lack of phone service. "Obstacles predicting lack of a regular
provider and delays in seeking care for patients at an urban public hospital." Kimberly J.
Rask, Mark V. Williams, Ruth M. Parker, Sally E. McNagny, JAMA, *The Journal of the
American Medical Association*, June 22, 1994, Vol. 271: No. 24; p. 1931. Fear of physical
harm at the neighborhood payphone is so extensive that people who need medical
attention will avoid the phone and hope their condition gets better. "Coverage is no
panacea for the poor," Bill Hendrick, *The Atlanta Journal and Constitution*, June 22,

1994, p. A7. Because there are so few public phones in some New York City neighborhoods residents cannot alert fire departments to the existence of a fire. "Phone Scarcity Complicates Fire Alarm Plan" Alan Finder, *The New York Times*, February 11, 1996, Sec. 1, p. 49, Col.3.

[15] "Telecommute America: New national survey reports sharp rise in telecommuting," M2 PRESSWIRE, July 3, 1997, "More than 11 million people reported working as telecommuters in 1997, compared to eight million in 1995. See also, "Wiring the countryside: Will it bring in new jobs; Trends in telecommuting in rural areas," *Telecommuting Review: The Gordon Report*, October 1, 1991, Vol. 8.

[16] *"A Census in Cyberspace,"* Amy Cortese, May 5, 1997, p. 85.

[17] Many are concerned "that large segments of the population could become technologically disenfranchised, including: low-income households that cannot afford either a computer or the ongoing costs of a connection to the Internet; rural residents with no local access to a network connection; those with disabilities, such as the blind, who are unable to use traditional computer equipment." "No universal agreement on 'Net Debate on need for access spirited," Dwight Silverman, *The Houston Chronicle*, July 5, 1996, p. 1; "Busting Barriers to Cyberspace," Jube Shiver, Jr., *Los Angeles Times*, March 29, 1995, p. A1; "Losing the Cyberspace Race," Peter Y. Hong, *Los Angeles Times*, February 26, 1995; "The haves and the have-nots; access to information technologies," Ed Rose, *Communication World*, November, 1994, p. 22; "Information Superhighway Bypasses Poor Neighborhoods," Manuel Mendoza, *The Times Union* (Albany, NY), July 24, 1994, p. H2; "Personal Technology: Info Highway May Bypass Poor," *The Atlanta Journal and Constitution*, June 12, 1994, p. H10; and "Data Highway Ignoring Poor, Study Charges," Steve Lohr, *The New York Times*, May 24, 1994, p. A1.

[18] "Nynex Accepts Plan to Freeze Phone Rates, *The Buffalo News*, July 4, 1995, p. B7. "All-Digital Phone Network Makes Its Way Across U.S.," David Butler, *The Columbus Dispatch*, February 10, 1996, p. H7.

[19] "United States: Minorities Look for Access on Information Highway," Farhan Haq, Inter Press Service, January 4, 1995; "Blacks In The Fast Lane of the Information Superhighway," Laura B. Randolph, *Ebony*, January 1995, p. B98; "Bell Companies Decry Consumer Groups' Claims of Discrimination," *Telco Business Report*, August 1, 1994, No. 15, Vol. 11; "Groups Petition FCC for Prohibition of 'Electronic Redlining' by RHCs," *Advanced Intelligent Network News*, June 1, 1994. Minority communities' concerns about being redlined electronically have historic precedent in the recent absence of cable service from forty percent of Brooklyn, New York and forty-five percent of Bronx,

New York. See "City Council tunes in on lagging cable television services," *United Press International*, February 2, 1993.

[20] "Development-Communications: Third Wave Hits Third World," Peter Constantini, Inter Press Service, October 9, 1995; "Avoiding a New Era of Redlining," Gwen Moore and Richard Polanco, *The San Francisco Chronicle*, July 3, 1995, p. A17; "Universal service-or regulated 'telewelfare'?" James Carlini, *Network World*, June 19, 1995, p. 51.

[21] The Office of Technology Assessment, Congress of the United States, The Technological Reshaping of Metropolitan America, (1995) at 81; "FCC Urged To Challenge Industry On Universal Access," Bill Pietrucha, *Newsbytes*, December 23, 1996; "Coalition Forms To Support Universal Telecom Service," *Newsbytes*, October 24, 1996.

[22] According to a study conducted by the U.S. Department of Commerce's National Telecommunications and Information Administration, 19 percent of both rural and urban residents with incomes under $10,000 don't have a phone. "No universal agreement on 'Net; Debate on need for access spirited," Dwight Silverman, *The Houston Chronicle*, July 5, 1996, p 1.

[23] For instance, at current market prices, a computer is the most expensive consumer purchase after a house and a car. "Job creation and the emerging home computer market," Laura Freeman, *Monthly Labor Review*, August, 1996, Vol. 119; No. 8; p. 46. "Roughly one-third of American households have personal computers. ... But analysts say that gaining ground from now on will be more difficult because so many affluent house holds already have personal computers and the less-affluent ones resist shelling out $2,000 or more for a computer. ... [A] ... report, based on a survey of 10,000 households, estimated that two-thirds of all the personal computers sold to households are bought by those with incomes of $40,000 or more. Yet census data show that only about one in three households have incomes of $40,000 or more. Unless prices drop drastically, some experts predict, the personal computer will be unlikely to find its way into more than 40 percent or 45 percent of American households." "Wired Life; The Great Unplugged Masses Confront the Future," Steve Lohr, *The New York Times*, April 21, 1996, Sec. 4; p. 1.

[24] "P&G's Artzt: TV Advertising in Danger: Remedy is to Embrace Technology and Return to Program Ownership," *Advertising Age*, May 23, 1994, p. 24.

[25] "The spinal cord, the brain's link to the rest of the body, is like a telephone trunk line with 31 pairs of individual lines extending from it to transmit messages from the brain to the rest of the body and to send sensory signals from organs and tissues along the lines back to the brain." "Paralysis may not be incurable; Studies suggest some 'dead' nerve cells can revive," Jane Brody, *Star Tribune*, September 4, 1994, p. E3.

[26] "...Alzheimer's [is]...a degenerative disease of the brain in which nerve cells stop communicating with one another. Ordinarily, brain cells communicate by releasing chemicals that allow the cells to receive and transmit messages for various types of behavior. In Alzheimer's the brain doesn't produce enough of these chemicals, so the cells can't communicate. Without the communication, they deteriorate and die. ... This degeneration happens only in the sections of the brain that affect memory, speech and personality, leaving parts that control other functions—such as heartbeat, breathing and sexual activity—intact." "The Long Goodbyes," Zaven Khachaturian, and Alicia Brooks, *People Magazine,* February 27, 1995, p. 40M. "Alzheimer's disease, for example, is a neural disaster in which cells in the cerebral cortex—the part of the brain involved in memory and cognition—mysteriously die off, taking with them a person's ability to think, reason and recall ..." *Diseases That Attack The Brain;* Scientists try A Novel Approach To Save Brain Cells," *The Washington Post,* April 4, 1995, p. Z10.

[27] "Amyotrophic lateral sclerosis, or ALS, the medical term for Lou Gehrig's disease, is a relentlessly progressive disorder caused by deterioration of the motor nerves (nerves that control the action of muscles) in both the brain and spinal cord. The first manifestations are typically weakness and clumsiness of one or both hands; but the symptoms may begin in almost any muscle, and most muscles are affected as the disease worsens. The muscle weakness is accompanied by a decrease in their size, stiffness and muscle twitches. There is no loss of sensation or pain except for possible muscle cramps. The disease eventually involves the tongue and muscles controlling swallowing and respiration. Death often results from respiratory failure. ALS is invariably fatal; the average lifespan after the onset of symptoms is two to five years." "Ripken streak brings a look at illness that felled Gehrig," Dr. Simon Margolis, *The Baltimore Sun,* September 26, 1995, p. E5; "Lou Gehrig's disease, or ALS, occurs when motor neurons—the nerve cells that run from the brain to the limbs—spontaneously degenerate, paralyzing victims and ultimately robbing them of the strength to breathe." "Diseases That Attack The Brain; Scientists Try A Novel Approach to Save Brain Cells," *The Washington Post,* April 4, 1995, p. Z10.

[28] See Margolis, op. cit. The Baltimore Sun, September 26, 1995, p. E5; and *The Washington Post,* op. cit. April 4, 1995, p. Z10.

[29] Zaven Khachaturian, and Alicia Brooks, op. cit. *People Magazine,* February 27, 1995, p. 40M; and The Washington Post, op.cit., April 4, 1995, p. Z10.

[30] Title to a song by Stevie Wonder.

[31] "If we build it, will it pay?" Ruth Thompson and Nancy Hunt-Coffey *Rural Telecommunications,* March/April 1996, Vol. 15, No. 2, pp. 44-51.

32 The Technological Reshaping of Metropolitan America, The Office of Technology Assessment, Congress of the United States, 1995.

33 "Electronic commerce combines EDI with the buying and selling that takes place via e-mail and among computers connected to the Internet and commercial subscription services, including CompuServe, America OnLine and Prodigy. "It's No Longer Too Early to Get In," T.C. Doyle, VARBusiness, May 1, 1995, p. 54. American Online recently surpassed the 2 million subscriber mark, having added more than a half-million subscribers in U.S. households since December; CompuServe stands at 1.82 million in the U.S. (claiming 2.7 million worldwide); and Prodigy can count at least 1.5 million subscribers. And with ... Microsoft establishing its own on-line Microsoft Network ..., the numbers are expected to continue to multiply. "Net results; sporting goods industry links up with the Internet," Hollee Actman, *Sporting Goods Business*, June, 1995, Vol. 28; No. 6, p. 36.

34 "An increasing number of major national retail companies and catalog firms are moving onto the Web—bringing with them name-recognition, established customer relationships, distribution networks and advertising budgets. Companies like L. L. Bean, Eddie Bauer, Lands' End, The Bombay Company, and even Wal-Mart now have Web sites where customers can browse the inventory and make purchases on-line." "More National Retailers Weave Web Sites into Sales Strategy, Wired For Shopping," *The Hartford Courant*, November 28, 1996, p. E1.

35 "Estimates of consumer spending on-line this year range from a low of $250 million to as high as $1 billion. While those numbers may seem impressive, they are in fact but a tiny sliver of overall retail sales. Most estimates put the value of on-line consumer spending at upwards of $6 billion by the year 2000." Moran, op. cit., p. E1.

36 According to the 1995 Consumer Online Services Report, approximately 30 million people are already communicating on the Internet. Although no one's quite sure exactly who these surfers are, recent studies indicate that the average Internet browser is an entertainment-oriented, educated male between 18 and 34, with an average household income of $ 85,000. Hollee Actman, op.cit., p. 36.

37 "Recent studies conclude that electronic commerce and complementary markets including electronic data interchange (EDI) are indeed poised for impressive growth ... the market for electronic commerce products and services totaled $4.8 billion in 1994. Given that the market is growing at approximately 30 percent annually, the total value of the market for electronic commerce products and services is anticipated to grow to roughly $13.7 billion by 1998. EDI, meantime, is expected to grow to $1.2 billion from $500 million during that same period." T.C. Doyle, op. cit., p. 54. Others predict that

Internet consumer purchases alone, will grow to as much as $4 billion by the year 2000. "AAMA [American Apparel Manufacturers Association] Web page still awaits 1st vendor WWD," Jim Ostroff, May 28, 1996, Vol. 171; No. 103; p. 3.

[38] By the year 2000, the federal government plans to use computers to conduct 75 percent of all practicable transactions. The Federal Acquisition Streamlining Act (FASA) of 1994 requires the government to implement this governmentwide system for electronic commerce—the Federal Acquisition Computer Network (FACNET)—by that year. This electronic commerce/electronic data interchange (EC/EDI)' system will be used first for small acquisitions; eventually, though, it will be broadened to include all practicable federal procurements. Christopher Yukins, op. cit., pp. 35-49.

[39] Moran, op. cit., p. E1; Doyle, op. cit., p. 54.

[40] Thompson, Hunt-Coffey, op. cit., pp. 44-51.

[41] "Manufacturers moving, shippers shipping out; Information-based companies, services rising industry stars in the Bay Area," David Lazarus, *The San Francisco Examiner,* February 16, 1997, p. W4; Federal Reserve Bank of New York Economic Policy Review, *ASAP,* February, 1997, No. 1, Vol. 3; p. 93; "Still the Best Places to Do Business, Inc.," July, 1996, p. 42.

[42] "Economic and Demographic Change: The Case of New York City," Samuel M. Ehrenhalt, *Monthly Labor Review,* U.S. Department of Labor, 1993, February 1993, p. 40; "Strains in the Family," Rochelle L. Stanfield, *National Journal,* September 28, 1991, p. 2316.

[43] Thompson, Hunt-Coffey, op. cit., pp. 44-51. "The technological Reshaping of Metropolitan America," The Office of Technology Assessment, Congress of the United States, 1995.

[44] *The Urban Challenge; Telecommunications Services Special Report: Approaching the 21st Century,* Steven Titch, Richard Karpinski Telephony, March 18, 1991, p. 88; "Rural Colorado seeks tech linkup, Dinah Zeigler, *Denver Post,* July 6, 1993, p. C1; "Pennsylvania Industry Report Says Telcos Not Selling Advantages of New Services, *Telephone News,* January 27, 1992, No. 2, Vol. 13.

[45] For instance, the Community Reinvestment Act, a 1977 federal law, mandates that banks provide credit to all segments of their communities. However, a bill making its way through Congress would exempt nearly 9 of 10 banks and thrifts from CRA requirements if it becomes law. "No Checks or Balances," Paul D'Ambrosio, *Asbury Park Press,* September 10, 1995, p. C1.

[46] D'Ambrosio, op. cit., C1. "Computer technology is scarce in poor neighborhoods, and some community activists worry that banks' community reinvestment commitments may get slighted if predictions about the industry's electronic future come to pass." "It's real difficult for the inner cities to keep up," she sighs. "We know this is where the country is going, but we won't have a work force to meet our needs" if school-age children and young adults—particularly those in the inner city—don't get trained with Internet-capable computers, on-line services and other new technologies. It's only in the last seven or eight years that the Community Reinvestment Act has had a noticeable impact on bank lending to low-income neighborhoods ... this has typically been done through physical presence—the brick-and-mortar branches that consultants and Wall Street analysts say banks must unload if they want to control their costs and remain competitive ... Right now, it doesn't look like there are any community reinvestment regulations related to electronic banking that will substantially affect the industry. But Washington has begun to focus on the issue, and legislators and officials with the key banking agencies have raised some of the same concerns that community activists have voiced.

[47] Id.

[48] A report from a House Banking Committee member noted that "inner-city households have the lowest percentage of telephone subscribers, and that inner-city African-American and Hispanic households have the fewest personal computers among all racial groups." "Moreover, there are neighborhoods that are so poor that 20% of the households still don't have telephones, according to a 1995 Commerce Department study." "Will Electronic Banking Ignore the Poor?" Joseph Radigan, *U.S. Banker*, December, 1996, p. 58.

[49] Id.

[50] Radigan, op. cit. p. 58.

[51] Public assistance programs include people receiving Aid to Families with Dependent Children, Emergency Aid to the Elderly, Disabled and Children, and food stamps. Nationally, African Americans make up 27 percent and Hispanics make up 22 percent of welfare recipients.

[52] Basic banking services, such as check cashing, are usually not accessible to those at the lowest end of the economic scale even though banks, by law, offer low-cost checking accounts. Banks will not cash a public assistance check unless the recipient has an account at the bank, or the government agency uses that bank to issue its checks.

[53] D'Ambrosio, op. cit., C1.

54 Many are finding that equitable access to credit and banking services is a crucial civil rights issue of the 1990s and 2000s, just as voting and housing rights were in the 1960s. Without the assurance that all individuals and communities have the opportunity to grow economically, the gulf between haves and have nots will widen.

55 "HISPANICS INCREASE ACCESS TO COMPUTERS," Rick Mendosa, *New America News Service*, May 5, 1997; "Blacks Step Up Their Computer Buying, Ernest Holsendolph, *The Atlanta Journal and Constitution*, January 5, 1997, p. F3.

56 At least one half of the fifty states have been involved in litigation over the constitutionality of their school financing schemes. See GAO Reports, December 19, 1995, GAO/HEHS-96-39 "School Finance: Three States' Experience with Equity in School Funding, Report to Congressional Requesters;" Linda G. Morra, Director, *Education and Employment Issues*, and "Preferences for school finance systems: voters versus judges," Colin D. Campbell and William A. Fischel, *National Tax Journal*, March 1996, p. 1; and "The School Finance Cases," Richard Briffault, *New York Law Journal*, August 10, 1995, p. 3.

57 An Education Conference With a Corporate Agenda," Peter Applebome, *The New York Times*, March 28, 1996, B10; "Clinton: Let's Raise Academic Standards," Jerry Markon, *Newsday*, March 28, 1996, p. A8.

58 "It's hard work; Inner cities struggle for employees," Dee DePass, *Star Tribune* (Minneapolis, MN), July 9, 1996, p. 1D; "Poor, Minority Students Lack Access to Computers; Report Also Suggests That Few Teachers Are Trained to Use PCs as Learning Tools," Rene Sanchez, *The Washington Post*, May 15, 1997, p. A13; Frerkingt, op. cit., p. D5. Also see "Tale of Two Schools, Just Miles Apart," John Gittelhorn, *The Orange County Register*, April 23, 1997, p. A6; "Tale of Two Schools Is Text For A Sermon On Class," *Sacramento Bee*, March 6, 1997, p. B7; Robert O'Harrow Jr., op. cit. p. B1, "Reading, 'Riting and ROMs: Computers Expand The Three R's, But Utah Schools Still Must Close The Cybergap Among the Classes," Katherine Kapos and Samuel A. Autman, *The Salt Lake Tribune*, January 28, 1996, p. A1.

59 Michael N. Milone, Jr. and Judy Salpeter, op. cit., p. 38

60 Ibid.

61 See Hammond, "Diversity and Equal Protection in the Marketplace: the Metro Case in Context," *44 Arkansas Law Review* 1063 (1992); "Wimmer, Deregulation and Market Failure in Minority Programming: The Socioeconomic Dimensions of Broadcast Reform," 8 Comm/Ent 329, pp. 334-388. (1986); Hammond, "Now You See it, Now You Don't:

Minority Ownership in an 'Unregulated' Video Marketplace," 32 Catholic Univ. L. Rev. pp. 633, 639-645 (1983).

[62] Ibid.

[63] Pursuant to 47 C.F.R. Section 73.2080, requires that a broadcast licensee refrain from engaging in employment discrimination and establish and maintain a positive and continuing effort to recruit, employ and promote qualified women and minorities. The Commission evaluates a licensee's EEO performance by analyzing the licensee's efforts to recruit, employ and promote qualified minorities and women. The Commission also examines and weighs any evidence of discrimination by the licensee. See Sections 73.2080(b) and (c) of the Commission's Rules, 47 C.F.R. Sections 73.2080 (b) and 73.2080 (c). Where Commission analysis of a licensee's renewal application indicates an absence of adequate EEO efforts, the Commission may impose a variety of sanctions or remedies, including reporting conditions, renewal for less than a full term, forfeiture, or a combination of the above. The Commission may also designate the renewal application for hearing. Amendment of Part 73 of the Commission's Rules Concerning Equal Employment Opportunity in the Broadcast Radio and Television Services, 2 FCC Rcd 3967 (1987) (Broadcast EEO), petition for recon. pending; see also 4 FCC Rcd 1715 (1989) (request for clarification by the National Association of Broadcasters). See In re Applications of Sun Mountain Broadcasting, Inc., "Memorandum Opinion And Order And Notice Of Apparent Liability," 9 FCC Rcd 2124, (1994) paragraphs 7 and 8; Beaumont Branch of the NAACP and the National Black Media Coalition v. FCC, 854 F.2d 501, 506 (D.C. Cir. 1988) (Beaumont); Bilingual Bicultural Coalition v. FCC, 595 F.2d 621 (D.C. Cir. 1978).

[64] See, "Red Lion Broadcasting V. FCC, 395 U.S. 367 (1969); Brandywine-Main Line Radio, Inc." 24 F.C.C. 2d 18 (1970) recon. denied 27 F.C.C. 2d 565 (1971); Public Media Center v. FCC, 587 F. 2d 1322 (D.C. Cir. 1978); In Re: Alan F. Neckritz, 29 F.C.C, 2d 807 (1971), reaffirmed, 37 F.C.C. 2d 528 (1972); sustained 502 F. 2d 411 (D.C, Cir. 1974); Wilderness Society, 30 F.C.C. 643 (1971). Also see, Fairness Report of 1974, 48 F.C.C. 2d 1 (1974); recon. denied 58 F.C.C. 691 (1976); affirmed, NCCB v. FCC, 567 F. 2d 1095 (D.C. Cir. 1977) cert. denied 436 U.S. 926 (1978). The FCC has been petitioned and ruled that a license should be denied due to the chronic and repeated refusal to present diverse minority oriented programming. See Alabama Educational Te. Comm'n, 50 FCC 2d 461 (1975); Leflore Broadcasting Co., 46 FCC 2d 980 (1974); Lomar Broadcasting Co., 38 FCC 1143 (1965), rev'd sub nom. Office of Communication of the United Church of Christ v. FCC, 425 F.2d 543 (D.C. Cir. 1969).

[65] UNITED CHURCH OF CHRIST v. FCC, 359 F.2d 99 (1966).

[66] "Diversity In The Media: For Minorities, Future In Media Looks Bleak," *Electronic Media*, August 21, 1995, p. 16; "Patrick Partially Dissents; FCC Adopts Cable EEO Rules Focusing on Efforts, Not Numbers," *Communications Daily*, September 19, 1985, p. 4.

[67] Adarand Constructors, Inc. v. Pena, 115 S. Ct. 2097, 2112-2117, (1995) (overuling Metro Broadcasting, 497 U.S. 547 (1990).

[68] "City Council tunes in on lagging cable television services," U.P.I., February 2, 1993.

[69] "We need a national public network", Mitch Kapor, Jerry Berman, Daniel Weitzner, *Whole Earth Review*, March 22, 1992, p. 72; "Electronic Democracy; The Great Equalizer," *Whole Earth Review*, June 22, 1991, p. 4; Hong, op. cit., p. 12.

[70] 'Updating electronic democracy; online election activity' Graeme Browning, *Database*, June 16, 1997, No. 3, Vol. 20; p. 47.

[71] It is estimated that in 1996, "more than ten million Americans had access to the Internet through commercial online services such as CompuServe and America Online, and several million more communicated via email and surfed the web regularly through direct Net connections either at work or at home. By the time Dole and President Bill Clinton went head-to-head on national TV in early October, both campaigns were actively soliciting votes through web sites, while hundreds of other candidates nation wide were doing the same ... Most political consultants agree that the Internet played a role at all levels of the [political election] campaigns last fall. Some candidates attribute their success at the polls to the impact of their web sites, and a few hardy political consultants even predict that cyberspace will be the prime political battleground in the year 2000.

[72] Rheingold, op. cit., p. 4.

[73] "New Georgia Voting Map Upheld by Supreme Court; 5-4 Ruling Calls 1 Majority-Black District Enough," Joan Biskupic, *The Washington Post*, June 20, 1997, p. A1.

[74] Ibid. The acute irony of the "High Court"'s rulings is made clear by the recent attempts by the conservative republican congress to block efforts to employ a revised census survey technique that would more accurately count and fairly reflect the number of minorities living in various states. The identification of previously undercounted minorities could cause a shift in the balance of power in states by possibly creating more districts and opportunities for minority political candidates who are not as likely to share the views of the conservatives.

[75] "Are we turning our backs on the poor?," John Disconsiglio, *Scholastic Update*, February 21, 1997, No. 10, Vol. 129; p. 2.

[76] "Some fundamental facts about welfare need to be grasped. The perception exists—widely—of hordes of welfare mothers sitting around with hordes of children, most of them conceived with the intent of getting a higher welfare payment. Such cases can be found, of course, but the far more typical case is much different. ... the numbers don't indicate that a large number of welfare mothers bear more children to boost their benefits ... ERRONEOUS PERCEPTIONS ABOUT welfare and welfare recipients abound ... across the nation. Nationally, some 42.5 percent of welfare families include one child, and another 30.2 percent include two children. The stereotypical huge welfare family simply isn't the norm. Nor are the welfare rolls filled primarily with inner-city minorities. Nationally, non-Hispanic whites make up 48 percent of welfare recipients, African-Americans 27 percent and Hispanics 22 percent. The point here is not to overdose on statistics, but rather to keep the reform debate grounded in reality ... Reform is important and necessary, but it must be based on accurate information about the system and the people in it." "Stick to Reality Perceptions Hamper Reform Effort," *The Montgomery Advertiser*, September 25, 1996, p. 16A.

[77] For instance, as one journalist has observed, even presidential candidates with the complicity of the press"... deal with race indirectly through hedged statements about, say, affirmative action, or through code words about their policies on such issues as crime, welfare, or immigration ... [For example] when candidates talk about welfare reform—far-reaching legislation that Clinton, after agonizing, decided to sign—race is implicit. Yet political reporters seldom call on candidates to address the law's racial repercussions. For example, tougher work rules have a disproportionate impact on blacks and Latinos, many in central cities long ago stripped of industrial jobs. Likewise, if reform hurls one million children into poverty, as critics allege, racial disparity looms. While one in eight American children receives welfare, roughly 60 percent of the recipients are black or Latino. Too few stories connect those dots." ""Where is race in the race?" Sig Gissler, *Columbia Journalism Review*, September, 1996/October, 1996, Vol. XXXV, No. 3; p. 34.

[78] Kapor, Berman and Weitzner, and Rheingold, op. cit.

[79] Rheingold, op. cit.,.

[80] Communication Act of 1934, 47 U.S.C. Title I, Section 1(a).

[81] "Ready for Prime Time - Universal Service Meets Universal Competition," Jerry Weikle, *Rural Telecommunications*, March/April 1995, pp. 50-53.

[82] Leveling The Field In Telecommunications," Richard Taylor, , *St. Louis Post-Dispatch*, February 21, 1995, p. 11B.

[83] "Paving The Way for Women On the Information Superhighway: Curbing Sexism Not Freedom, Keith A. Ditthavong, 4 Am. U. J. Gender & Law 455, (1996) "Telephony, because of its point-to-point isolation, is also shielded from burdensome content regulation—arising essentially from the telephone companies' lack of editorial control ...;" Jeffrey E. Faucette, The Freedom of Speech at Risk in Cyberspace: Obscenity Doctrine and a FrightenedUniversity's Censorship of Sex On The Internet, 44 Duke L.J. 1155, 1173, 1995. "Common carriers such as telephone companies ... and other non-content providers ... also lack substantial editorial control and generally are considered immune from liability for the statements of others;" Henry H. Perritt, Jr. Tort Liability, The First Amendment, And Equal Access To Electronic Networks. 5 Harv. J. Law and Tec 65, 1992; "Under the common law of defamation, a republisher of defamatory material and its author are equally liable, but only so long as the republisher exercises control over content. "Telephone and telegraph companies are not liable for defamatory communications transmitted on their facilities, and newsstand operators are not liable absent notice of defamatory material; Allen S. Hammond, *Private Networks, Public Speech: Constitutional Speech Dimensions Of Access To Private Networks*, 55 U. Pitt. L. Rev. 1085, 1115, 1994; "Regulated Monopolies: Lesson from Around 1915," 39 FED. COM. L.J. 171, pp. 171-76 (1989). "As a further means of assuring non-discrimination, the telephone companies were not allowed any control over the content of information they transmitted."

[84] In July 1994, the national telephone penetration rate was almost 94 percent of U.S. house holds. Although this percentage gives the appearance of universal service coverage, in fact there are 21 states at or below the average penetration rate. There are still 6.2 million homes without telephone service. Thus, universal service is not yet nationwide. Weikle, op. cit., pp. 50-53.

[85] According to a 1993 study, in some poor neighborhoods of New York City, as much as 25 percent of the households lack phones. The absence of working payphones can undermine fire protection in the absence of local alarm boxes. Research by Rutgers University shows that about six million U.S. homes have no direct access to a telephone, including 50 percent of households headed by single women with children who are at or below the poverty level and 21 percent of those living in public housing. See"Access denied; inequality in access to information networks," Barbara Ruben, Environmental *Action Magazine*, September 22, 1995, p. 18.

[86] According to the 1990 Census for Chicago, "1.8 percent of single-family homes and 12.1 percent of renters do not have telephones." "Daley: Ban Pay Phones From Private Property," Mary A. Johnson and Fran Spielman, *Chicago Sun-Times*, July 13, 1994, p. 4.

A survey by *The New York Times*, covering more than 450 public telephones in 15 New York City neighborhoods from Jan. 23 to Feb. 2, 1996 found that nearly one-third were broken. "Phone Scarcity Complicates Fire Alarm Plan," Alan Finder, *The New York Times*, February 11, 1996, p. 49. To combat their use in facilitating drug dealing, and other illicit activities such as phone fraud and computer hacking, payphones have been removed from many poor neighborhoods or restricted to outbound calls only or returned to rotary dialing. "New Stab At Lifeline of Dealers; Pay Phones Face 2nd Daley Attack," Robert Davis ,*Chicago Tribune*, July 13, 1994, p. 1, "Press "R" for Rip-Off," Michael Moss, *Newsday*, March 19, 1995, p. A5.

[87] In a recently published study of obstacles which predict a lack of a regular medical provider and delays in seeking medical care for patients at an urban public hospital, 20% of respondents cited a lack of phone service., "Obstacles predicting lack of a regular provider and delays in seeking care for patients at an urban public hospital," Kimberly J. Rask, Mark V. Williams, Ruth M. Parker, Sally E. McNagny, JAMA, *The Journal of the American Medical Association*, June 22, 1994, Vol. 271: No. 24; p. 1931. For example, "many people in public housing who responded to the surveys said they don't want to go to a pay phone on the corner because it's simply too dangerous, so they will wait until morning[.]... So they hope their problem gets better, or goes away." Hendrick, op. cit., A7.

[88] Because there are an insufficient number of phones on the street in some New York City neighborhoods, residents have no way to let fire departments know if there's a fire. See "Phone Scarcity Complicates Fire Alarm Plan," Alan Finder, *The New York Times*, February 11, 1996, p. 49.

[89] "Black children logging on less," Noreen Seebacher, *The Detroit News*, July 10, 1996, p. J4.

[90] "Integrating Cyberspace; Web Developers Aim to Get Blacks More in Tune with High Technology," *Sun-Sentinel* (Fort Lauderdale, FL), February 21, 1997, p. 1D.

[91] http.www.ntia.doc.gov/ntiahome/tables.htm (1997).

[92] Holsendolph, op. cit., p. F3; "Winning The Fight Against 'Electronic Apartheid:' Programs Give Low- and Middle-Income Ohioans A Chance To Log On To The Computer Revolution," Anjetta McQueen, *The Plain Dealer*, January 21, 1996, p. 1A.

[93] For families with income of $75,000 per year and up, 76.4 percent of black families were computer owners, vs. 74.6 percent of white families. And among families with incomes of $ 15,000 and less, the ownership percentage for black families and white were 12 percent and 10.7 percent, respectively. Holsendolph, op. cit., p. F3.

[94] "One area where the Net still trails the general population is race. The Internet remains a medium dominated by whites, who make up 85% of Internet and Web users, according to the Harris Poll. Blacks and Hispanics each account for 6% of Net users—up just slightly from a year ago. The Net population is also still skewed toward the affluent: 42% of Internet and Web users have household incomes of more than $ 50,000 a year, while only 18% take in $ 25,000 or less. But since the lower-income category probably includes many students, it may overstate Net participation by the country's poorest households." Cortese, op. cit., p. 85. For an in depth analysis of internet usage and an assessment of the reliability of recent studies on such usage, see "Internet and Web use in the U.S," Donna L. Hoffman, William D. Kalsbeek, Thomas P. Novak, *World Wide WebCommunications of the ACM*, December 1996, No. 12, Vol. 39; p. 36. Also see "Segmenting the Internet," Thomas E. Miller, *American Demographics*, July, 1996, p. 48, and "For African Americans: Community On-Line," Kate McKee, *News & Record* (Greensboro, NC), May 20, 1996, p. D1.

[95] Freeman, op. cit., p. 46.

[96] Lohr, op. cit., Sec.4, p. 1.

[97] "The Haves and the Have-nots: Access to Information Technologies," Ed Rose, *Communication World*, November 1994, p. 22.

[98] "The Quest For a More Diverse Online World," *PR Newswire*, January 27, 1997,

[99] Katherine Kapos and Samuel A. Autman, op. cit., p. A1; Miloneand Salpeter, op. cit., *Technology & Learning*, January, 1996, Vol. 16 ; No. 4 ; p. 38.

[100] "The Quest For a More Diverse Online World," *PR Newswire*, January 27, 1997.

[101] It is undisputed that much of what we know about ourselves and others is acquired through electronic sources of communication. To the extent that such information serves as a basis for determining how we define ourselves as individuals, groups and communities, and, how we determine who is valuable in our society, our very notions of individual self worth, equality and equity are subject to change as well.

[102] Section 254 (j) provides that "Nothing in this section shall affect the collection, distribution, or administration of the Lifeline Assistance Program provided for by the Commission under regulations set forth in section 69.117 of title 47, Code of Federal Regulations, and other related sections of such title. "Reduced Fees Available To Needy," Christine Arpe Gang, *The Commercial Appeal* (Memphis), August 2, 1991, p. C3.

[103] The limited, evolutionary focus of the Universal Service policy stands in stark contrast to the Congressional decision to liberalize the broadcast multiple ownership rules. The Act increases the number of broadcast stations that any one person or company can own to such a great extent that small broadcasters are being driven out of the industry by the new economics of multiple owner competition. The virtual repeal of the broadcast multiple ownership rules means very few Americans can afford to own a radio or television station. Meanwhile, government auction of the spectrum has resulted in the sale of vast public resources to private interests—a sale in which most Americans have played virtually no part. As a result, Americans are left even further behind as the courts uphold the private speech and editorial rights of media owners, often to the exclusion of the public.

[104] "Teleco Act is Year Old: Many are Willing to Wait for Results," *Communications Daily*, Feb. 5, 1997.

[105] Ibid.

[106] "Consumer Organization Fires Shot in David and Goliath Battle," *Business Wire*, Jan. 21, 1997.

[107] Common Carrier Action Commission Implements Telecom Act's Universal Service Provisions; Adopts Plan to Ensure Access to Affordable Telecommunications Services for All Americans" (CC Docket No. 96-45), Report No. CC 97-24; CC Docket No. 96-45, May 7, 1997.

[108] FCC 96093, In the Matter of CC Docket No. 96-95.

[109] See *Communications Daily*, June 27, 1997 , *Communications Daily*, June 20, *Communications Daily*, June 19, 1997.

[110] *Communications Daily*, July 28, 1997.

[111] Ibid.

[112] Section 254 (j) provides that "Nothing in this section shall affect the collection, distribution, or administration of the Lifeline Assistance Program provided for by the Commission under regulations set forth in section 69.117 of title 47, Code of Federal Regulations, and other related sections of such title.

[113] Gang, op. cit., p. C3.

[114] "Competition in the Local Loop," *Telecom Perspectives*, July 1996, p. 73; also see Statement of Jonathan B. Sallet, MCI Communications Corporation, before the Senate Commerce, Science, and Transportation Committee Subcommittee on Communications, Federal News Service, June 3, 1997.

[115] Silverman, op. cit.

[116] Ibid.

[117] "Do Lifeline Programs Promote Universal Telephone Service for the Poor?" Christopher Garbacz and Herbert G. Thompson, Jr., *Fortnightly*, March 15, 1997, p. 30.

[118] Ibid.

[119] "Total access; universal telecommunications services," Andrew L. Shapiro, *The Nation*, January 6, 1997, p. 5; Gang, op. cit.

[120] Gang, op. cit.

[121] Shapiro, op. cit.

[122] Telecommunications Act of 1996, Title I, Subtitle A-Telecommunications Services, Sec. 104. Nondiscrimination Principle.

[123] (CC Docket No. 96-45), Report No. CC 97-24; CC Docket No. 96-45, May 7, 1997.

[124] "Ameritech: we don't redline," Ted Hearn, *Multichannel News*, July 29, 1996, p. 3; "U.S. West's Long March," John J. Oslund, *Star Tribune*, July 17, 1995, p. 1D; and "Cable Accuses Bells of Targeting Only Wealthy," Ted Hearn, *Multichannel News*, April 17, 1995, p. 18 Rose, op. cit.

[125] This is one of the legislation's true shortcomings. While it establishes a technology fund to underwrite the development of new telecommunications businesses, the criteria for funding will necessarily entail the adoption of monetary and market disciplines similar to those employed by firms currently entering or competing in the more desirable markets. Even with liberal interconnection requirements, resale protection, and short-term entry barriers for network based competitors, absent the creation of an incentive structure favoring investment, deployment and service provision in less developed markets, entrepreneurs entering such markets will still find raising capital and providing service at a profit more difficult.

[126] Section 254 (j) provides that "nothing in this section shall affect the collection, distribution, or administration of the Lifeline Assistance Program provided for by the Commission under regulations set forth in section 69.117 of title 47, Code of Federal Regulations, and other related sections of such title.

[127] SEC. 254 (b)(6), SEC. 254 (c)(3) and SeC. 254 (h)(1)(B).

[128] COMMON CARRIER ACTION COMMISSION IMPLEMENTS TELECOM ACT'S UNIVERSAL SERVICE PROVISIONS; Adopts Plan to Ensure Access to Affordable Telecommunications Services for All Americans (CC Docket No. 96-45), Report No. CC 97-24; CC Docket No. 96-45, May 7, 1997.

[129] SEC. 254 (h)(1)(B).

[130] At least one half of the fifty states have been involved in litigation over the constitutionality of their school financing schemes. See GAO Reports, December 19, 1995, Tuesday, GAO/HEHS-96-39 December 19, 1995, School Finance - Three States' Experience with Equity in School Funding, Report to Congressional Requesters, Linda G. Morra, Director, Education and Employment Issues. Inequalities in State Based School Financing Schemes Continue to Spark Controversy and Litigation Over Their Questionable Constitutionality; and Colin D. Campbell and William A. Fischel, Preferences for school finance systems: voters versus judges, National Tax Journal, March, 1996, p. 1; and Richard Briffault The School Finance Cases, , New York Law Journal, August 10, 1995, p. 3.

[131] Federal and state government efforts to fund education have also been subject to increasing budgetary pressure. "National Education Association (NEA) Statement On Final Agreement For FY'96 Education Budget," U.S. Newswire, April 25, 1996; "Cutting Where It Hurts: Federal aid slashed for city schools," *Newsday*, February 2, 1996, p. A3; "In Search of Solutions for Troubled Schools," Rick Green and Robert A. Frahm, The Hartford Courant, May 22, 1996, p. A1; "Special-Ed Cuts Draw Fire," Robert Polner, *Newsday*, May 21, 1996, p. A3.

[132] COMMON CARRIER ACTION COMMISSION IMPLEMENTS TELECOM ACT'S UNIVERSAL SERVICE PROVISIONS; Adopts Plan to Ensure Access to Affordable Telecommunications Services for All Americans (CC Docket No. 96-45), Report No. CC 97-24; CC Docket No. 96-45, May 7, 1997.

[133] "Wired Life: The Great Unplugged Masses Confront the Future," Steve Lohr, *The New York Times*, April 21, 1996, Sec. 4, p.1.

134 "Ministry Programs, Churches Are Launching Computer Classes In Effort To Empower The Disadvantaged," Charlise Lyles, *Dayton Daily News*, June 22, 1997, p. E1; "Computer Upgrades: Program Helps Poor People Help Themselves by Offering Secondhand Computers, Classes, *The Plain Dealer*, July 1, 1997, p. 1B.

135 O'Malley, op. cit.

136 "NTIA's Telecommunications Information Infrastructure Assistance Program (TIIAP) provides matching grants to schools, libraries, hospitals, state and local governments and other non-profit entities. Last year, TIIAP leveraged $35.7 million in federal funds with $60 million in private, state and local funding. We awarded 117 grants to projects in 47 states, and the District of Columbia. More than 75 percent of the funds went to projects serving rural America or traditionally underserved Americans living in urban areas." FDCH Federal Department and Agency Documents, May 7, 1996, Testimony of Larry Irving, Assistant Secretary for Communications and information, National Telecommunications and Information Administration Administration, U.S. Department of Commerce, May 7, 1996.

137 "California regulators Pass Universal Service Program, *Washington Telecom Newswire*, October 25, 1996.

138 Rulemaking on the Commission's Own Motion into Universal Service and to Comply with the Mandates of Assembly Bill 3643; Investigation on the Commission's Own Motion into Universal Service and to Comply with the Mandates of Assembly Bill 3643; Decision No. 96-10-066, Rulemaking No. 95-01-020 (Filed January 24, 1995), Investigation No. 95-01-021 (Filed January 24, 1995); California Public Utilities Commission, 1996 Cal. PUC LEXIS 1046, October 25, 1996.

139 Citing as authority, Assembly Bill [AB] 3643 which established inter alia, the following principles: "(1) Essential telecommunications services should be provided at affordable prices to all Californians regardless of linguistic, cultural, ethnic, physical, geographic, or income considerations. "(6) Because of their economic and social impact, education, health care, community, and government institutions must be positioned to be early recipients of the benefits of the information age.

140 "PSC Should Ease Accessibility To Information Highway," Louise Trubek and Caleb Keller, *Wisconsin State Journal*, July 23, 1997, p. A9.

141 Dr. Bernard C. Watson, *Changes and Choices*, (c) 1991, National Urban League, Inc.

The State of African-American Politics

By   M a r t i n   L .   K i l s o n

I. DYNAMICS OF THE BLACK POLITICAL CLASS

The patterns of the African-American political class have been both similar to and different from those of that Irish-Americans, Jewish-Americans, Italian-Americans, and other white ethnic groups. True, the political class of both black Americans and white ethnic groups have undergone three rather distinct stages of political development—namely, a Protest Stage, an Electoral Empowerment Stage, and a Power Consolidation Stage.

Irish-Americans, for example, experienced a Protest Stage between the 1870s and the 1920s that worked on two levels. On one level it was driven by cultural cleavages between the Catholic Irish and the White Anglo-Saxon Protestant (WASP) majority that dominated American life. Militant pro-Celtic groups like the Fenian Brotherhood and Sinn Fein, which functioned among Irish-Americans throughout the late 19th century and well into the 20th century, were concerned with protesting WASP anti-Catholic patterns and Anglo-Britain's domination of Ireland. At the other level, the Irish-dominated trade unions located in the country's major industrial areas fought fiercely to gain greater social mobility and political power for Irish-Americans.

Among Irish-Americans, electoral political power and protest politics occurred simultaneously—which was not the case at all for African Americans. Why? Because the massive use of racist or white supremacist mechanisms (legal, political, social, and economic) almost completely excluded blacks from mainstream American processes. Between the 1890s and 1960s, that dynamic of exclusion—often sustained through white violence—was, of course, fiercest in the South, where the over-whelming majority of blacks lived: 80 percent of African Americans resided there as late as 1950.

This rigid exclusion from mainstream social and political processes had an enormous, distorting impact on the development of the African-American political class. For one thing, it meant that, during this era, electoral politics was an available activity only for the tiny minority of blacks in the North and West. And, of course, even in those areas, de facto racism severely restricted African Americans' use of electoral politics. One result of this: by 1960 only five African-Americans were seated in the U.S. Congress (Adam Clayton Powell from New York City; William O. Dawson, from Chicago; Charles Diggs, from Detroit; and Robert N.C. Nix, from Philadelphia).

In a broader sense, the exclusion blacks endured meant that African-Americans and their leadership had to employ the tactics of protest politics for a much longer time than did white ethnic groups. Irish-Americans, for example, had virtually discarded protest politics by the 1920s—a decade in which they elected governors in Ohio, Illinois, and New York, and won the Democratic Party's presidential nomination.

Thus, from the 1920s to the 1960s white ethnic groups were pursuing Electoral Empowerment Policies and advancing to Power Consolidation Politics (or what can also be called Systemic Incorporation Politics). The African-American community, on the other hand—12 million strong by 1930, 20 million by 1950—was largely confined to protest politics. During that period, the NAACP, the National Urban League, black professional associations, and religious and trade union organizations such as A. Philip Randolph's Brotherhood of Sleeping Car Porters launched and sustained the major protest activities.

While these groups practiced what can be called a pragmatic-activist political protest style, there was another leadership sector involved in protest politics who practiced an ethnocentric militancy. This black ethnoradical protest style focused on black cultural pride and on autonomous black-group development. Before World War II, its leading practitioner was Marcus Garvey's Universal Negro Improvement

Association (UNIA). From the late 1950s onward, black ethnoradicalism leading proponent has been the Nation of Islam. While its official leader was Elijah Muhammad, its key political figure was Malcolm X, and today the key political figure in the Nation of Islam is Minister Louis Farrakhan. These groups' very popularity was dramatic proof of how necessary it was that blacks as a group continue a full-blown pattern of protest politics right up to the emergence of the more mature pattern of Electoral Empowerment Politics in the late 1960s.

The latter was made possible by the massive intervention of the federal government through the Voting Rights Act of 1965 and subsequent legislation—spurred, of course, by the Civil Rights Movement. That intervention broke the violence-riddled barriers the White South had had in place against African Americans for almost a century.

Conservative analysts such as Abigail Thernstrom and Stephen Thernstrom argue (in their recent book, *America In Black And White* that the Federal intervention which brought blacks full electoral participatory capability was wrong. There is little doubt, however, that that intervention was necessary—and productive. In the mid-1960s, there were fewer than 300 black elected officials in the United States (for a black population of about 20 million), and only six black members of Congress (five in the House of Representatives and one in the Senate—Edward Brooke of Massachusetts). Seven years after the passage of the Voting Rights Act of 1965, there were about 4,000 Black elected officials. By 1989, there were around 7,000; and by the mid-1990s, some thirty-years after the Voting Rights Act, there were around 8,000 Black elected officials—a figure representing about 1.5 percent of all elected officials. By including the much larger number of appointed and civil service officials and administrative technicians, the full size of the African-American political class might total 30,000 to 40,000 persons nationwide.

Finally, to understand the rise of a viable Black Electoral Empowerment Politics, one must underscore the importance of middle-size and big cities: The black voting age population reached a critical-mass position in some 20 or more cities by the early 1970s, setting in motion a two-decade long period of political maturation.

II. PROBLEMS OF CONSOLIDATING POWER

It's one thing to successfully establish Electoral Empowerment Politics for one's ethnic community, but quite another matter to translate it into viable political clout and public-policy outcomes. That's what's required to produce what I call the Power Consolidation Stage in an ethnic group's political development.

In general, most white ethnic groups' political class achieved a moderate-to-high level of viable political clout and public-policy outcomes through electoral politics. First, electoral politics enabled them to significantly dissipate the negative status and social attitudes that WASPs held about them, for in general terms American democratic politics involves cross-cutting electoral and legislative alliances among groups that differ along ethnic lines and class lines. Above all, the development of effective electoral politics among white ethnic groups occurred at a time when government's role in advancing social mobility was expanding, That period of a social welfare-oriented American governance—at the city, state, Federal level—was from about 1870 to 1950 according to the two major scholars of this process, John Buenker and Steven Erie. [1]

Buenker identifies a kind of breakthrough rise of social welfare-oriented American governance that he dates from around the 1890s into the 1930s, a period he labels the "Era of urban liberalism and reform." Both Buenker and Erie show that the social welfare-oriented dynamic advanced through key stages during the rise of liberal and progressive American presidencies—those of Woodrow Wilson (1913-1921), Franklin D. Roosevelt (1933-1945), and Harry S. Truman (1945-1952). And It can be said that the moderate Republican politics of Dwight Eisenhower (1953-1960), especially in building the inter-state highway and massively assisting American farmers, continued the main thrust of social welfare-oriented American governance.

The result of tilting public policy toward advancing citizens' social mobility and welfare—either of the forceful type under Roosevelt's New Deal and Truman's Fair Deal or the moderate type under Eisenhower—was a major transformation affecting most white Americans. They advanced from weak working-class conditions from 1870 to 1930 to stable working-class and some middle-class conditions in the 1940s, 1950s, and 1960s.

But by the time blacks entered effective Electoral Empowerment Politics, such use of public policy had fallen from favor—to be partially replaced by so-called White Backlash, which opposed the active use of federal power to end white-supremacist patterns and bring blacks fully into the American mainstream. This reaction, which gathered force with Governor George Wallace's electoral campaigns in 1964, 1968, and 1972, was a special form of American conservatism, in that it combined both anti-Civil Rights (and thus was anti-Black) and anti-Federal government activism. The anti-Federal government aspect of "Wallaceism"—a rightwing phenomenon that by the mid-1970s would carry the name 'Neoconservatism'—was jingoistically labeled "Big Government" by Wallace's followers. Professor Seymour Martin Lipset diagnosed the core rightwing purposes of "Wallaceism" as follows:

> It could certainly be seen as "hidden racism;" and it could be seen as serving the subsurface anti-Negro hostility of bigots. But as an illuminator of the common aspects of rightwing extremism, it [Wallaceism] can be seen as a backlash against change in which there is an almost absolute congruence between the backlash against dreaded change and the backlash targetry, that is, the change-bearers [Black Americans and Federal government]? [2]

Thus, from anti-Civil Rights conservatism of the late 1960s to the more theoretical Neoconservatism discourse fashioned by conservative intellectuals during the early 1970s onward (supply-side economic and thus anti-government intervention policy), a qualitatively different American political Climate (American governance climate) surrounded the emergence of Black electoral empowerment. Steven Erie employed the term "rainbow's end" to characterize this phenomenon. During most of the 1970s, this resulted in the election of relatively-moderate conservative Republican Administrations under Nixon and Gerald Ford, and in the 1980s the ultra-conservative Republican Administrations under Reagan and Bush. Even when Democratic presidents squeezed into the White House, as Jimmy Carter did in 1976 and Bill Clinton in 1992 and 1996, they had neither much ideological commitment to the Federal interventionist policy profile of past Democratic Administrations nor much room for electoral maneuvering vis-a-vis those white voters who, as a minority of overall white voters, gave these Democratic presidents their votes. Black voters, thus, were the key to these presidents' victories.

Of course, an equally significant constraint limiting the full development of Black Electoral Empowerment Politics was the steady decline of once-vibrant medium industrial cities in which millions of working-class African Americans had settled after World War II.

Thus, the resources blacks had to translate Black Electoral Empowerment into Power Consolidation Politics has been at best problematic, and at worse, non-existent, especially for poor and weak working-class (the so-called working poor) African Americans.

In other words, the new Black political class spawned by Black Electoral Empowerment Politics has achieved only a low-level of Power Consolidation Politics for some 40 percent of African-American households who fall into the weak-working-class and poor categories, and just a moderate level of Power Consolidation Politics to push the interests of blacks in the stable working class, middle-class, and upper-class sectors.[3] The inability of the black political class and its allies among white groups to alter the 1996 Welfare Act to aid the black and Hispanic poor—the two ethnic groups with the largest proportion of poor families—graphically underlined the black leadership's political failure to secure political benefits for the poor.

There has been one other important cause of what I call the black political class' low-to-moderate success in achieving Power Consolidation Politics: its weak coalition status compared to the moderate-to-strong-coalition status legitimacy of white politicians and their voters. This matter of the weak-coalition legitimacy that's accorded black politicians and voters by white Americans is a way of saying that as a group black politicians and leaders are not accorded the high political authoritativeness—respect—that white leaders and politicians get. Even so, this contempo-

rary aspect of America's white-supremacist legacy is riddled with paradoxes. For example, when black American politicians bid for offices that
require a significant amount of white votes—offices at the state and federal levels—they seldom get them. But when white politicians and white
voters' interest groups require the strategic cluster of votes controlled by
African-American legislators (black legislators at both state and Federal
legislative levels have historically built up a disproportionately high rate
of legislative seniority, thereby giving them strategic power positions on
legislative committees and in intricacies of legislative maneuverings and
log-rolling), they rather easily, momentarily, put aside their lack of respect
for black politicians.

A keener understanding of the paradoxes surrounding the interactions
of white politicians and interest groups, on the one hand, and black politicians on the other hand (legislators in this instance) can be derived from
looking at black/Jewish political relations.

In general, the past 25 years or so have witnessed discord in
black/Jewish relations. But even the most conservative Jewish interest
groups and politicians do not shun the African-American members of
Congress sitting on the House Foreign Affairs Committee (nearly 15 percent black representation) and on the Appropriations Committee (8 percent black representation). Such Jewish groups and politicians require
the annual support of these black representatives for the billions of dollars in aid the United States gives to Israel. And, in fact, the Congressional
Black Caucus has one of the steadiest and strongest pro-Israel voting
records among Congressional voting blocks. Yet, while treating black legislators as politically authoritative for a selected area of Jewish groups'
interests, these same groups do not give African-American candidates for
Congress and state legislators anywhere near a fair share of electoral
support—financial and voting—compared with what they give Irish-
American, Italian-American, and other white candidates.

Though this contradictory relationship between black legislators and
white interest groups and voters requires further study, I am reasonably
sure that this kind of white-voter hypocrisy toward the African-American
political class (like the Jewish voters' contradictory interface with black

Congresspersons) has been widespread. This situation finds white interest groups and voters claiming disproportionate public policy benefits for
themselves, on the one hand, but rendering to black politicians and black
Interests generally a minimal exchange in votes for black politicians or
for policies basic to African-American interests. Further study of what I
call white-voter hypocrisy toward the African-American political class—
especially of such white constituencies who rely on public policy allocations for a crucial segment of their wherewithal or living standards the
white elderly, small businesses, white farmers, and white ethnic groups
who have ethnic-linked foreign policy interests—is needed.

Thus, it might be said, that in the era of the 1990s— some 30-odd years
following black Electoral Empowerment—the major issue facing the
African-American leadership in general and the political class especially
is how to gain more viable political clout and more effective public-policy capability. This is what the stage of Power Consolidation Politics is all
about for the political class of any American ethnic group or general interest group. It is the mature stage of the political development of any
group's politician class. There is little doubt, I think, that the continued
unwillingness of white American interest groups and of white voters generally to accord black politicians the same degree of political authoritativeness that they accord white politicians lies at the heart of the low-to-
moderate Power Consolidation capability available to the African-
American political class. White interest groups and voters, then, carry the
key responsibility for correcting this persistent white-supremacist practice toward African-American politicians.

THE POWELL PHENOMENON AND BIRACIAL POLITICS

Interestingly enough, there has been growing evidence during the past
decade that a small-but-growing segment of white American voters has
assisted, through voting, the movement of American politics along bi-
racial lines—that is, along political lines that involve equal opportunity
for African Americans to hold offices that white voters control through
their votes, not just offices that black voters control. A beginning of a bi-
racializing dynamic with whites electing black officials has occurred in

several medium-sized cities during the 1990s. For example, in Saginaw, Michigan in 1993 (40 percent black); in Pontiac, Michigan in 1993 (42 percent black); in Evanston, Illinois in 1993 (22 percent black); in Roanoke, Virginia, in 1992 (24 percent black); in New Haven in 1993 (36 percent black); in Denver in 1995 (13 percent black); and in Dayton in 1993 (48 percent black).[4] Indeed, black officials were elected in three Congressional Districts in the South in 1996 (Sanford Bishop and Cynthia McKinney in Georgia and Corrine Brown in Florida) after, owing to a U.S. Supreme Court decision, their Congressional Districts had changed from black-majority Districts to white-majority ones. However, on closer analysis of these 1996 black Congressional victories in White-majority Districts, the victories of Bishop, McKinney, and Brown depended squarely upon having gained the vast majority of African-American votes, while in no case did these black Congresspersons gain more than between 30 percent and 40 percent of the white votes.

Again, it seems to be a very difficult cultural sea-change for white Americans to accord black American politicians and candidates the same level of political authoritativeness as white politician and candidates. Professor Kenneth Reeves, of Harvard's Kennedy School of Government, has conducted surveys among white voters which showed that their view of Black politicians and candidates exhibit "deeply rooted racial stereotypes." The research led him to conclude that "not only that black candidates chances of victory [in Congressional elections] are not improving but that the future of minority representation may be bleak unless race can remain an acceptable consideration in drawing [Congressional] district lines." [5]

What does the evidence of a few African-American politicians gaining office through white-majority legislative districts, on the one hand, and the persistent evidence of racial stereotypes about blacks influencing most whites' responses to black politicians, on the other hand, tell us about the generic character of the place of racial issues in American politics today?

It tells us that African-Americans still inhabit a kind of schizophrenic status in American life, being both "insiders" in certain key respects and especially for the 50 percent of blacks who are in the middle class, and "outsiders," especially those 40 percent of black households who are in the weak working-class and poor categories.)

Under the best possible interpretation, this Janus-faced status for African Americans, compared with the pervasive white supremacist patterns of the past, suggests that more and more African-American politicians should appeal to white voters and interest groups, along with their primary supporters, African-American voters and interest groups.

However, in this era when ultra-conservatism dominates both the national Republican Party and the Congress, it's hardly possible to wax gloriously about the future prospects for serious bi-racial politics development. That requires that black politicians and voters have substantive access to bipartisan electoral and legislative mechanisms. But it has been precisely the national Republican Party that has denied blacks a fair bipartisan option for more than 50 years. This denial of access to bipartisan mechanisms in American politics—first offered white ethnic groups by the Republicans back in the 1940s and 1950s and massively since the late 1960s—has persisted during the past 30 years when a sizeable African-American middle-class has come into being. Indeed, the GOP has preferred to indulge in cynical backlash politics in its appeal to white voters, thereby becoming in the past decade the dominant party among Southern white voters, with about 70 Southern Congressmen and women compared to 54 Southern Democratic members of Congress.

Then, quite out of the blue, a unique thing happened on the way to the 1996 presidential election. An African American—in the person of a brilliant military figure, General Colin Powell—led the field of contenders in the polls, whether matched against hopefuls for the Republican nomination or against President Clinton. Colin Powell's potential Presidential campaign—which he prematurely aborted—represented the best opportunity blacks have ever had to normalize, in bi-partisan terms, its electoral status.

Two of the attributes that Powell possessed would have made him unique as a presidential candidate in this regard. First, Powell was "pro-black" without being viewed as "white-averse." Although a Republican, Powell expressed solid commitment to the core pillars of the mainline black leadership's Civil Rights agenda, including support for affirmative action. Powell's stance brought him sharp rebukes from such black Republicans as Congressman J. C. Watts of Missouri and such conservative black intellectuals as Thomas Sowell, Shelby Steele, Robert Woodson, and Alan Keyes.[6] Yet, Powell's broad appeal to White voters persisted despite his commitment to the mainline black leadership's Civil Rights agenda. Why? Whatever the full answer to this question is, it is clear that for the majority of white voters who in polls supported Powell's candidacy believed he possessed a certain magical quality as an African-American. Derrick Z. Jackson, the Boston Globe's astute black columnist best characterized this magical quality. Powell was "the Whites' Great Black Hope," Jackson observed, pinpointing the fact that for many whites, Powell as a black candidate radiated an aura of discipline, moral uplift, an up-by-the-bootstrap ethos and sentimentality that white Americans place great store by. That perception of Powell contrasted sharply with the attitude that still enables many whites, a majority perhaps, to view African-Americans through the prism of the weakest and most distressed segment of the African-American community. Thus the idea of Powell as "Whites' Great Black Hope" takes on a possible transformative meaning: Powell as president just might have, through his exceptional leadership qualities, devised ways to transform the social disorder and distress found among the black poor.

Of course, since Powell declined to run, it will remain one big historical question whether enough white voters could have been mobilized to give him the chance to act out that transformative role. It will also remain a historical question whether Powell, as the first African-American president, would have had the political strength to liberalize the GOP's dominant form of conservatism. Put another way, would Powell's ability in regard to what I call Power Consolidation Politics (translating black electoral successes into viable legislative or public policy outcomes for African Americans) have proved significantly superior to that which the African-American political class has generated since the early 1970s?

And what in substance has been the dominant form of conservatism of the Republican Party in our era? It is a conservatism that functions by cynically attacking trade unions, feminists, the welfare system and other issues relating to the poor (and the black and Hispanic poor especially), and to key aspects of blacks' Civil Rights agenda. Of course, as moderate and liberal Republicans who are a minority in that party know well, there could be what I call a pro-active conservatism the GOP could pursue, an approach that would mobilize both public policies and private-sector practices to address in a serious way the problem of poverty and joblessness among blacks and Hispanics.

I have often challenged conservatives who talk about their concern for the black and Hispanic poor to act to fashion a conservatism with a human face. Even small pro-active conservative responses such as a system of scholarships funded by right-wing foundations for high-achieving poor black and Hispanic schoolchildren or a set of grants to assist significant programs of neighborhood development would make a difference. Thus, another question we'll likely never know is whether Colin Powell, as the first African American to become president, would have generated a conservatism with a human face.

Bob Herbert, the New York Times columnist, who is African-American, observed that Powell was a good man "hanging out with the wrong crowd ... in Powell's case, the wrong crowd is a political party that believes deeply in policies deliberately crafted to hurt the poor, racial and ethnic minorities, and the working classes." [7]

There would have been then, some very problematic dimensions of a Powell candidacy, dimensions which did not go unnoticed by black voters.

Most polls showed that, in a matchup with President Clinton, only about one-third of blacks favored Powell, compared to about 55 percent of whites. This African-American response to Powell reflected a certain political realism toward someone they otherwise viewed in heroic terms, someone they intrinsically trusted as a high-achieving black American—who nonetheless sustained broad and deep commitments to African-American realities and interests. Powell was "a brother!" Of course, had Powell actually gained the Republican nomination and gained about one-third of the African-American vote, that would have been sufficient to win the Presidency.

CONSERVATISM AND BIRACIAL POLITICS

There is no doubt whatever that African-American political development must be conducted along bi-racial political lines. Of course, though most white conservative commentators on black politics like George Will, Joe Klein, Jim Sleeper, and Nat Hentoff, among others don't seem to know it, the goal of biracial or interracial political patterns has always been firmly held by the African-American political class and leadership groups generally. This has been so since the days of Frederick Douglass and W. E. B. DuBois, down to our very era. Nevertheless, hard-line white conservatives have persistently argued that the black nationalist strand of African-American political activity is the preferred political pattern among blacks. This is the fundamental reason white conservatives give for the lack of significant bi-racial political patterns in American Politics. This conservative argument is, I need hardly add, both empirically wrong and an affront to African-Americans .[8]

While there is no denying that proponents of the ethno-radical, or black nationalist, outlook, have a presence among African-Americans and, as such, make movement toward bi-racial politics problematic, white conservatives are totally wrong in identifying this ethno-radical strand among blacks as the main obstacle to greater biracial politics. The greatest obstacle to biracial political patterns in American politics is and has been for many decades the refusal of whites to accord blacks the same coalition legitimacy status that white groups accord each other.

The most brilliant analysis of the reasons underlying what I call African Americans' politically low-level entry into electoral and legislative coalitions in American politics was written by Jerry Watts, a political scientist at Trinity College (Conn.). According to Watts, there are two generic types of coalition processes in American politics. One he calls "disjointed coalitions" and the other he calls "shared coalitions." The former are the typical coalition patterns that governed the classic American urban political machines from the late 19th century to the 1960s—the machines that Steve Erie studied in his book. In such disjointed coalitions, the goals are disparate, governed by the unique situations faced by a given ethnic group in its particular urban subcommunity.

Thus, the party leaders of a given city political machine (say, the Irish in Tammany Hall—the Democratic party organization in New York—from the 1880s to the 1960s) could satisfy some of one group's goals by giving them a good share of street construction jobs, in the case of the Italian-American community, or a share of school teacher jobs, in the case of the Jewish-American community. In satisfying these two key numerically-important groups, the Irish politicians controlling Tammany could act as they pleased in regard to a whole series of broader governmental functions, putting their own Irish-American group in control of them and/or ignoring other, politically weaker groups.[9] Because of our country's white-supremacist values, blacks were one of the politically weak groups who gained only a marginal status in disjointed coalitions. So, ever since black politicians first entered such coalitions, first in Chicago under Congressmen Oscar DePriest's and William G. Dawson's leadership during the 1930s and 1940s, and since the late 1960s, their public policy and patronage benefits were distinctly fewer than what the quality of their votes were to the white-controlled city machines.

On the other hand, what Watts calls "the shared core coalitions" are fundamentally different, for, according to Professor Watts, "A shared core coalition exists when various disparate groups come together because they support a common issue agenda." In other words, while under the usual "disjointed coalitions," disparate groups emphasize their localized or subcommunity interests, under "shared core coalitions," American groups minimize their subcommunity concerns for broader region-wide or nation-wide concerns. It is, says Watts, these kind of coalitions that surround great periods of social movement politics in American society. As Watts put it: "Perhaps the best examples of shared core coalitions are those coalitions that arise as social movements."[10] Key examples of such social-movement generated coalitions were those associated with agrarian radicalism among American farmers in the late 19th and early 20th century, and the white working class activism associated with the rise of the trade union movement from the 1870s to the 1950s. The coalitions at the electoral and legislative level associated with the social-movement processes produced a qualitatively different kind of political benefit for millions-on-millions of American citizens—benefits that fundamentally advanced their social mobility from weak and poor working class to stable working class and middle-class standing. The John Buenker book mentioned earlier is the best study of the kind of fundamental public policy benefits associated with such "shared core coalitions."

It is typically forgotten today among the new middle-class white American families who became middle class from the 1930s onward that the explicit use of federal public policy played a major role in their development. This was especially the case in regard to the expansion of home ownership among white Americans from the 1930s onward through Federal government subsidization of home mortgages. In fact, a recent study that attempts to explain the extensive wealth gap between white and black families—by Melvin Oliver and Tom Shapiro titled *Black Wealth, White Wealth: A New Perspective on Racial Inequality*—found that the place of Federal government affirmative assistance in facilitating home ownership for white families goes back to the homestead acts during the post-Civil War era. In a summary of the Oliver-Shapiro study, the Boston Globe columnist Derrick Jackson observed that "the unequal results [in Black/White wealth today] are caused by an unbroken 132-year legacy of government affirmative action in asset building to white Americans. White Americans received far more land for homesteading at the end of the Civil War than African Americans. In the 1930s, federal programs and tax policies promoted housing and business expansion in the suburbs for white Americans while the Federal Housing Authority denied loans to African-American neighborhoods. ..." Then, in the post-World War II era, two key developments impacted disfavorably upon African Americans in regard to enhancing family financial asset and favorably upon white American families. One was the racist banking practices that continued throughout the postwar era, and the other involved natural market patterns that favorably inflated housing values. As Derrick Jackson put it: "Banking redlining [racist loan practices] lasted into this decade [the 1990s]. The damage done was tremendous. The wealth of white families, enhanced by a rise in home equity twice that of African Americans from 1967-1977, are in a far better position to transfer wealth to kin, start up businesses, and make other long-term invest-ments." [11] In regard to figures on the wealth gap differential, the median net wealth-worth of African Americans is presently only 8 percent of the median net wealth-worth of white Americans—$3,700 compared with $43,800. The net wealth-worth gap contrasts sharply with the black/white income gap, for black median income is about 60 percent of whites— $15,630 and $25, 384, respectively.

This, then, is the kind of interplay between public policy processes, on the one hand, and the facilitation of major social mobility advances for American citizens, on the other hand, that those kinds of political coali-tions sparked by social-movement politics like that of the New Deal era can produce. Professor Jerry Watts calls these coalitions "shared core coalitions," and in fact the first time black Americans ever participated in such a coalition was during the period of the Civil Rights Movement of the late 1950s and 1960s. Just enough liberal participation by white Americans in the labor movement and in liberal white interest groups helped to give the Civil Rights Movement the attributes of a shared core coalition. As Watts put it:

> The civil rights movement was, for the most part, a shared core coalition. Individuals from various backgrounds, ethnicities, loca-tions, came together in the movement to help better the socio-political, economic plight of blacks.... More often than not, shared core coalitions emerge in response to a political crisis. It is the heightened sense of crisis that often allows diverse people to scut-tle their parochial interests on behalf of something greater. [12]

Thus, Professor Watts' analysis strongly suggests that it should be a high-priority goal of the black political class and of black leadership groups generally to facilitate conditions for a new wave of shared core coalitions related to African-American issues. But Watts' analysis also informs us that a primary condition for the development of a new wave of shared core coalitions falls on the shoulders of conservative groups, both among Republicans and Democrats. Conservative groups, Watts says, must assist significantly in countering the massive demonization of the black poor that conservatives have been responsible for during the past 25 years or so. Today, says Watts, "Blacks are often seen as a foreign group of some sort: as inauthentic citizens." He continues:

> It was one of the ideological masterpieces of the Reagan admin-
> istration and contemporary conservative political posturing to
> create an image of the black poor as wards of their ethnic group.
> The black poor came to be seen as the responsibility of the black
> non-poor. In effect, they have ceased to be viewed as American cit-
> izens, that is, as persons who had linkages to the broader
> American community. This image and the resultant ideological
> discursive marginalization of the black poor ... are manifestations
> of a broader problem confronting black politics at present within
> the national electoral arena. ... It appears that large numbers of
> white voters are not very concerned about the plight of blacks.
> That is, at the national level, it appears that a candidate's position
> on blacks is important to the majority of the white voting populace
> only if the candidate is imagined as appealing too much to the
> black vote. The white voting populace seems quite capable of vot-
> ing for a candidate who appears to be not only indifferent but
> antagonistic to the peculiar needs of blacks.[13]

There is, then, an indisputably clear need to find the political means and will required to fashion new shared core coalitional patterns in American politics, especially in regard to the needs of many African Americans. The road back to biracial political patterns demands, as Professor Watts intimates, that dominant conservative forces in American life and politics begin to redress their massive demonization of the black poor in particular, and by extension this has had a negative impact on whites' perceptions of African-American patterns in general.

BLACK NATIONALIST AND BIRACIAL POLITICS

It is important to recognize that in a democratic political system like our American system, xenophobic or ethnocentric organizations like the White Citizens Councils of the 1960s and 1970s, or the Militia and Patriot groups today are not illegal. Nor are xenophobic groups among African Americans, like the Nation of Islam, illegal. For those of us who oppose xenophobic behavior and favor a cosmopolitan orientation or interracial outlook, our goal is to reduce the influence of xenophobic groups and thereby, hopefully, render them political pariahs.

However, the process of reducing the influence of xenophobic organizations has never been an easy one, as witnessed by the longstanding influence of anti-Black and anti-Semitic xenophobic groups among White Anglo-Saxon Protestants (WASPs) in the South like the Ku Klux Klan (from the 1880s to the 1970s), or the influence today among WASPs of the Militia and Patriot groups. Similarly, although African Americans have suffered enormous victimization from xenophobic anti-black organizations among us, blacks nevertheless have themselves produced ethnocentric organizations like the Garvey Movement during the 1920s to 1940s and the Nation of Islam today.

Why, one might ask, have some African Americans exhibited sympathy toward ethnocentric organizations? For a rather basic and simple reason. Namely, owing to America's long-standing racist denigration of African Americans as a group and as individuals—stripping many millions of blacks of a viable self-esteem—many African Americans have required a kind of countervailing catharsis, which is to say, a kind of ideological response which enables them to vent anger and even rage, on the one hand, and to feel an inner-self-wholeness, (to "feel like somebody"), on the other hand. This, then, was the function of the Garvey Movement among millions of African Americans during the 1920s to 1940s—despite the xenophobic dimension of this Movement—and it is the function today of the Nation of Islam.

It is important to note, however, that the mainline African-American leadership groups from the 1920s onward have persistently criticized ethnocentric and xenophobic patterns among blacks, consistently favoring a cosmopolitan approach to interethnic and interracial relations. Furthermore, although many African Americans have, in any given period since the 1920s, exhibited interest in and some sympathy for ethnocentric groups like the Nation of Islam, this sympathy always had a clear limit to it. This sympathy was never translated—and is not so translated today— into real political support for xenophobic organizations. For example, black American voters have always reserved their real, viable political support for politicians associated with the mainline African-American leadership groups—the NAACP, the National Urban League, the National Conference of Negro Women, the numerous black professional organizations, etc. In other words, since the World War I era onward, the typical African-American citizen preferred to trust what might be called black operational leadership hegemony only to leaders associated with the mainline black organizations. Black communities have almost never elected supporters of militant ethnocentric organizations to political office. This cannot be said for WASPs, who have elected followers and leaders of xenophobic white groups like the Ku Klux Klan and the White Citizens Councils to offices during this century in the South and elsewhere, too.

Thus, one might say there has been a kind of schizophrenic attitude among African-American citizens toward two leadership patterns—the mainline, pragmatic-oriented leadership pattern, on the one hand, and the ethnocentric-oriented leadership pattern,on the other. Blacks have turned to the xenophobic leadership pattern when seeking a catharsis or therapeutic defense for themselves—for their inner soul, so to speak—against the vicious vagaries of American racism. But these very same blacks have, when push came to shove in political terms, only given their political authority, or operational leadership hegemony, to the mainline black leadership groups.

Some recent data, from a major poll of African-American attitudes, illustrate what I call African Americans' schizophrenic relationship with black nationalist, or ethnoradical groups, on the one hand, and the mainline, pragmatic-oriented groups, on the other hand. The findings by the Yankelovich Survey in February 1994 for *Time* magazine—shown in Table III—represent what I call the political-cathartic outlook of African Americans toward the Nation of Islam. For example, blacks' responses in this poll reveal that many of them lend an "attentive ear" to Minister Louis Farrakhan's ethnocentric leadership style. Thus, when asked whether Farrakhan "says things the country should hear," some 70 percent of blacks said "yes." When asked "whether Farrakhan speaks the truth," some 63 percent of blacks said "yes." When asked "whether Farrakhan is good for the black community," some 63 percent of blacks said "yes."

On the other hand, when we look at other responses by blacks in the same Yankelovich poll, we find responses that represent what I call the political-substantive outlook of African Americans toward the Nation of Islam. In regard to the issue of letting followers of Farrakhan hold office in city councils, state legislatures, and federal offices, African Americans clearly do not give that level of acceptbility to the Nation of Islam or any other black nationalist organization. Thus, in the Yankelovich survey, some 74 percent of African Americans preferred the NAACP over Farrakhan's organization; only 31 percent favored the Nation of Islam. When asked if they have generally favorable or unfavorable attitudes toward any given African-American leader, blacks overwhelmingly chose Reverend Jesse Jackson, leader of the Rainbow Coalition, not Farrakhan (86 percent to 48 percent). Illinois Senator Carol Moseley Braun came in close to Farrakhan, with a 42 percent rating, while then black Secretary of Commerce, Ron Brown, gained 38 percent of blacks' approval, as did Colin Powell. Finally, when asked "who is the most important black leader today?," a strong 34 percent of African Americans selected Jesse Jackson—as shown in Table IV—compared with only 9 percent who selected Farrakhan.

Thus, there is very good evidence to illustrate that while many black Americans give an "attentive ear" or a "cathartic ear" to black nationalist groups and their leaders, African Americans, in regard to their political substantive outlook, overwhelmingly give political or electoral support to mainline black leadership groups. Even so, most of the leaders of these mainline black political organizations have persistently endeavored to rein in and tame the influence of black ethnocentric groups such as the Nation of Islam. Mainline African-American leaders like Jesse Jackson, Leon Sullivan, Andrew Young, Benjamin Hooks, Hugh Price, Julian Bond, John Lewis, Charles Rangel, Eleanor Holmes Norton, among many others, have often criticized black nationalist organizations. And at the same time some mainline black leaders have tried to discipline black nationalist groups through organizational or coalition ties.

Although the process of taming ethnocentric groups like the black nationalist organizations is a protracted one, the idea of linking organizations like the Nation of Islam with broader and liberal events among the mainline black community is a workable one. The first serious effort to do this—which was heavily criticized by whites and by some blacks, too— was the Million Man March in the fall of 1995. While the media emphasized the role of ethnocentrist Farrakhan in the leadership of the March, what was important, from a long-run political standpoint, was, I think, the overwhelmingly black middle-class organizational control of the event. The march's organizational mechanism was the work of the black middle-class networks, which were based on professional associations among black lawyers, engineers, computer scientists, doctors, scholars, accountants, money managers, businessmen, architects, and many other professionals. These networks attracted more than 800,000 persons to the march—an unprecedented number in the history of marches to Washington, D.C.

From the Philadelphia area, for example, my nephew, Thomas Kilson Queenan, who is an architect and holds an MBA from the Wharton School of Business, participated in the massive middle-class groundswell for the Million Man March. As deputy treasurer of Philadelphia, he helped persuade Mayor Richard Rendell and other city officials to support the organizational effort for the march. The result was that some 60,000 persons attended the march from the Philadelphia area—the largest single regional contingent. So, despite Farrakhan's high visibility as a leading figure in the march, in the black communities around the country, it was black middle-class professionals like Queenan who actually controlled the mobilization of the march. And their purposes were not to celebrate the ethnocentric views of Farrakhan, but to help millions of black Americans—black males in the first instance—to take more care about the needs and concerns of black families, in particular, and of the black community, in general.

One major consequence of the 1995 Million Man March occurred during the 1996 presidential election. About 1.4 million more black males voted than in the 1992 presidential election. Post-Million Man March activity in black communities all around the country contributed to this greater electoral participation by black males.

CONCLUSION

One general goal associated with the Million Man March was to bring into closer relationship that segment of African-American leadership that concerns itself with the egalitarian needs of the black community (its civil rights needs), and that segment of the African-American leadership that concerns itself with black pride and community-uplift needs. This is just another way of characterizing the black mainline leadership, such as the NAACP and black elected politicians, on one side, and the black nationalist leadership element, on the other.

That the Million Man March successfully brought these two branches of African-American leadership into a new, though cautious, working relationship was reflected in the selection of Congressman Kweisi Mfume as the new executive officer of the NAACP in early 1996. Mfume was one of the most skillful African-American members of the Congress, where he served a term as head of the Congressional Black Caucus. Mfume, while still in Congress, supported the Million Man March—as did the caucus as a group—and in the state of Maryland a major organization was a force behind the march. Mfume is above all a pragmatic-activist in his political style (which is also the dominant style of the whole mainline African-American leadership). He has set for himself the goal of facilitating the emergence of new patterns of the shared core coalitions Professor Watts describes. Hugh B. Price, president of the National Urban League, who participated in the Summit Conference that followed the march, has also emerged as a skillful proponent of new biracial coalition patterns in African-American politics.

If the conservative forces in the Republican Party follow Watts' suggestion and retreat from backlash politics, then the chances for new biracial patterns are very good. Another situation that can contribute to the rise of new biracial patterns is the growing activism and progressivism among some middle-class whites. This is especially so among blue-collar workers and some middle-class white-collar workers who have recognized the growing wealth gap between themselves, on the one hand, and the almost plutocratic level of wealth among America's business and corporate class, on the other. The bitter strike of United Parcel Service workers last summer was directly related to that gap—now the largest between the middle-and top-income sectors in any democratic nation-state. Indeed, it might be approaching crisis levels. If so, such crises have often been the stuff of the kind of social-movement activism that produced all of the major periods of progressive coalition politics in national 20th century American politics. There are, then, some grounds currently for a more hopeful outlook in regard to new biracial political patterns in the years ahead.

REFERENCES

1. See John Buenker, *Urban Liberalism and Progressive Reform*, New York, Scribner's, 1973, and Steve Erie, *Rainbow's End: Irish-Americans and Dilemmas of Urban ....*, 1840-1985.

2. Seymour Martin Lipset and Earl Raab, *Politics Of Unreason: Rightwing Extremism In America 1790-1970* (New York. Harper & Row, 1970), p.741.

3. The kind of data to support my view of a moderate-level Power Consolidation Politics relative to middle-class and elite African-American households relate significantly to the use of Affirmative Action policies and Practices at city, state, and federal levels. See, for example, data in Christopher Edley, *Not All Black And White.*

4. These data were culled from the bulletin of the Joint Center For Political And Economic Research, Washington, D.C., called Focus for years 1992, 1993, and 1995.

5. See Mary K. Garber, "Future Clouded For Majority-Black Districts," *Focus: Bulletin Of Joint Center For Political And Economic Research* (Washington, D.C., February - March, 1997), p. 4.

6. See Shelby Steele, *The Content of Our Character: A New Vision of Race in America*, HarperCollins, 1991.

7. See Bob Herbert, "The Wrong Crowd," *New York Times*, November 10, 1995, A18.

8. I have an extended critique of these conservative arguments in a forthcoming book, Martin Kilson, *Dilemmas Of Black Intellectuals*.

9. See Jerry Gafio Watts, "Blacks and Coalition Politics: A Theoretical Reconceptualization," in Wilbur Rich, ed., *Politics of Coalitions and Ethnic Minorities*, Westport: Praeger Publishers, 1996, pp. 43-45.

10. Ibid., p. 43.

11. Derrick Z. Jackson, "The Money Gap for Blacks," *The Boston Globe*, September 17, 1997.

12. Watts, op. cit., p. 44.

13. Ibid., p. 45.

A History of the National Urban League

The National Urban League, which has played so pivotal a role in the 20th-Century Freedom Movement, grew out of that spontaneous grassroots movement for freedom and opportunity that came to be called the Black Migrations. When the U.S. Supreme Court declared its approval of segregation in the 1896 Plessy v. Ferguson decision, the brutal system of economic, social and political oppression the White South quickly adopted rapidly transformed what had been a trickle of African Americans northward into a flood.

Those newcomers to the North soon discovered they had not escaped racial discrimination. Excluded from all but menial jobs in the larger society, victimized by poor housing and education, and inexperienced in the ways of urban living, many lived in terrible social and economic conditions.

Still, in the degree of difference between South and North lay opportunity, and that difference African Americans clearly understood.

But to capitalize on that opportunity, to successfully adapt to urban life and to reduce the pervasive discrimination they faced, they would need help. That was the reason the Committee on Urban Conditions Among Negroes was established in 1910 in New York City. Central to the organization's founding were two remarkable people: Mrs. Ruth Standish Baldwin and Dr. George Edmund Haynes, who would become the Committee's first executive secretary. Mrs. Baldwin, the widow of a railroad magnate and a member of one of America's oldest families, had a remarkable social conscience and was a stalwart champion of the poor and disadvantaged. Dr. Haynes, a graduate of Fisk University, Yale University, and Columbia University (he was the first African American to receive a doctorate from that institution), felt a compelling need to use his training as a social worker to serve his people.

A year later, the Committee merged with the Committee for the Improvement of Industrial Conditions Among Negroes in New York (founded in New York in 1906), and the National League for the Protection of Colored Women (founded in 1905) to form the National League on Urban Conditions Among Negroes. In 1920, the name was later shortened to the National Urban League.

The interracial character of the League's board was set from its first days. Professor Edwin R. A. Seligman of Columbia University, one of the leaders in progressive social service activities in New York City, served as chairman from 1911 to 1913. Mrs. Baldwin took the post until 1915.

The fledgling organization counseled black migrants from the South, helped train black social workers, and worked in various other ways to bring educational and employment opportunities to blacks. Its research into the problems blacks faced in employment opportunities, recreation, housing, health and sanitation, and education spurred the League's quick growth. By the end of World War I the organization had 81 staff members working in 30 cities.

In 1918, Dr. Haynes was succeeded by Eugene Kinckle Jones who would direct the agency until his retirement in 1941. Under his direction, the League significantly expanded its multifaceted campaign to crack the barriers to black employment, spurred first by the boom years of the 1920s, and then, by the desperate years of the Great Depression. Efforts at reasoned persuasion were buttressed by boycotts against firms that refused to employ blacks, pressures on schools to expand vocational opportunities for young people, constant prodding of Washington officials to include blacks in New Deal recovery programs and a drive to get blacks into previously segregated labor unions.

As World War II loomed, Lester Granger, a seasoned League veteran and crusading newspaper columnist, was appointed Granger's successor.

Outspoken in his commitment to advancing opportunity for African Americans, Granger pushed tirelessly to integrate the racist trade unions, and led the League's effort to support A. Philip Randolph's March on

Washington Movement to fight discrimination in defense work and in the armed services. Under Granger, the League, through its own Industrial Relations Laboratory, had notable success in cracking the color bar in numerous defense plants. The nation's demand for civilian labor during the war also helped the organization press ahead with, greater urgency, its programs to train black youths for meaningful blue-collar employment. After the war those efforts expanded to persuading Fortune 500 companies to hold career conferences on the campuses of Negro Colleges and place blacks in upper-echelon jobs.

Of equal importance to the League's own future sources of support, Granger avidly supported the organization of its volunteer auxiliary, the National Urban League Guild, which, under the leadership of Mollie Moon, became an important national force in its own right.

The explosion of the civil rights movement provoked a change for the League, one personified by its new leader, Whitney M. Young, Jr., who became executive director in 1961. A social worker like his predecessors, he substantially expanded the League's fund-raising ability—and, most critically, made the League a full partner in the civil rights movement. Indeed, although the League's tax-exempt status barred it from protest activities, it hosted at its New York headquarters the planning meetings of A. Philip Randolph, Martin Luther King, Jr., and other civil rights leaders for the 1963 March on Washington. Young was also a forceful advocate for greater government and private-sector efforts to eradicate poverty. His call for a domestic Marshall Plan, a ten-point program designed to close the gap between the huge social and economic gap between black and white Americans, significantly influenced the discussion of the Johnson Administration's War on Poverty legislation.

Young's tragic death in 1971 in a drowning incident off the coast of Lagos, Nigeria brought another change in leadership. Vernon E. Jordan, Jr., formerly Executive Director of the United Negro College Fund, took over as the League's fifth Executive Director in 1972 (the title of the office was changed to President in 1977).

For the next decade, until his resignation in December 1981, Jordan skillfully guided the League to new heights of achievement. He oversaw a

273

major expansion of its social-service efforts, as the League became a significant conduit for the federal government to establish programs and deliver services to aid urban communities, and brokered fresh initiatives in such League programs as housing, health, education and minority business development. Jordan also instituted a citizenship education program that helped increase the black vote and brought new programs to such areas as energy, the environment, and non-traditional jobs for women of color—and he developed *The State of Black America* report.

In 1982, John E. Jacob, a former chief executive officer of the Washington, D.C. and San Diego affiliates who had served as Executive Vice President, took the reins of leadership, solidifying the League's internal structure and expanding its outreach even further.

Jacob established the Permanent Development Fund in order to increase the organization's financial stamina. In honor of Whitney Young, he established several programs to aid the development of those who work for and with the League: The Whitney M. Young, Jr. Training Center, to provide training and leadership development opportunities for both staff and volunteers; the Whitney M. Young, Jr. Race Relations Program, which recognizes affiliates doing exemplary work in race relations; and the Whitney M. Young, Jr. Commemoration Ceremony, which honors and pays tribute to long term staff and volunteers who have made extraordinary contributions to the Urban League Movement.

Jacob established the League's NULITES youth-development program and spurred the League to put new emphasis on programs to reduce teenage pregnancy, help single female heads of households, combat crime in black communities, and increase voter registration.

Hugh B. Price, appointed to the League's top office in July 1994, has taken its reins at a critical moment for the League, for Black America, and for the nation as whole. A fierce market-driven dynamic, described by the rubric of "globalization," is sweeping the world, fundamentally altering economic relations among and within countries. Within the United States that dynamic is re-shaping the link between the nation's citizenry and its economy, and at least for the moment, fostering enormous uncertainty among individuals and tensions among ethnic and cultural groups.

This economic change, and the efforts of some to rollback the gains African Americans have fashioned since the 1960s, have made the League's efforts all the more necessary. Price, a lawyer by training, with extensive experience in community development and other public policy issues, has intensified the organization's work in three broad areas: in education and youth development, in individual and community-wide economic empowerment, and in the forceful advocacy of affirmative action and the promotion of inclusion as a critical foundation for securing America's future as a multi-ethnic democracy.

African-Americans Then and Now
A Statistical Overview

Since its inception, *The State of Black America* has rigorously monitored and assessed the conditions of African Americans. During this time, we have observed significant shifts in the composition of the population as well as changes in various indicators of socioeconomic well being. While important improvements in status have come about, the movement toward racial equality is best described as problematic. Indeed, on some key indicators, the relative position of African Americans has stagnated or worsened over the past two decades or so.

The selected statistical data in this appendix section document some of the developments that have occurred during this general time frame and reflect the mixed pattern of African-American progress. The presentation covers three main areas of interest—demographics and vital statistics, education, and employment and earnings. (Coverage periods vary because of differences in the availability of data.) Some narrative highlights preface each set of data tables.

DEMOGRAPHICS AND VITAL STATISTICS

■ African Americans number about 32 million persons. Between 1975 and 1993 their share of the total U.S. population increased from 11.5 percent to 2.5 percent and it is projected to rise to 12.8 percent of the total by the year 2000. By contrast, the white populations will continue to decline as a proportion of the total.

■ The African-American population continues to be heavily concentrated inside the central cities. As of 1992, they were 2.2 times as likely as whites to be central-city residents. Also, a majority of African Americans continue to live in the southern region of the country compared to, less than a third of whites.

■ The average life expectancy of African Americans remains more than six years lower than that of whites. Projections suggest that this disparity might increase slightly as we move through the next century. Also, the racial gap in infant mortality rates has widened over the years. In 1991, the African-American infant mortality rate was 2.4 times that of whites, up from 1.8 in 1975.

■ The racial disparity in births to unmarried mothers has narrowed. In 1991, African Americans were 3.1 times as likely as whites to give birth out-of-wedlock, which was less than half the 6.7 ratio in 1975.

■ The proportion of married-couple families among African Americans has decreased sharply—from about 58 percent in 1975 to 40 percent in 1993. In 1993, African-American families were only 67 percent as likely as white families to be a married-couple, down from 83 percent in 1975. The percent of female-headed households among African Americans jumped from 35 percent to about 48 percent during this time.

RESIDENT POPULATION BY RACE AND SEX

1975, 1993 and projections to 2050 (in thousands)

Table **1**

Total Population	Year	Both Sexes	Male	Female
	1975	215,973	105,366	110,670
	1993	257,908	125,896	132,010
	2000	276,241	135,101	141,140
Projected	2010	300,421	174,187	153,245
	2050	329,031	192,098	199,933

African American	Year	Both Sexes	Male	Female	% of total pop.
	1975	24,778	11,806	12,927	11.5
	1993	32,168	15,253	16,972	12.5
	2000	35,469	16,802	18,667	12.8
Projected	2010	40,224	19,027	21,197	13.4
	2050	61,586	29,279	32,307	15.7

White American	Year	Both Sexes	Male	Female	% of total pop.
	1975	187,629	91,806	95,823	86.9
	1993	214,765	105,283	109,482	83.3
	2000	226,267	111,245	15,022	81.9
Projected	2010	240,297	118,505	121,792	80.0
	2050	285,591	140,947	144,644	72.8

Source: U.S. Bureau of the Census, *Preliminary Estimates of the Population of the United States by Age, Sex, and Race: 1970 to 1981*, Current Population Reports, Series P2S-917, Table I, and Series P25-1104, *Population Projections of the United States, by Age, Race, and Sex: 1993 to 2020*, Table 2, Washington, DC, U.S. Government Printing Office, 1981 and 1993.

PERCENT DISTRIBUTION OF THE AFRICAN AMERICAN POPULATION
by Sex and Age – 1975 and 1993

Table 2

Age	Both Sexes 1975	Both Sexes 1993	Male 1975	Male 1993	Female 1975	Female 1993
Under 5 years	9.7	9.7	10.3	10.4	9.1	9.1
5-9 years	10.3	8.8	10.8	9.5	9.7	8.3
10-14 years	11.8	8.8	12.5	9.4	11.2	8.3
15-19 years	11.6	8.3	12.2	8.9	11.1	7.8
20-24 years	9.5	8.3	9.5	8.7	9.5	8.1
25-29 years	7.5	8.3	7.3	8.4	7.6	8.3
30-34 years	6.1	8.8	5.9	8.7	6.3	8.9
35-44 years	9.9	15.2	9.5	14.9	10.3	15.4
45-54 years	9.1	9.1	8.7	8.7	9.4	9.5
55-64 years	7.0	6.4	6.8	5.9	7.4	6.9
65 years and over	7.5	8.3	6.6	6.7	8.3	9.6
Median Age	23.5	28.7	22.2	27.0	24.7	30.1

Source: *U.S. Bureau of Census, Preliminary Estimates of the Population of the United States by Age, Sex, and Race, 1970 to 1981*, Series P25-917, Table 2, and Series PPL-8, *U.S. Population Estimates by Age, Sex, and Race, and Hispanic Origin: 1990 to 1993*, Table 1, U.S. Government Printing Office, Washington, DC, 1982 and 1994.

TEN METROPOLITAN STATISTICAL AREAS
WITH THE LARGEST AFRICAN-AMERICAN POPULATIONS

1970 and 1990

Table **3**

MSA 1970*	African-American Population	Percent African-American
1. New York, NY MSA	1,885,303	16.3
2. Chicago, IL MSA	1, 230,919	17.6
3. Philadelphia, PA MSA	944,300	24.4
4. Los Angeles, CA MSA	762,844	10.8
5. Detroit, MI MSA	757,083	18.0
6. Washington, DC MSA	703,745	24.6
7. Baltimore, MD MSA	490,012	23.7
8. Houston, TX CMSA	382,302	19.3
9. St. Louis, MO MSA	378,816	16.0
10. Newark, NJ MSA	348,342	18.8

MSA 1990	African-American Population	Percent African-American
1. New York, NY CMSA	3,455,594	17.7
2. Chicago, IL CMSA	1,561,270	18.9
3. Los Angeles, CA CMSA	1,226,477	8.4
4. Philadelphia, PA CMSA	1,083,070	18.4
5. Washington, DC PMSA	1,072,591	25.4
6. Detroit, MI CMSA	1,059,432	20.4
7. Atlanta, GA MSA	746,440	25.2
8. Houston, TX CMSA	666,669	17.9
9. Baltimore, MD PMSA	615,218	25.8
10. Miami, FL CMSA	591,784	18.5

* 1970 figures are for "Negro and other races."

Source: U.S. Bureau of the Census, Population Estimates by Race, for States: July 1,1973 and 1975, Series P-23, No. 67, Table 67, and Metropolitan Areas as Defined by the Office of Management and Budget, June 30, 1993, 1990 Census of Population & Housing Supplementary Reports, Series CPH-S-l-1, Table 8, U.S. Government Printing Office, Washington, DC, 1973 and 1993.

METROPOLITAN AREAS
WITH THE HIGHEST PERCENTAGE OF AFRICAN AMERICANS
1970 and 1990

Table 4

Metro Area 1970	Percent African American
1. Pine Bluff, AR	40.8
2. Memphis, TN-AR-MS	37.8
3. Jackson, MS	37.4
4. Montgomery, AL	35.1
5. Albany, GA	34.7
6. Savannah, GA	34.3
Metro Area 1990	Percent African American
1. Albany, GA	45.8
2. Sumter, SC	43.2
3. Pine Bluff, AR	43.1
4. Jackson, MS	42.5
5. Rocky Mount, NC	41.9
6. Memphis, TN-AR-MS	40.7

Source: U.S. Bureau of the Census, *1970 Census of Population: General Population Characteristics – United States*, Table 66, and "Metropolitan Areas," Statistical Brief SB/94-9, U.S. Government Printing Office, Washington, DC, U.S., 1971 and April 1994.

CITIES WITH THE LARGEST AFRICAN-AMERICAN POPULATIONS
1970 and 1991

Table 5

1970*	African-American Population	Percent African-American
1. New York	1,668,000**	21.1
2. Chicago	1,103,000	32.7
3. Detroit	660,000	43.7
4. Philadelphia	654,000	33.6
5. Washington	538,000	71.1
6. Los Angeles	504,000	17.9
7. Baltimore	420,000	46.4
8. Houston	317,000	25.7
9. Cleveland	288,000	38.3
10. New Orleans	267,000	45.0

1991	African-American Population	Percent African-American
1. New York	2,103,000 **	28.7
2. Chicago	1,088,000	39.1
3. Detroit	778,000	75.7
4. Philadelphia	632,000	39.9
5. Los Angeles	488,000	14.0
6. Houston	458,000	8.1
7. Baltimore	436,000	59.2
8. Washington	400,000	65.8
9. Memphis	335,000	54.9
10. New Orleans	308,000	61.9

*1970 figures are for "Negro and other races."

**Populations rounded to nearest thousand.

Source: U.S. Bureau of the Census, *Statistical Abstract of the United States 1977 (98th edition)*, Table 23, *Statistical Abstract of the United States 1993 (113th edition)*, Table 46, and Statistical Brief SB/94-9, "Metropolitan Areas," U.S. Government Printing Office, Washington, DC, 1977, 1993, and April 1994, respectively.

PERCENT DISTRIBUTION OF POPULATION
by Residence – 1976 and 1992

Table 6

Residence	1976 African American	1976 White American	1992 African American	1992 White American
Total	100.0	100.0	100.0	100.0
Metropolitan	73.7	66.3	84.8	76.2
Central Cities	55.0	24.4	56.6	25.5
Outside Central Cities	18.7	41.9	28.2	50.6
Non-Metropolitan	26.3	33.7	15.2	23.8

Source: U.S. Bureau of the Census, Current Population Reports, Series P60-107, *Money Income and Poverty Status of Families and Persons in the United States: 1976(Advance Report)*, Table 19, and Series P60-185, Poverty in the United States: 1992, Tables 1 and 8, U.S. Government Printing Office, Washington, DC, 1977 and 1993.

PERCENT DISTRIBUTION OF POPULATION
by Region and Race – 1975 and 1992

Table 7

African Region	1975 African American	1975 White American	1992 African American	1992 White American
United States	100.0	100.0	100.0	100.0
South	52.4	29.5	54.8	32.0
Northeast	19.4	23.9	16.5	20.6
Midwest	20.2	28.2	20.5	25.1
West	8.0	18.3	8.1	22.2

Source: U.S. Bureau of the Census, *Statistical Abstract of the United States: 1977 (98th edition)*, Table 35, and Current Population Reports, Series P60-185. Poverty in the United States: 1992, Tables 1 and 8, U.S. Government Printing Office, Washington, DC, 1977 and 1993.

LIFE EXPECTANCY AT BIRTH

by Race and Sex – 1975, 1992
and projections to 2050

Table 8

Both Sexes		African American	White American	AA/WA
Year	1975	66.98	73.4	.91
	1992	69.8	76.5	.91
	2000	70.2	77.6	.90
Projected	2010	71.3	78.8	.90
	2050	75.5	83.3	.90

Male		African American	White American	AA/WA
Year	1975	62.4	69.5	.90
	1992	65.5	73.2	.89
	2000	65.3	74.3	.88
Projected	2010	66.5	75.6	.88
	2050	71.3	81.0	.88

Female		African American	White American	AA/WA
Year	1975	71.3	77.3	.92
	1992	73.9	79.7	.93
	2000	75.1	80.9	.93
Projected	2010	76.0	82.0	.93
	2050	79.6	86.5	.92

Source: U.S. Bureau of the Census, *Statistical Abstract of the United States 1994 (114th edition)*, Table 114, and Current Population Reports, Series P25-1104, *Population Projections of the United States, by Age, Sex, Race, and Hispanic Origin: 1993 to 2050*. Table B-I. U.S. Government Printing Office, Washington, DC, 1993 and 1994.

INFANT MORTALITY RATE

by Race – 1975 and 1991

Table 9

Year	African American	White American	AA/WA
1975	26.2*	14.2	1.85
1991	17.6	7.3	2.41

Source: Louise L. Hornor, *Black Americans: A Statistical Sourcebook, 1994*, Information Publications Palo Alto, CA, 1994, Table 2.11, and National Center for Health Statistics, *Advance Report of Final Mortality Statistics 1991*, U.S. Government Printing Office, Washington, DC, 1991, p. 11.

BIRTH RACE

by Race – 1975 and 1991

Table 10

Year	African American	White American	AA/WA
1975	20.7*	13.6	1.52
1991	21.9	15.4	1.42

*Births per 1,000 population.

Source: U.S. Bureau of the Census, *Statistical Abstract of the United States: 1993 on CD-ROM*, Table 93, and *Statistical Abstract of the United States: 1994 (114th edition)*, Table 92, U.S. Government Printing Office, Washington, DC, 1993 and 1994.

BIRTHS TO UNMARRIED MOTHERS

by Race – 1975 and 1991

Table 11

Year	African American	White American	AA/WA
1975	49.0	7.3	6.71
1991	68.0	22.0	3.09

*As a percent of all live births.

Source: Hornor, *Black Americans, op. cit.*, Table 2.03, and U.S. Bureau of the Census, *Statistical Abstract of the United States: 1994 (114th edition)*, U.S. Government Printing Office, Washington, DC, 1994, Table 100.

MARITAL STATUS
by Race and Sex – 1975 and 1993

Table 12

Both Sexes	1975			1993		
	African American	White American	AA/WA	African American	White American	AA/WA
All statuses	100.0	100.0		100.0	100.0	
Single	24.2	16.7	1.45	41.9	24.2	1.73
Married	58.7	70.8	.83	40.4	60.5	.67
Spouse present	47.1	68.4	.69	33.1	58.0	.57
Spouse absent	11.6	2.4	4.83	7.3	2.5	2.92
Widowed	10.7	8.1	1.32	8.0	6.9	1.16
Divorced	6.5	4.4	1.48	9.8	8.4	1.17

Male	1975			1993		
	African American	White American	AA/WA	African American	White American	AA/WA
All statuses	100.0	100.0		100.0	100.0	
Single	27.2	20.0	1.36	45.5	28.2	1.61
Married	62.7	74.0	.85	42.4	62.3	.68
Spouse present	53.7	71.9	.75	37.0	59.9	.62
Spouse absent	9.0	2.1	4.29	5.4	2.4	1.71
Widowed	5.0	2.4	2.08	4.1	2.4	1.71
Divorced	5.1	3.6	1.42	8.0	7.1	1.13

Female	1975			1993		
	African American	White American	AA/WA	African American	White American	AA/WA
All statuses	100.0	100.0		100.0	100.0	
Single	21.7	13.7	1.58	38.9	20.5	1.90
Married	55.5	68.0	.82	38.6	58.9	.66
Spouse present	41.8	65.3	.64	29.9	56.2	.53
Spouse absent	13.7	2.7	5.07	8.8	2.7	3.26
Widowed	15.2	13.3	1.14	11.2	11.1	1.01
Divorced	7.5	5.0	1.50	11.3	9.5	1.19

Source: U.S. Bureau of the Census, Current Population Reports, *Marital Status and Living Arrangements: March 1975*, Table 1, and *Marital Status and Living Arrangements: March 1993*, Table 1, U.S. Government Printing Office, Washington, DC, 1975 and 1993.

PERCENT DISTRIBUTION OF HOUSEHOLDS
by Family Type and Race – 1975 and 1993

Table 13

Type of Family	1975			1993		
	African American	White American	AA/WA	African American	White American	AA/WA
All Families	100.0	100.0		100.0		
Married Couple	61.1	87.1	.70	47.5	82.3	.58
Female Householder No Spouse Present	35.0	10.4	3.37	46.7	13.6	3.43
Male Householder No Spouse Present	3.9	2.5	1.56	5.8	4.2	1.38

Source: U.S. Bureau of the Census, Current Population Reports, Series P20-411, *Household and Family Characteristics: March 1985*, and Series P20-477, *Household and Family Characteristics: March 1993*, U.S. Government Printing Office, Washington, DC, 1986 and 1994, Table E.

DEATH RATE
by Race and Sex – 1975 and 1992

Table 14

Sex	1975			1992		
	African American	White American	AA/WA	African American	White American	AA/WA
Both	8.9*	6.0	1.48	7.7	4.8	1.60
Male	11.6	8.0 ·	1.45	10.3	6.3	1.63
Female	6.7	4.4	1.52	7.5	3.6	2.08

*Deaths per 100,000 population. Age-adjusted.

Source: U.S. Bureau of the Census. *Statistical Abstract of the United States: 1993 on CD-ROM*, U.S. Government Printing Office, Washington, DC, 1993, Table 118, and National Center for Health Statistics, *Annual Summary of Births, Deaths, Marriages, Divorces, and Deaths in the United States: 1992*, National Center for Health Statistics, Hyattsville, MD, 1994, Table 9.

HOMICIDE RATE
by Race and Sex – 1975 and 1992

Table 15

Sex	1975			1992		
	African American	White American	AA/WA	African American	White American	AA/WA
Both	40.4*	5.8	6.97	41.8	6.2	6.74
Male	68.5	9.0	7.61	71.7	9.5	7.55
Female	14.9	2.9	5.14	14.3	2.8	5.11

*Homicides per 100,000 population.

Source: U.S. Bureau of the Census, Current Population Reports.
Series P25-917, *Preliminary Estimates of the Population of the
United States by Age, Sex, and Race: 1970 to 1981*, Table I, National
Center for Health Statistics, *Vital Statistics of the United States:
Volume II Mortality*, Table 1-22, *Final Mortality, Monthly Vital
Statistics: 1992* (Advance Report), Table 1-25, U.S. Government
Printing Office, Washington, DC, Table 9, 1981, 1979, and 1994.

EDUCATION

■ The education attainment of African Americans has improved markedly over the past two decades. In 1975, only 27 percent of African Americans ages 25 and older had completed high school. In 1993, the figure was 36 percent. Similarly, the proportion of African Americans with some college education increased from 9 percent to 22 percent. Significant gains occurred in every region of the country.

■ While there continues to be a considerable racial disparity in high school dropout rates, the gap has narrowed. In 1975, African Americans were about twice as likely as whites to drop out of high school. By 1993, they were just 1.3 times as likely to drop out.

■ The racial disparity in college enrollment rates has widened. African Americans ages 18 to 24 are 70 percent as likely as their white counterparts to be in college, down from 77 percent in 1975. On the other hand, the rate of college completion among African Americans has increased faster than the rate among whites.

EDUCATIONAL ATTAINMENT
OF PERSONS 25 YEARS OLD AND OVER
by Race and Sex – 1975 and 1993

Table 16

Both Sexes	1975			1993		
	African American	White American	AA/WA	African American	White American	AA/WA
Less than high school	57.4	35.5	1.62	29.6	18.5	1.60
High school graduate	27.1	37.3	.73	36.3	35.6	1.02
Some college	9.0	12.8	.70	22.0	23.3	.94
Bachelor's degree or more	6.4	14.5	.44	12.2	22.6	.54

Male	1975			1993		
	African American	White American	AA/WA	African American	White American	AA/WA
Less than high school	58.3	34.9	1.67	30.3	18.2	1.66
High school graduate	25.2	33.1	.76	36.9	33.1	1.11
Some college	9.7	13.6	.71	20.7	23.0	.90
Bachelor's degree or more	6.7	18.4	.36	11.9	25.7	.46

Female	1975			1993		
	African American	White American	AA/WA	African American	White American	AA/WA
Less than high school	56.7	35.9	1.58	28.9	18.7	1.55
High school graduate	28.6	41.1	.70	35.8	38.0	.94
Some college	8.5	12.1	.70	23.0	23.6	.97
Bachelor's degree or more	6.2	11.0	.56	12.3	19.7	.62

Source: U.S. Bureau of the Census, *Statistical Abstract of the United States 1977(98th edition)*, U.S. Government Printing Office, Washington, DC, 1977, Table 217, and Current Population Reports, Series P20-476, *Educational Attainment in the United States: March 1993 and 1992*, U.S. Government Printing Office, Washington, DC, 1994, Table 1.

EDUCATIONAL ATTAINMENT
OF PERSONS 25 YEARS OLD AND OVER
by Race and Region – 1975 and 1993

Table 17

Education	1975			1993		
	African American	White American	AA/WA	African American	White American	AA/WA
Less than high school	57.4	35.5	1.62	29.6	18.5	1.60
High school graduate	27.1	37.3	.73	36.3	35.6	1.02
Some college	9.0	12.8	.70	22.0	23.3	.94
Bachelor's degree or more	6.4	14.5	.44	12.2	22.6	.54

South	1975			1993		
	African American	White American	AA/WA	African American	White American	AA/WA
Less than high school	67.4	39.8	.69	32.9	21.2	1.55
High school graduate	20.8	33.9	.61	36.6	34.0	1.08
Some college	5.7	12.7	.45	18.9	23.4	.81
Bachelor's degree or more	6.1	13.6	.45	11.6	21.4	.54

Northeast	1975			1993		
	African American	White American	AA/WA	African American	White American	AA/WA
Less than high school	47.6	36.5	1.30	26.2	17.6	1.49
Bachelor's degree or more	5.5	15.2	.36	13.7	24.8	.55

Midwest	1975			1993		
	African American	White American	AA/WA	African American	White American	AA/WA
Less than high school	50.7	35.0	1.45	28.9	16.7	1.73
High school graduate	32.1	40.2	.80	33.9	40.8	.83
Some college	11.2	11.5	.97	25.4	22.0	1.15
Bachelor's degree or more	6.2	13.3	.47	11.8	20.5	.58

continued on next page

EDUCATIONAL ATTAINMENT
OF PERSONS 25 YEARS OLD AND OVER continued

West	1975 African American	1975 White American	AA/WA	1993 African American	1993 White American	AA/WA
Less than high school	37.8	27.8	1.36	16.5	17.3	.95
High school graduate	30.9	37.1	.83	32.1	29.8	1.08
Some college	20.5	18.5	1.11	37.7	28.4	1.33
Bachelor's degree or more	10.7	16.7	.64	13.7	24.5	.56

Source: U.S. Bureau of the Census, Current Population Reports, Series P20-295, *Educational Attainment in the United States: March 1975*, Table 3, and Series P20-476, *Educational Attainment in the United States: March 1993 and 1992*, Table 1, U.S. Government Printing Office, Washington, DC, 1976 and 1994.

HIGH SCHOOL DROPOUT RATE FOR PERSONS 18-24 YEARS OLD
by Race and Sex – 1975 and 1993

Table 18

Sex	1975 African American	1975 White American	AA/WA	1993 African American	1993 White American	AA/WA
Both	20.7	26.9	.77	24.5	34.8	.70
Male	20.3	30.1	.67	22.8	34.0	.67
Female	21.1	23.9	.88	26.1	35.2	.74

Source: U.S. Bureau of the Census, Current Population Reports, Series P20-479, *School Enrollment – Social and Economic Characteristics of Students: October 1993*, U.S. Government Printing Office, Washington, DC, 1994, Table A-5.

COLLEGE ENROLLMENT RATE
FOR PERSONS 18-24 YEARS OLD

by Race and Sex – 1975 and 1993

Table **19**

Sex	1975 African American	1975 White American	1975 AA/WA	1993 African American	1993 White American	1993 AA/WA
Both	27.3	13.9	1.96	16.4	12.2	1.34
Male	27.8	13.3	2.06	15.6	12.9	1.21
Female	26.9	14.2	1.89	17.2	11.5	1.50

Source: U.S. Bureau of the Census, Current Population Reports, Series P20-479, *School Enrollment – Social and Economic, Characteristics of Students: October 1993*, U.S. Government Printing Office, Washington, DC, 1994, Table A-5.

COLLEGE COMPLETION RATE
FOR PERSONS 25 YEARS OLD AND OVER

by Race and Sex – 1975 and 1993

Table **20**

Sex	1975 African American	1975 White American	1975 AA/WA	1993 African American	1993 White American	1993 AA/WA
Both	6.4	14.5	.44	12.2	22.6	.54
Male	6.7	18.4	.36	11.9	25.7	.46
Female	6.2	11.0	.56	12.3	19.7	.62

Source: U.S. Bureau of the Census, *Statistical Abstract of the United States: 1977 (98th edition)*, Table 217, and Current Population Reports, Series P20-276, *Educational Attainment in the United States: March, 1993 and 1992*, U.S. Government Printing Office, Washington, DC, 1977 and 1994, Table 1.

EMPLOYMENT AND EARNINGS

■ The racial unemployment gap has widened since 1975, when African Americans were 1.8 times as likely as whites to be unemployed. The ratio climbed to 2.2:1 in 1993. African-American teenagers were 2.4 times as likely as their white counterparts to be jobless, up from 2.0 in 1975. An increased racial unemployment gap occurred in every region of the country.

■ African-American employment in the manufacturing sector of the economy declined notably between 1975 and 1993, while the proportion of the African-American work force employed in most other industries grew—led by wholesale and retail trade. These changes parallel the equally noteworthy shift from blue-collar to white-collar occupations.

■ The earnings of African-American workers have not kept pace with the earnings of whites. In 1993, African-American workers earned just 77 percent as much as their white counterparts, down from 82 percent in 1975. The drop in relative earnings position was particularly pronounced in the Northeast and Midwest.

■ The per capita income of African Americans was less than 60 percent that of whites in both 1975 and 1993. Moreover, there was a widening of the racial income gap among families.

■ Although there continues to be a disproportionate incident of poverty among African Americans, the racial disparity in poverty rates has narrowed over the past two decades or so. Nonetheless, in 1993, 46 percent of all African-American children were poor as were more than half of all African Americans living in female-headed families.

OFFICIAL UNEMPLOYMENT RATE BY RACE

Sex and Age – 1975 and 1993

Table 21

Sex	1975			1993		
	African American	White American	AA/WA	African American	White American	AA/WA
Total	13.8	7.8	1.77	12.9	6.0	2.15
Male	13.6	7.2	1.89	13.8	6.2	2.22
Female	13.9	8.6	1.62	12.0	5.7	2.11
Teenagers	36.7	17.9	2.05	38.9	16.2	2.40
Male	35.2	18.3	1.92	40.1	17.6	2.28
Female	38.3	17.4	2.20	37.5	14.6	2.57

Source: U.S. Bureau of Labor Statistics, *Labor Force Statistics Derived From The Current Population Survey: A Databook*, Table A–28, and *Employment and Earnings*, Volume 41, No. 1, January, 1994, Table 3, U.S. Bureau of Labor Statistics, Washington, DC, 1982 and 1994.

OFFICIAL UNEMPLOYMENT RATE

by Race and Region – 1975 and 1993

Table 22

Sex	1975			1993		
	African American	White American	AA/WA	African American	White American	AA/WA
United States	13.9	7.7	1.81	12.9	6.0	2.15
South	13.4	6.5	2.06	11.9	5.2	2.29
Northeast	13.6	9.1	1.49	13.0	6.6	1.97
Midwest	16.3	7.2	2.26	15.1	5.1	2.96
West	12.8	8.8	1.45	14.2	7.6	1.87

* 1975 figures for "Black and Other Races."

Source: U.S. Bureau of Labor Statistics, *Geographical Profile of Employment and Unemployment, 1993*, Table 1, U.S. Bureau of Labor Statistics, Washington, DC, 1994, and unpublished U.S. Bureau of Labor Statistics data.

LABOR FORCE PARTICIPATION RATE
by Race, Sex, and Age – 1975 and 1993

Table 23

Sex	1975			1993		
	African American	White American	AA/WA	African American	White American	AA/WA
Total	59.6	61.5	.97	62.4	66.7	.94
Male	71.9	78.7	.91	68.6	76.1	.90
Female	49.4	45.9	1.07	57.4	58.0	.99
Teenagers	39.2	56.7	.69	37.0	55.1	.67
Male	42.9	61.9	.69	39.5	56.5	.70
Female	35.6	51.5	.69	34.5	53.7	.64

Source: U.S. Bureau of Labor Statistics, *Labor Force Statistics Derived From The Current Population Survey: A Databook*, Table E-2, and *Employment and Earnings*, Volume 41, No. 1, January, 1994, Table 1, U.S. Bureau of Labor Statistics, Washington, DC, 1982 and 1994.

LABOR FORCE PARTICIPATION RATE
by Race and Region – 1975 and 1993

Table 24

Sex	1975			1993		
	African American*	White American	AA/WA	African American	White American	AA/WA
United States	59.3	61.6	.96	62.4	66.7	.94
South	59.7	61.0	.98	64.3	65.6	.98
Northeast	56.4	60.0	.94	60.3	65.0	.93
Midwest	58.2	62.9	.95	59.5	69.4	.86
West	62.6	62.0	1.01	61.9	67.0	.93

*1975 figures for "Black and Other Races."

Source: Calculated by the National Urban League from unpublished U.S. Bureau of Labor Statistics data, and U.S. Bureau of Labor Statistics, *Geographical Profile of Employment and Unemployment, 1993*, Table 1, U.S. Bureau of Labor Statistics, Washington, DC, 1994.

PERCENT OF EMPLOYED CIVILIANS IN SELECTED INDUSTRY
by Race and Sex – 1975 and 1993

Table 25

Both sexes	1975			1993		
	African American	White American	AA/WA	African American	White American	AA/WA
All Industries	100.0	100.0		100.0	100.0	
Agriculture	3.1	4.1	.76	1.2	2.8	.43
Mining	0.2	0.9	.22	0.2	0.6	.33
Construction	4.6	6.1	.75	3.8	6.4	.59
Manufacturing	23.7	22.8	1.04	16.2	16.4	.99
Transport & Pub. Util.	7.1	6.6	1.08	9.6	6.8	1.41
Wholesale & Retail Tr.	13.6	21.3	.64	17.1	21.1	.81
Fin., Ins., & Real Est.	3.8	5.8	.66	5.5	6.8	.81
Services	36.5	27.2	1.34	39.3	34.4	1.14
Public Administration	7.4	5.4	1.37	7.1	4.6	1.54

Male	1975			1993		
	African American	White American	AA/WA	African American	White American	AA/WA
All Industries	100.0	100.0		100.0	100.0	
Agriculture	4.8	5.5	.87	2.1	4.0	.53
Mining	0.4	1.4	.29	0.4	0.9	.44
Construction	8.1	9.3	.87	7.2	10.7	.67
Manufacturing	29.9	26.7	1.12	19.8	20.6	.96
Transport & Pub. Util.	10.4	8.4	1.24	13.6	9.0	1.51
Wholesale & Retail Tr.	14.8	19.6	.76	18.8	20.4	.92
Fin., Ins., & Real Est.	3.2	4.6	.70	4.3	5.2	.83
Services	19.9	18.3	1.09	27.1	24.2	1.12
Public Administration	8.4	6.3	1.33	6.7	4.9	1.37

continued on next page

PERCENT OF EMPLOYED CIVILIANS IN SELECTED INDUSTRY continued

Female	1975 African American	1975 White American	AA/WA	1993 African American	1993 White American	AA/WA
All Industries	100.0	100.0		100.0	100.0	
Agriculture	1.0	1.8	.56	0.2	1.3	.15
Mining	0.1	0.2	.50	0.1	0.2	.50
Construction	0.3	1.0	.30	0.5	1.2	.42
Manufacturing	16.2	16.4	.99	12.7	11.3	1.12
Transport & Pub. Util.	3.3	3.7	.89	5.9	4.2	1.40
Wholesale & Retail Tr.	12.3	23.9	.51	15.5	21.9	.71
Fin., Ins., & Real Est.	4.5	7.5	.60	6.6	8.9	.74
Services	56.1	41.3	1.36	51.1	46.9	1.09
Public Administration	6.2	4.1	1.51	7.5	4.1	1.83

*1975 figures for "Black and Other Races."

Source: Calculated by the National Urban League from unpublished U.S. Bureau of Labor Statistics data, and U.S. Bureau of Labor Statistics, *Employment and Earnings*, Volume 41, No. 1, Table 26, U.S. Bureau of Labor Statistics, Washington, DC, 1994.

PERCENT OF EMPLOYED CIVILIANS AT SELECTED OCCUPATION
by Race and Sex – 1975 and 1993

Table 26

Both sexes	1975			1993		
	African American*	White American	AA/WA	African American	White American	AA/WA
All Occupations	100.0	100.0		100.0	100.0	
White Collar**	34.8	51.7	.67	45.7	59.3	.77
Blue Collar**	37.2	32.4	1.48	29.0	25.1	1.15
Services	25.4	12.3	2.07	23.6	12.6	1.87
Farm	2.6	3.5	.74	1.7	3.0	.57

Male	1975			1993		
	African American	White American	AA/WA	African American	White American	AA/WA
All Occupations	100.0	100.0		100.0	100.0	
White Collar	26.7	42.9	.62	32.7	47.9	.68
Blue Collar	53.2	44.4	1.20	44.6	38.4	1.16
Services	16.2	7.8	2.08	19.4	9.3	2.09
Farm	3.8	4.9	.78	3.2	4.5	.71

Female	1975			1993		
	African American	White American	AA/WA	African American	White American	AA/WA
All Occupations	100.0	100.0		100.0	100.0	
White Collar	44.4	65.6	.68	58.3	73.2	.80
Blue Collar	17.9	13.6	1.32	14.0	9.0	1.56
Services	36.6	19.4	1.89	27.5	16.8	1.64
Farm	1.0	1.4	.71	0.3	1.0	.30

*1975 figures for "Black and Other Races."

**"White Collar" includes professional and technical workers, managers, administrators, sales workers, and other clerical workers. "Blue Collar" includes craft and kindred workers, operatives, transport equipment operatives, and nonfarm laborers.

Source: Calculated by the National Urban League from U.S. Bureau of Labor Statistics, *Labor Force Statistics Derived From the Current Population Survey: A Databook*, Table B-18, and *Employment and Earnings*, January, 1994, Table 21, U.S. Bureau of Labor Statistics, Washington, DC, 1982 and 1994.

MEDIAN WEEKLY EARNINGS
OF FULL-TIME WAGE AND SALARY WORKERS
by Race and Sex – 1975 and 1993

Table 27

Sex	1975			1993		
	African American	White American	AA/WA	African American	White American	AA/WA
Both	401*	489	.82	370	478	.77
Male	445	579	.77	392	531	.74
Female	334	355	.94	349	403	.86

*In constant 1993 dollars.

Source: U.S. Bureau of Labor Statistics, *Labor Force Statistics Derived From the Current Population Survey: A Databook*, Table C-19, and *Employment and Earnings*, January 1994, Table 54, U.S. Bureau of Labor Statistics, Washington, DC, 1982 and 1994.

MEDIAN WEEKLY EARNINGS OF EMPLOYED WORKERS
by Race and Region – 1979 and 1993

Table 28

Region	1979			1993		
	African American*	White American	AA/WA	African American	White American	AA/WA
United States	406*	496	.82	370	478	.77
South	358	461	.78	332	439	.76
Northeast	434	493	.88	410	512	.80
Midwest	473	520	.91	397	468	.85
West	478	542	.88	456	502	.91

*In constant 1993 dollars.

Source: Calculated by the National Urban League from unpublished U.S. Bureau of Labor Statistics data.

PER CAPITA INCOME BY RACE

1975 and 1993

Table 29

Year	African American	White American	AA/WA
1975	7,642*	13,041	.59
1993	9,806	16,576	.59

*In constant 1993 dollars.

Source: U.S. Bureau of the Census, *1993 Statistical Abstract of the United States on CD-ROM*, Table 732, and Current Population Reports, Series P60-188, *Income, Poverty, and Valuation of Noncash Benefits: 1993*, Table A, U.S. Government Printing Office, Washington, DC, 1993 and 1995.

PERCENT DISTRIBUTION OF HOUSEHOLDS

by Total Money Income and Race – 1975 and 1993

Table 30

Income	1975 African American	1975 White American	1975 AA/WA	1993 African American	1993 White American	1993 AA/WA
Total	100.0	100.0		100.0	100.0	
Under $5,000	8.5	3.4	2.50	10.9	3.6	3.03
$5,000-9,999	19.1	9.5	2.01	18.0	8.6	2.09
10,000-14,999	14.0	9.2	1.52	11.8	8.9	1.33
15,000-24,999	19.7	16.9	1.17	19.2	16.6	1.16
25,000-34,999	15.2	16.8	.90	13.8	14.9	.93
35,000-49,999	13.9	20.4	.68	12.0	17.0	.71
50,000-74,999	7.7	16.4	.47	9.3	17.0	.55
75,000-99,999	1.4	4.5	.31	3.3	7.1	.46
100,000 and over	0.5	3.0	.17	1.9	6.3	.30

*In constant 1993 dollars.

Source: U.S. Bureau of the Census, Current Population Reports, Series P60-188, *Income, Poverty, and Valuation of Noncash Benefits: 1993*, Table G, U.S. Government Printing Office, Washington, DC, 1995.

MEDIAN FAMILY INCOME
by Race and Region – 1975 and 1992

Table 31

Region	1975 African American*	1975 White American	1975 AA/WA	1992 African American	1992 White American	1992 AA/WA
United States	21,916*	35,619	.62	21,161	38,909	.54
South	19,213	32,648	.59	20,429	36,279	.56
Northeast	24,944	37,080	.67	23,364	43,302	.54
Midwest	26,225	37,070	.71	20,181	38,995	.52
West	24,293	36,196	.67	24,827	39,502	.63

*In constant 1992 dollars.

Source: U.S. Bureau of the Census, Current Population Reports, Series P60-103, *Money Income and Poverty Status of Families and Persons in the United States: 1975 and 1974 Revisions (Advance Report)*, Table 1, and *Statistical Abstract of the United States 1994*, Table 718, U.S. Government Printing Office, Washington, DC, 1976 and 1994.

PERCENT OF PERSONS BELOW THE POVERTY LEVEL
by Race and Region – 1976 and 1993

Table 32

Region	1976 African American*	1976 White American	1976 AA/WA	1993 African American	1993 White American	1993 AA/WA
United States	31.1	9.1	3.42	33.1	12.2	2.71
South	33.1	10.8	3.06	33.6	12.8	2.63
Northeast	29.5	8.3	3.55	31.2	11.0	2.84
Midwest	29.7	7.9	3.76	35.9	10.3	3.49
West	25.8	9.0	2.87	25.9	14.6	1.77

Source: U.S. Bureau of the Census, Current Population Reports, Series P60-103, *Money Income and Poverty Status of Families and Persons in the United States: 1975 and 1974 Revisions (Advance Report)*, Table 20 and Series P60-185, *Income, Poverty, and Valuation of Noncash Benefits: 1993*, Table 20, U.S. Government Printing Office, Washington, DC, 1976 and 1995.

CHILD POVERTY RATE
by Race – 1975 and 1993

Table 33

Year	African American	White American	AA/WA
1975	41.7*	12.7	3.28
1993	46.1	17.8	2.59

*Percent of children under the age of 18 in poverty.

Source: U.S. Bureau of the Census, Current Population Reports, Series P60-188, *Income, Poverty, and Valuation of Noncash Benefits: 1993*, U.S. Government Printing Office, Washington, DC, 1995, Table K.

POVERTY RATE FOR PERSONS IN FEMALE-HEADED FAMILIES
by Race – 1975 and 1993

Table 34

Year	African American	White American	AA/WA
1975	54.3	29.4	1.85
1993	53.0	31.0	1.71

*Percent of persons in female-headed families below the poverty level.

Source: U.S. Bureau of the Census, Current Population Reports, Series P60-188, *Income, Poverty, and Valuation of Noncash Benefits: 1993*, U.S. Government Printing Office, Washington, DC, 1995, Table J.

Index of Authors and Articles, 1987-1998

In 1987, the National Urban League began publishing *The State of Black America* in a smaller, typeset format. By so doing, it became easier to catalog and archive the various essays by author and article name.

The 1998 edition of *The State of Black America* is the fifth to contain an index of the authors and articles since 1987. The articles have been divided by topic and are listed in alphabetical order of their authors' names.

Reprints of the articles catalogued herein are available through the National Urban League, 120 Wall Street, New York, New York 10005; 212-558-5316.

BUSINESS

Glasgow, Douglas G., "The Black Underclass in Perspective," 1987, pp. 129-144.

Henderson, Lenneal J., "Empowerment through Enterprise: African-American Business Development," 1993, pp. 91-108.

Tidwell, Billy J., "Black Wealth: Facts and Fiction," 1988, pp. 193-210.

DIVERSITY

Bell, Derrick, "The Elusive Quest for Racial Justice: The Chronicle of the Constitutional Contradiction," 1991, pp. 9-23.

Cobbs, Price M., "Critical Perspectives on the Psychology of Race," 1988, pp. 61-70.

——————————, "Valuing Diversity: The Myth and the Challenge," 1989, pp. 151-159.

Watson, Bernard C., "The Demographic Revolution: Diversity in 21st Century America," 1992, pp. 31-59.

ECONOMICS

Alexis, Marcus, and Henderson, Geraldine R., "The Economic Base of African-American Communities: A Study of Consumption Patterns," 1994, pp. 51-82.

Bradford, William D., "Money Matters: Lending Discrimination in African-American Communities," 1993, pp. 109-134.

Burbridge, Lynn C., "Toward Economic Self-Sufficiency: Independence Without Poverty," 1993, pp. 71-90.

Carson, Emmett D., "Black Philanthropy in the New Millenium," 1998, pp. 71-88.

Edwards, Harry, "Playoffs and Payoffs: The African-American Athlete as an Institutional Resource," 1994, pp. 85-111.

Henderson, Lenneal J. "Blacks, Budgets, and Taxes: Assessing the Impact of Budget Deficit Reduction and Tax Reform on Blacks," 1987, pp. 75-95.

——————————, "Budget and Tax Strategy: Implications for Blacks," 1990, pp. 53-71.

—————————————, "Public Investment for Public Good: Needs, Benefits, and Financing Options," 1992, pp. 213-229.

Jeffries, John M., and Schaffer, Richard L., "Changes in the Labor Economy and Labor Market State of Black Americans," 1996, pp. 12-77.

Jones, Vinetta C., "Improving Black Student Performance on a Large Scale: The Lessons of the EQUITY 2000 Program," 1998, pp. 173-194

Malveaux, Julianne M., "The Parity Imperative: Civil Rights, Economic Justice, and the New American Dilemma," 1992, pp. 281-303.

—————————————, "The Future of Work and Who Will get It," 1998, pp. 53-70.

National Urban League Research Staff," African Americans in Profile: Selected Demographic, Social and Economic Data," 1992, pp. 309-325.

Oliver, Melvin L., and Shapiro, Thomas N., "Closing the Asset Gap," 1998, pp. 15-36.

Schorr, Lisbeth B., "A Common Purpose: Putting It All Together to Transform Neighborhoods," 1998, pp. 37-52.

Swinton, David H., "Economic Status of Blacks 1986," 1987, pp. 49-73.

—————————————, "Economic Status of Black 1987," 1988, pp. 129-152.

—————————————, "Economic Status of Black Americans," 1989, pp. 9-39.

—————————————, "Economic Status of Black Americans During the 1980s: A Decade of Limited Progress," 1990, pp. 25-52.

——————————, "The Economic Status of African Americans: 'Permanent' Poverty and Inequality," 1991, pp. 25-75.

——————————, "The Economic Status of African Americans: Limited Ownership and Persistent Inequality," 1992, pp. 61-117.

——————————, "The Economic Status of African Americans During the Reagan-Bush Era: Withered Opportunities, Limited Outcomes, and Uncertain Outlook," 1993, pp. 135-200.

Tidwell, Billy J., "Economic Costs of American Racism," 1991, pp. 219-232.

Webb, Michael B., "Programs for Progress and Empowerment: The Urban League's National Education Initiative," 1993, pp. 203-216.

EDUCATION

Bradford, William D., "Dollars for Deeds: Prospects and Prescriptions for African-American Financial Institutions," 1994, pp. 31-50.

Comer, James P., Haynes, Norris and Hamilton-Lee, Muriel, "School Power: A Model for Improving Black Student Achievement," 1990, pp. 225-238.

Darling-Hammond, Linda, "New Standards, Old Inequalities: The Current Challenge for African-American Education," 1998, pp. 109-171.

Dilworth, Mary E. "Historically Black Colleges and Universities: Taking Care of Home," 1994, pp. 127-151.

Edelman, Marian Wright, "Black Children In America," 1989, pp. 63-76.

McBay, Shirley M. "The Condition of African American Education: Changes and Challenges," 1992, pp. 141-156.

McKenzie, Floretta Dukes, with Evans, Patricia, "Education Strategies for the 90s," 1991, pp. 95-109.

Robinson, Sharon P., "Taking Charge: An Approach to Making the Educational Problems of Blacks Comprehensible and Manageable," 1987, pp. 31-47.

Sudarkasa, Niara, "Black Enrollment in Higher Education: The Unfulfilled Promise of Equality," 1988, pp. 7-22.

Watson, Bernard C., with Traylor, Fasaha M., "Tomorrow's Teachers: Who Will They Be, What Will They Know?" 1988, pp. 23-37.

Willie, Charles V., "The Future of School Desegregation," 1987, pp. 37-47.

Wilson, Reginald, "Black Higher Education: Crisis and Promise," 1989, pp. 121-135.

Wirschem, David, "Community Mobilization for Education in Rochester, New York: A Case Study," 1991, pp. 243-248.

EMPLOYMENT

Darity, William M. Jr., and Myers, Samuel L., Jr., "Racial Earnings Inequality into the 21st Century," 1992, pp. 119-139.

Tidwell, Billy J., "A Profile of the Black Unemployed," 1987, pp. 223-237.

————, "The Unemployment Experience of African Americans: Some Important Correlates and Consequences," 1990, pp. 213-223.

——————————, "African Americans and the 21st Century Labor Market: Improving the Fit," 1993, pp. 35-57.

Thomas, R. Roosevelt, Jr., "Managing Employee Diversity: An Assessment," 1991, pp. 145-154.

Wilson, William Julius, "Jobless Ghettos: The Impact of the Disappearance of Work in Segregated Neighborhoods," 1998, pp. 89-108.

FAMILIES

Billingsley, Andrew, "Black Families in a Changing Society," 1987, pp. 97-111.

——————————, "Understanding African-American Family Diversity," 1990, pp. 85-108.

Hill, Robert B., "Critical Issues for Black Families by the Year 2000," 1989, pp. 41-61.

Willie, Charles V., "The Black Family: Striving Toward Freedom," 1988, pp. 71-80.

HEALTH

Christmas, June Jackson, "The Health of African Americans: Progress Toward Healthy People 2000," 1996, pp. 95-126.

Leffall, LaSalle D., Jr., "Health Status of Black Americans," 1990, pp.121-142.

McAlpine, Robert, "Toward Development of a National Drug Control Strategy," 1991, pp. 233-241.

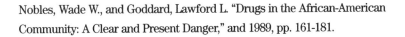

Nobles, Wade W., and Goddard, Lawford L. "Drugs in the African-American Community: A Clear and Present Danger," and 1989, pp. 161-181.

Primm, Beny J., "AIDS: A Special Report," 1987, pp. 159-166.

——————————, "Drug Use: Special Implications for Black America," 1987, pp. 145-158.

HOUSING

Calmore, John O., "To Make Wrong Right: The Necessary and Proper Aspirations of Fair Housing," 1989, pp. 77-109.

Clay, Phillip, "Housing Opportunity: A Dream Deferred," 1990, pp. 73-84.

Leigh, Wilhelmina A., "U.S. Housing Policy in 1996: The Outlook for Black Americans," Ph.D., 1996, pp. 188-218.

POLITICS

Coleman, Henry A., "Interagency and Intergovernmental Coordination: New Demands for Domestic Policy Initiatives," 1992, pp. 249-263.

Hamilton, Charles V., "On Parity and Political Empowerment," 1989, pp. 111-120.

——————————, "Promoting Priorities: African-American Political Influence in the 1990s," 1993, pp. 59-69.

Henderson, Lenneal J., "Budgets, Taxes, and Politics: Options for the African-American Community," 1991, pp. 77-93.

Holden, Matthew, Jr., "The Rewards of Daring and the Ambiguity of Power: Perspectives on the Wilder Election of 1989," 1990, pp. 109-120.

Kilson, Martin L., "The State of African-American Politics," 1998, pp. 247-270.

McHenry, Donald F., "A Changing World Order: Implications for Black America," 1991, pp. 155-163.

Persons, Georgia A., "Blacks in State and Local Government: Progress and Constraints," 1987, pp. 167-192.

Pinderhughes, Dianne M., "Power and Progress: African American Politics in the New Era of Diversity," 1992, pp. 265-280.

——————————, "Civil Rights and the Future of the American Presidency," 1988, pp. 39-60.

Tidwell, Billy J., "Serving the National Interest: A Marshall Plan for America," 1992, pp. 11-30.

RELIGION

Lincoln, C. Eric. "Knowing the Black Church: What It Is and Why," 1989, pp. 137-149.

Richardson, W. Franklyn, "Mission to Mandate: Self-Development through the Black Church," 1994, pp. 113-126.

TECHNOLOGY

Hammond, Allen S., "Standing at the Edge of the Digital Divide," 1998, pp. 195-246.

URBAN AFFAIRS

Bates, Timothy, "The Paradox of Urban Poverty," 1996, pp. 144-163.

Bell, Carl C., with Jenkins, Esther J. "Preventing Black Homicide," 1990, pp. 143-155.

Bryant Solomon, Barbara, "Social Welfare Reform," 1987, pp. 113-127.

Brown, Lee P., "Crime in the Black Community," 1988, pp. 95-113.

Bullard, Robert D., "Urban Infrastructure: Social, Environmental, and Health Risks to African Americans," 1992, pp. 183-196.

Chambers, Julius L., "The Law and Black Americans: Retreat from Civil Rights," 1987, pp. 15-30.

—————————, "Black Americans and the Courts: Has the Clock Been Turned Back Permanently?" 1990, pp. 9-24.

Edelin, Ramona H., "Toward an African-American Agenda: An Inward Look," 1990, pp. 173-183.

Fair, T. Willard, "Coordinated Community Empowerment: Experiences of the Urban League of Greater Miami," 1993, pp. 217-233.

Gray, Sandra T., "Public-Private Partnerships: Prospects for America ... Promise for African Americans," 1992, pp. 231-247.

Hill, Robert B., "Urban Redevelopment: Developing Effective Targeting Strategies," 1992, pp. 197-211.

Henderson, Lenneal J., "African Americans in the Urban Milieu: Conditions, Trends, and Development Needs," 1994, pp. 11-29.

Jones, Dionne J., with Greg Harrison of the National Urban League Research Department, "Fast Facts: Comparative Views of African-American Status and Progress," 1994, pp. 213-236.

Jones, Shirley J., "Silent Suffering: The Plight of Rural Black America," 1994, pp. 171-188.

Massey, Walter E. "Science, Technology, and Human Resources: Preparing for the 21st Century," 1992, pp. 157-169.

Mendez, Jr. Garry A., "Crime Is Not a Part of Our Black Heritage: A Theoretical Essay," 1988, pp. 211-216.

Miller, Warren F., Jr., "Developing Untapped Talent: A National Call for African-American Technologists," 1991, pp. 111-127.

Murray, Sylvester, "Clear and Present Danger: The Decay of America's Physical Infrastructure," 1992, pp. 171-182.

Pemberton, Gayle, "It's the Thing That Counts, Or Reflections on the Legacy of W.E.B. Du Bois," 1991, pp. 129-143.

Pinderhughes, Dianne M. "The Case of African-Americans in the Persian Gulf: The Intersection of American Foreign and Military Policy with Domestic Employment Policy in the United States," 1991, pp. 165-186.

Robinson, Gene S. "Television Advertising and Its Impact on Black America," 1990, pp. 157-171.

Schneider, Alvin J., "Blacks in the Military: The Victory and the Challenge," 1988, pp.115-128.

Stewart, James B., "Developing Black and Latino Survival Strategies: The Future of Urban Areas," 1996, pp.164-187.

Stone, Christopher E., "Crime and Justice in Black America," 1996, pp. 78-94.

Tidwell, Billy J., with Kuumba, Monica B., Jones, Dionne J., and Watson, Betty C., "Fast Facts: African Americans in the 1990s," 1993, pp. 243-265.

Wallace-Benjamin, Joan, "Organizing African-American Self-Development: The Role of Community-Based Organizations," 1994, pp. 189-205.

Walters, Ronald, "Serving the People: African-American Leadership and the Challenge of Empowerment," 1994, pp. 153-170.

YOUTH

Fulbright-Anderson, Karen, Ph.D., "Developing Our Youth: What Works," 1996, pp.127-143.

Hare, Bruce R., "Black Youth at Risk," 1988, pp. 81-93.

Howard, Jeff P., "The Third Movement: Developing Black Children for the 21st Century," 1993, pp. 11-34.

McMurray, Georgia L. "Those of Broader Vision: An African-American Perspective on Teenage Pregnancy and Parenting," 1990, pp. 195-211.

Moore, Evelyn K., "The Call: Universal Child Care," 1996, pp. 219-244.

Williams, Terry M., and Kornblum William, "A Portrait of Youth: Coming of Age in Harlem Public Housing," 1991, pp. 187-207.

About the Authors:
The State of Black America 1998

EMMETT D. CARSON is President of The Minneapolis Foundation and an authority on the history of philanthropy.

LINDA DARLING-HAMMOND is Professor of Education at Teachers College, Columbia University. Her books include *The Right To Learn: A Blueprint for Creating Schools That Work*.

ALLEN S. HAMMOND IV is Professor of Law at New York Law School.

VINETTA C. JONES, PH.D., is Executive Director of the College Board EQUITY 2000 program.

MARTIN L. KILSON is Frank M. Thompson Professor of Government at Harvard University and a member of the editorial board of *The State of Black America*.

JULIANNE MALVEAUX, PH.D., is a widely-published author and syndicated columnist specializing in economic affairs.

MELVIN L. OLIVER is vice president in charge of the asset building and community development program at the Ford Foundation, in New York, and Professor of Sociology and Policy Studies at the University of California at Los Angeles. He is the co-author, with THOMAS M. SHAPIRO, of *Black Wealth/White Wealth*, which was published in 1995.

HUGH B. PRICE is President and Chief Executive Officer of the National Urban League.

LISBETH B. SCHORR is a Lecturer in Social Medicine at Harvard University who has written widely on efforts to improve the lives of impoverished children and families.

THOMAS M. SHAPIRO is Professor of Sociology and Anthropology at Northeastern University. He is the co-author, with MELVIN L. OLIVER, of Black Wealth/White Wealth, which was published in 1995.

WILLIAM JULIUS WILSON is the Malcolm Wiener Professor of Social Policy at the Malcolm Wiener Center for Social Policy of the John F. Kennedy School of Government, Harvard University. He is the author of numerous books, including, most recently, *When Work Disappears: The World of the New Urban Poor.*